The
Risk It Takes
to Bloom

The
Risk It Takes
to Bloom

ON LIFE AND
LIBERATION

RAQUEL WILLIS

ST. MARTIN'S PRESS
NEW YORK

Library of Congress Cataloging-in-Publication Data

Names: Willis, Raquel, author.
Title: The risk it takes to bloom : on life and liberation / Raquel Willis.
Description: First edition, | New York : St. Martin's Press, 2023. |
    Includes bibliographical references.
Identifiers: LCCN 2023025379 | ISBN 9781250275684 (hardcover) |
    ISBN 9781250275691 (ebook)
Subjects: LCSH: Willis, Raquel. | Transgender women—United States—Biography. |
    African American transgender people—Biography. | Transgender people—Civil
    rights—United States. | Gay rights—United States. | Civil rights—United States.
Classification: LCC HQ77.8.W555 A3 2023 | DDC 306.76/8082 [B]—dc23/
    eng/20230620
LC record available at https://lccn.loc.gov/2023025379

First Edition: 2023

10 9 8 7 6 5 4 3 2 1

To all who have ever doubted their place
in the garden of liberation.

And the day came,
when the risk
to remain tight
in a bud
was more painful
than the risk
it took
to blossom.

—Elizabeth Appell[1]

CONTENTS

Introduction

January 21, 2017

Nothing could settle my nerves as I stood at the national Women's March podium just after Donald Trump's presidential inauguration. This moment, at the dawn of a new era slated to be considerably more oppressive than the previous one, injected a mix of frustration and stage fright into my veins. It didn't help that the legendary Angela Davis had just addressed the audience to thunderous applause. *How would I follow the brilliance this social justice titan had just shared? And did I even belong here?* A twenty-something Black transgender activist from the South who had only recently expanded her local community-organizing lens to a more national one. *And what do I make of this crowd?* A sea of woolen pink "pussy" hats and varying protest signs nodded to the overarching *femaleness* of the audience. Most attendees believed that what drew them together was a laundry list of experiences I hadn't had. I was little more than a mythical creature to them: a woman who, upon emerging from her mother's womb, hadn't been assigned a vagina by nature nor designated female by a doctor.

Despite having traveled a different path to my womanhood,

I trusted that we mostly shared similar values and concerns about the direction the United States was heading. Indeed, millions around the world were joining us in protesting the ascent of a most threatening bigot. But I yearned for clarification that people knew Trump and his ilk weren't animated just by misogyny. No, they drew sustenance from numerous systems of oppression: white supremacy, ableism, queerphobia, transphobia, classism, and so much more. This Women's March couldn't rebuke just a sliver of his dehumanizing worldview; it needed to address all of it and demonstrate what's possible when folks across the margins assemble. And the voices of women who had historically been sidelined and undervalued had to serve that purpose. My voice had to serve that purpose.

I wasn't alone, though. My mother's grounding presence helped dissipate the fog of uncertainty that surrounded me. She was a reminder of the radical power of transformation herself—a Southern Black woman born during the Civil Rights Era who had just witnessed a major recall on progress. Bundled up against the frigidity of this new era, her smile had been a source of warmth throughout the morning. That her child would address scores of people had enlivened her. Her love was a given after witnessing every iteration of myself that had ever existed: the observant gender-nonconforming child, the gay teenager who came out despite years of constant bullying, the genderqueer college student first exposed to the complexity of identity, the hopeful trans woman embarking on a journalism career, and now the activist in action. Momma would witness me tell the world what I'd told her many times throughout my life: "I have something to say."

I'd racked my brain over every syllable to include in this monumental address, attempting to present a pristine politick. I believed in an intersectional feminism that was anti-colonial, anti-carceral, anti-cisheteropatriarchal, anti–white supremacist, and anti-everything that the United States had recently showed that it still was. My feminism was some unique concoction that could only come from a generation half a century removed from the Stonewall riots, the Black Power era, and the schisms of the second feminist wave. If Alice Walker once said, "Womanist is to feminist as purple is to lavender," the ideology that sprang forth from my generation of Black trans folks was some deeper undefined tone. Those beliefs fueled me to amplify many who couldn't tell their stories: Black folks murdered by the State, trans women of color often killed by lovers before the State had their turn, trans youth who couldn't be their selves at home or at school, and elders who lived in a time when people like us would have been heckled out of such a rally—not invited to address it. But this was a new moment.

"Give it up for Raquel Willis." The announcer's booming voice tore through my reverie, and I relinquished my worries into the harsh January air. With determination, I rooted my feet, cleared my throat, and grabbed on to the podium for dear life.

"Alright, everyone . . . I won't take up too much of your time. I know you are amped and ready." I served up as quick an introduction as I could per guidance from the event organizers. I explained how my father's death was the jolt I needed to embrace my gender identity, I nodded to my Southern roots, my mother's presence, and the *trancestors*—trans ancestors—who made it possible for me to live authentically. Gratifying bursts of applause merged with my resounding voice, emboldening me.

I want to stress the importance of us being intentional about inclusion. I think about, historically, trans women of color like Sylvia Rivera and Marsha P. Johnson, who lit the fire on the LGBTQIA rights movement, and they were quickly kicked out and erased. They share a common thread with Sojourner Truth, another revolutionary woman, and just like her, Black women, women of color, queer women, trans women, disabled women, Muslim women, and so many others are still asking many of y'all, "Ain't I a woman?" So as we commit to build this movement of resistance and liberation, no one can be an afterthought anymore. We must hold each other in love and accountability . . .

Then, just before I hit the core of my speech, my voice stopped reverberating. Half of the audience's attention was diverted elsewhere. *What's going on?* I whipped my head toward the other side of the stage where an event organizer had been standing. I caught the tail end of her flashing "go ahead" gestures to another staffer. I quickly realized that my microphone had been cut! Panic, rage, uncertainty—I felt it all as I retreated from the podium and the stage.

As Momma and others tried to soothe me afterward, my mind raced for a solution. My immediate thought, as I absorbed social media posts inquiring about the abrupt end to my speech, was to call out the organizers in real time. But I didn't per the supportive and wise suggestion of author and activist Janet Mock. Because she was a Black trans woman in the media that I'd admired for years, I knew she was familiar with the resolve it took to control your own narrative. Her words reminded me that I didn't want to be in the position of being defined by or reduced to this humiliation. So I gleaned whatever lessons I could from the experience: that I needed to look more critically at the movements of which I was a part, that I needed to ensure that I wasn't relying too heavily on anyone else to platform my voice. Mostly, though, I never forgot the ordeal, I tucked it in my pocket. Whenever I was asked about the event for the next few years, I'd trap the disappointment behind a smile. Nodded whenever anyone mentioned how impressive it was that I'd been asked to speak. As with countless moments throughout my life, I resisted showing the cracks and being—as filmmaker and activist Tourmaline has said—*disrespectable*, that is intentionally centering my own desires over fitting others' expectations.

* * *

WHEN I STARTED writing *The Risk It Takes to Bloom: On Life and Liberation*, I set out to craft an irrefutable tome about my journey as a Black trans activist navigating progressive social justice movements. Imperceptibly, my fear of being disrespectable crept back up, placing a barrier between me and the page. However, family and friends reminded me that I'd need all the sides and fixin's for this story to resonate. That guidance sparked a grueling and therapeutic writing experience that required extending much more grace to myself and others. This process gave me permission to be angry, messy, solemn, unresolved, unrighteous, and unsure. It encouraged me to speak and write even when I didn't have the most flawless take. In fact, throughout this memoir, there are times when all I can do is ask questions with the hope that answers will find me at some other time.

A well-known short poem influenced the title *The Risk It Takes to Bloom*. I first heard it as a college freshman when Alicia Keys adapted and recited it for the opening of her fourth studio album, *The Element of Freedom*. I felt seen by the words. They transported me to my childhood, reminding me of the branches of a neighbor's Southern magnolia tree that sprawled over our wire fence. When I was out of sight, I'd pull off the velvety flowers and deeply inhale their scent. Sometimes I'd look at the still-closed buds that were more viridescent than porcelain. Like them, I longed for the ability to bloom, opening beautifully

and delicately beyond the social expectations that already stifled me.

While researching this poem, I learned it is often misattributed
to writer Anaïs Nin. However, Sky Blue Press, a key publisher of
Nin's works, agrees that Elizabeth Appell maintained a credible
claim to the poem in 2013. She'd produced evidence of crafting
the piece for a widely published John F. Kennedy University class
bulletin while serving as its director of public relations in 1979.
Later, the poem appeared on a widely distributed poster in San
Francisco through the Bay Area Rapid Transit system and journeyed further from the source for decades.

Beyond the title, Part I: Rooting is set in Augusta and Athens, Georgia, and delves into my attempts to honor my inner
voice regarding gender, race, and sexual orientation. Like many
in the LGBTQ+ community, isolation was a key feature of my
earliest years. Affirming and authentic narratives about gender-
nonconforming, queer, and transgender people eluded me. So
I hid my truth, trying to shred up any map that could lead me
back to it. In college, I instinctually gravitated toward others
whose unapologetically queer natures served as gateways to crucial epiphanies. Experiences of grief, ignorance, and uncertainty
seeped into the soil of my life, serving as fertilizer for growth.
This is when I most bloomed within.

Part II: Budding, Part III: Pruning, and Part IV: Blooming
couch the personal within the political, traversing my migra-
tions to Monroe and Atlanta, Georgia; Oakland, California; and
New York City. Upon graduating from the University of Georgia, I gained my professional footing with a rural newspaper reporter job. There I worked stealth, that is, closeted as a queer
trans woman. It wasn't until I moved to Atlanta and found others
in Atlanta's Black LGBTQ+ community that I became an organizer. Those formative organizing experiences fueled my thirst

for embracing authentic storytelling as a critical aspect of collective liberation. There is where I most bloomed beyond.

Each journey in my life has required an openness to the possibility of transformation. Death and tragedy, in particular, have most activated me, defining the hardest and inspiring the most hopeful moments. Throughout the book, I write "letters" to people whose earthly departures have most impacted my life and work. Unfortunately, I could not capture an exhaustive list of those losses. Still, the death of my father, Chester Willis Sr.; the killings of other Black people like Michael Brown, Trayvon Martin, Sandra Bland, George Floyd, Breonna Taylor, and Tony McDade; the suicides of trans teens like Leelah Alcorn and Blake Brockington; and the deaths of Black trans women like Islan Nettles, Chyna Gibson, Layleen Polanco, Dominique "Rem'mie" Fells, Riah Milton, and countless others forever changed me.

In this book, I share many of the moments that required taking the thrilling risk of listening to, trusting my convictions. It's often been daunting and seemingly impossible, but belief in myself and in better conditions has often given me opportunities to bloom. I hope my thoughts and words will encourage you to do the same.

PART I

Rooting

1

Four Blue Walls

I was five years old the last time I felt precious and pure, unencumbered by the restrictions of the world or my hometown of Augusta, Georgia. It was before the world began shouting at me to straighten up, walk differently, speak differently, *be* different. Then, I was just a child with light-brown, wannabe hazel eyes drawing attention with quiet wonder. On this April evening, the Windsor Spring Elementary School talent show coaxed this seedling from the earth. Onstage in front of a darkened crowd in a lunchroom that doubled as an auditorium, the spotlights shone as I confidently recited a monologue about what I could be when I grew up.

"And the crowd goes wiiiiiiiiiiiiild!" I screamed. In this hypothetical future, I might be a renowned basketball player who'd just made a game-winning shot. *Space Jam* had recently further cemented Michael Jordan as the main possibility model for little Black boys, so it felt apt. But I was nobody's athlete in real life. Fright was my natural reaction to objects hurled in my direction. Still, I attempted my best fake layup. Just before the ball whacked the floor, my sister, Jessica, caught it just out of sight backstage. She smiled, encouraging me to keep going. And I turned, realizing that the crowd was waiting for the next line. *How could all these people be listening to me?* As the soft-spoken youngest of three, I spent most of my time observing older folks' lives. I loved making sense of them, questioning the motives behind everything they did. I never fought to be heard at home because someone would inevitably address my needs before I ever had to say anything. The most I needed to do was nod.

My mother, Marilyn, panicked a bit when I brought home the event flyer from school. I can only imagine what she was thinking. After all, I wasn't some musical prodigy, nor did I fancy performing like the musicians I saw at any moment on MTV in the nineties. The most impressive thing I could do was ride a bike with no training wheels. Of course, that wasn't a stage-worthy talent. So, Jessica intervened, lending her Virgo insights to craft a concise script. She also cast herself as my mother in the opening and closing sequences. It wasn't the most outrageous idea. At twelve years my senior, Jessica was frequently mistaken as my mother when we ran errands, probably because she had a way of speaking that left little room for rebuttal. It didn't bother me because I revered her. She was the one who often shielded me from the teasing of my brother, Chet. Ever the goofball of the family, he showed his love in small, tender moments like when he cracked open Gobstoppers with his molars before I had my own. I loved them both, but I bonded more with Jessica. The connection was easier. I didn't feel like I was being tested, as if I had to prove something. Whatever she liked, I liked, and it was OK. Spending time with her practicing the monologue and nailing down the blocking was thrilling. Even though my wild mind kept me from meeting my sister's standards of perfection, I knew I could just look in the wings for support if I got stuck.

Looking out as the heads of strangers disappeared in the distance, I felt determined to deliver an excellent performance. Five minutes felt like forever, but a little voice in my head gave me a pep talk. "You can do this. It's easy." Jessica concocted a genius plan to lay out all the props, in order, on the folding table behind me to keep me on track. "Just go down the line. Throw the ball. Next is the briefcase. Okay, talk about the stethoscope." With just a glance at each item, the right words sprang into my mind, and my body followed the simple choreography associated with it. I rattled off lines about becoming an actor, athlete, lawyer, or pediatrician (as my paternal grandmother, Inez, wanted), and the illuminated grown-up faces in the front responded with mesmerized joy. I fed on the warmth of their affirmation. All I wanted to do was make everyone proud.

By the time Jessica and I received our final applause, I didn't want to leave the stage. I wanted this feeling that I was doing things right to stay, but I followed the hem of my sister's long, dark flowy church dress anyway. "You did great," she whispered through her bright, adrenaline-fueled smile. I beamed as the show host's voice resounded. With her hands on my shoulders, Jessica guided me to an opening in the back of the auditorium. Along the way, the men in the audience nodded, the women beamed, and a few kids pointed, having just realized I had been the source of the activity onstage. In the meantime, our family hustled from their seats to greet us, and I peered up at them as they gathered around.

"That was so good, Suga Plum," Momma said, bending her padded shoulders down to hug me and plant a sloppy kiss on my plump cheek. She swiped away the pigment she'd left with her thumb and stepped aside. Grandma Inez agreed, following the kiss protocol and engulfing me in a spicy cloud of her signature scent, Estée Lauder Youth-Dew. In his baseball team uniform, Chet hugged me and pinched a little too hard as he said, "Good job, bro." If annoying me was an art, he had perfected it. But I didn't dare do more than wince as he pulled the skin on my arm, because I knew I'd lose out on the validation that was coming. With a smirk, my father, Chester, shot out his hand as if we were in a business meeting. "That's my little man," his gruff voice boomed, and my tiny fingers disappeared in his firm, rough handshake. There's no trophy, no evidence, no nothing that I won the talent show that night, but I always felt like I did.

* * *

WHEN I WAS young, so much seemed to revolve around me in our family. It was most noticeable during holidays and birthdays. By the time I was old enough to remember them, my siblings were teenagers, as invested in keeping the magic alive for me as our parents. We were something like the Huxtables from *The Cosby Show*, albeit steeped in Southernness and seared in Roman Catholicism. Of course, I was Rudy with all eyes on me, because my parents had me so much later than my siblings. Chet, the nearest in age, was nine years older, and for years I was the youngest on both sides of my family. Momma swore that my birth was not the result of an accidental pregnancy. She prided herself on remembering that she and Dad conceived me during the sticky summer of the 1990 Devoe Family Reunion. Then, she'd claim she wanted another child after me, but I "broke the mold." Did that mean I was special or too much to handle?

Often relatives on my dad's side described my birth as transformational for him and Grandma Inez. They would whisper about their alcoholism, claiming they were capable of such bouts of belligerence that folks would count down until the festivities ended. On more than one occasion, my birth was described as if I'd performed some Jesus-like miracle I couldn't remember. I experienced just a bit of Dad's vice-fueled era in the stacks of old Heineken and Budweiser boxes used for storage and the cigarette butts that often littered the floor of his crimson Ford F-150. I don't think my grandma, a retired medical technician, ever stopped drinking, but she lessened the frequency. Sometimes I'd be seated in the back of her car as she drove to a nearby liquor store. After pulling up to a window 'round back, she'd exchange a few words with an older gentleman, then grab a brown paper bag like it was a McDonald's Happy Meal. Neither Grandma nor Dad ever directly spoke of this aspect of their lives. It lived in asides and murmurs like many of their other similarities.

While my parents forged their professional lives, Grandma Inez served as a third parent to me. She'd pick me up from the bus stop every day in elementary school while my siblings delivered on their extracurricular-laden schedules. Hours later, Dad would pick me up and they'd exchange small talk while I zipped up my backpack. Grandma might complain about something she'd watched on CNN that inspired her to exclaim, "Aww, hell," and Dad might chastise her about some safety hazard in her house. There was love between them, but I always sensed Dad tense up during these quick exchanges. They never spoke about why he went off to live with his grandparents for most of his formative years. The most I heard was that Grandma was a hot commodity and a spitfire in her youth. Dad said an uncle had nicknamed "Spider" for the way she ensnared boys, and later men, in her web. Older relatives gushed with astonishment at how her beauty turned the heads of Black and white men in a time when Black beauty was even more stigmatized. It wasn't surprising to me because I'd seen her woo them at the bank and the grocery store with just a few words. In their presence, she'd flaunt her café au lait complexion, immaculately applied cosmetics, and adopt a Southern debutante lilt that could easily turn into a foul-mouthed drawl once they were out of earshot.

Life had demanded an unexpected ferocity from our petite

matriarch. She was the oldest of four children born during the Great Depression. In her late teens, she married my grandfather and they moved to Brooklyn, prompted by his work for a railroad company. She told every story of this time matter-of-factly, including the loss of her youngest sister, who was twelve years old, to pneumonia. That same year, in 1953, Grandma gave birth to Dad. And Auntie Robyn came into this world not long after. Somewhere in there, the small family moved back to Augusta and my grandparents separated for reasons that were never fully explained. But this is where extended family became crucial in raising the kids.

* * *

DAD EMERGED AS a golden child to his relatives. As the first-born, he benefited from the patriarchy when boys were even more openly prized. This allowed him to be, in his own words, mischievous and rambunctious. But the aged version I knew, a railroad dispatcher turned risk management inspector for the local government, was often tight-lipped, with a furrowed brow and a dark mustache speckled with silvery strands. He was a serious man who didn't have to say anything for you to know that he was in control and had a particular way of seeing the world. A deep thinker, he always read books about religion or philosophy before his nightly slumber. There seemed to be a vibrant world underneath his often solemn demeanor that he refused to give away in more than spurts. From my earliest years, I felt him analyzing me. Dad would scold Momma for "babying" me, his earliest crusade against my burgeoning "softness." I'd have to "pick up" my feet whenever I wasn't walking fast enough or with perceived purpose. He'd also monitor my responses to other adults, ensuring they were a particular brand of clear and confident demanded of Black men in the United States. Dad's corrections were out of love, serving as stakes in cruel earth to guide my otherwise aimless growth. I didn't quite know what I was supposed to fear; in fact, it seemed like I was a threat to myself. He claimed his main lot in life was to make sure I grew up to be a smart, strong, and successful man who could take care of his family. His father and namesake, who died three years before I was born, was nothing like that, or so I heard. He was absent from my father's and aunt's lives after separating from Grandma Inez. All I knew was that he ultimately remarried and had another son.

After the split, some of Dad's earliest years were spent staying with Grandma in various housing projects. Then, he went to live with my great-grandparents Novella and Clarence in their shot-gun house on downtown Augusta's Luckey Street. He described them as "his life" and the reason he became the man he did. They were humble hard workers who ensured Dad had everything he needed. Papa Clarence died before I was born, and Grandma No's life span overlapped mine by about three years. Dad de-scribed the former as a hunter, fisherman, and, most of all, Clark Gable's twin. As a manual laborer who couldn't read or write, Papa Clarence made do with signing an X for any official busi-ness. He relied on other forms of intelligence. Whenever Dad took Chet and me fishing, he'd remind us he learned everything he knew about nature from his grandfather. Grandma No, on the other hand, was the crown jewel of the family. Whenever older relatives talked about her, they lit up as if her sparkling spirit had just sauntered into the room. She was a seamstress and dry cleaner who made sure Dad wore immaculately pressed clothing when he attended the local Catholic school, described as the best education for Negro children in Richmond County his heyday.

Dad's school image was a far cry from life at home as "Butch." He would reminisce about running around the neighborhood barefoot, dodging shards of glass with a ragtag crew of friends dubbed the "Children of the Ditch." Love surrounded him in the adjacent houses on Luckey Street where aunts and uncles lived. They'd come together at Grandma No and Papa Clarence's nexus of a home to congregate for meals, play Spades, and drink illegal whiskey that they called *scrap iron*. But it wasn't all gravy. They draped a comical lens and idyllic nostalgia over instances of domestic abuse and infidelity in scattered stories. But overall, Dad fashioned himself into a generational bridge between their wisdom and his children's potential. He described his formative years as free from the constraints of the world, so much so that he claimed to not know that his family wasn't wealthy until he went off to Morris Brown College (MBC) in Atlanta, Georgia, where he met Momma.

The second of four girls, Momma was born in Jacksonville, Florida, to two grade-school educators, Grandma Ida and Granddaddy Marion. The latter, an army veteran, died a few months before my third birthday in a tragic countryside house fire. I don't remember him, but I have many memories of Grandma Ida. Most summers, our family would hop into my mom's teal Oldsmobile sedan, my siblings would blast Outkast in the car's cassette player, and we'd travel to see her. Grandma would plead to keep her grandkids for the summer, so we could steal away to theme parks like Busch Gardens and Universal Studios. One time, her synthetic churchy wig flew off during a roller-coaster ride. We couldn't help but chuckle, but she didn't stress, as if it happened all the time.

Momma had a similar way of warding off difficult moments. Ever cheery and encouraging, she always stressed family, volunteerism, and "making the grade." She was pretty low-key as a kid, often allowing Auntie Thelma, her brazen older sister by eleven months and twenty-three days, to take the lead. Those two were particularly close, seeing their selves as the calmer, more mature foils to their younger sisters. But as a unit they were known as the Devoe Girls, and I took pride in carrying on Momma's maiden name as my middle one. Her side of the family held the Devoe history close, ensuring we were able to trace our heritage back as far as possible. Thanks to their diligence, I grew up knowing about Isaac Devoe Sr., one of our first enslaved ancestors, who started a sprawling line of descendants.

There were so many Devoes that I couldn't keep our extended relatives' names straight at our annual reunions. Barnwell, South Carolina, the origin of my maternal lineages, was a recurring site every few years, but typically reunions were held in different locations by different relatives every year. What rarely changed was the schedule: a kickoff fish fry with older relatives playing card games and frolicking little cousins; a formal banquet where my mom and her sisters sang a stirring selection and others would share milestones that their families had achieved that year; and a Sunday service presided over by one of several Protestant pastors in our bloodline. The latter would induce anxiety because of its differing rituals and hymns than the ones I was accustomed to in Catholic church. The gospel numbers, remixed with hoots and hollas from elders, were always a refreshing reprieve from the Gregorian chants I'd hear in the front pew of our masses. And the saving grace of the longer Protestant services were the repasts. My eyes would dilate as aunties piled Styrofoam plates with heaps of the crispiest fried chicken imaginable, golden cornbread, macaroni and cheese, and savory collard greens with ham hocks. Of course, they could never hold a candle to Momma's soul food extravaganzas back home. But whew, chiiile! I'd leave our reunions feeling cut off from the Black church experience, wondering if our family was returning to the wrong denomination when we went home. At St. Joseph's Catholic Church, we were one of only a few Black families (most others had migrated from West Africa) surrounded by white folks. But I didn't press my parents with these concerns. I reserved my energy for the big ones, like "How do you know God is real?" and "How do we know our religion is the right one?"

Though I had my doubts, I admired Momma's steadfastness. Her faith blew past Dad's and she was single-handedly why our family sat in the front pew every Sunday. Momma converted to the Catholic denomination upon marrying Dad, living up to one of her favorite mantras, "The family that prays together, stays together." By the nineties, she was about as close to a saint as a Southern Black woman could have been. Grandma Inez even nicknamed her "Sister Mary" for her commitment to community service and religion. Every Sunday, much to the disappointment of my dad's grumbling stomach, she'd talk to what seemed like everyone in our congregation, including the priest and deacons, who revered her immensely.

Everything Momma did was covered in a sheen of excellence, including her ambitious professional life. She'd finished a specialist degree in education while pregnant with me, then earned a doctorate at the University of Georgia. For years, she'd taught business and office technology at the local technical school before becoming director of the institution's adult literacy program. Anytime we went to Walmart or the mall we'd see one of her former students. "Dr. Willis! Dr. Willis!" they'd exclaim, and she'd deftly extoll advice for the next stage of their careers. She was the epitome of a boss, a quality that shone through long before she met my father.

As a teenager, Momma found a love for playing the flute and flexed those skills for a band scholarship to MBC. This determination bucked against Granddaddy Marion's desire for her to go to school in her hometown, and in college she spread her wings.

It became clear that education would be her route toward fufill-ment and upward mobility. Besides winter and spring band du-ties, she also became a majorette during football season. Every few years, she'd pull out photos of her in shimmering, fringed bodysuits with her bright, magazine-worthy smile. Some of those photos featured my dad as her escort when she was sashed as first runner-up for Miss MBC 1978, the college's homecoming pageant. Just a few months after that, my mother graduated and married my father. She swears she didn't know for sure that she was ready to be a wife, but she couldn't think of a concrete reason to decline the man she loved. The following year, they'd add my sister to the Willis family portrait, then my brother, and after that noticeable pause, me.

My baby boomer parents' lives revolved around raising well-adjusted children. Their script required heeding what they taught us until we left their home. Then, a particular future would un-fold including college, a career, marriage, a house, and children. It seemed easy to accomplish. After all, our middle-class family had it pretty cushy. There was never a worry about not having food or healthcare or somewhere to live, nor any worries that we'd run out of unique outfits to wear to school each day or that anything could threaten our familial unit. God had blessed us. All I needed to do was measure up to my parents', and even more so my dad's, expectations. But the summer that I turned six, something changed.

* * *

WEEKS AFTER THE talent show, when school hadn't quite let out for the season, my parents decided it was OK to go home with another family in our cul-de-sac. Usually Grandma Inez picked me up from the bus stop but this time she had a doctor's ap-pointment. Our neighborhood was full of kids near my age, but

I was closest to Jerry Dobson and his brothers. He was almost exactly a year younger than me, and I knew we were best friends the day we both agreed to take the training wheels off our first bicycles. We sprinted to our respective fathers, asking them to help us. Mine couldn't contain his pride, pulling out his ol' well-worn toolbox from the rusted brown shed in our backyard. After Jerry rode back to my house to show off his accomplishment, we became, as adults always said, "like two peas in a pod." During the summer, we darted all over our lush green neighborhood. I loved our breaks between adventures, especially when I could inhale the magnolia blooms that reached over a fence separating my family's backyard from some other neighbors. Of course, I'd never say that. I was already aware that flowers were forbidden, like Barbies or the color pink. Being rough-and-tumble, having chlorophyll-stained shorts, and taking on outside odors was how I was supposed to bond with the other boys.

Jerry and his older brothers, Jamal and Joshua, had lost their parents at a young age and lived with their aunt and uncle. Dad encouraged our camaraderie, seeing the care and love that emanated from their home. Portly and jovial Joshua was a year older than me. He'd been held back a grade, which often made him the butt of jokes. Other kids, sometimes even his brothers, would make fun of his belly and intellect. It always felt wrong when I heard the insults. But when he'd tease me, I'd regurgitate what other kids said. Jamal was three years older than me. His slender, leggy frame intimidated most other kids when he stared down at them as they played basketball. As the eldest of our bunch, he often asserted his power to decide our activities for the day. Today would be no different.

After the bus dropped us off from school, their uncle corralled us into the back of his enormous black Ford F-150. He was a man of few words, but always nice. Their aunt took the lead in disciplining the boys, so things always felt smoother around him. As the wind blasted our faces, I threw my head back as the boys squealed about Pokémon and our forthcoming after-school snacks. When we arrived in their driveway, their uncle let down the truck's hatch, and we all maneuvered off the hot metal. I looked over at my family's beige and bricked two-story home, feeling the weirdness of having no keys to enter it. Nevertheless, Jerry and I followed his uncle inside as the older boys lingered in the sun. After we grabbed crinkling bags of sweetness, we ran back to the front porch.

"Man, stop it," Joshua screamed in between chuckles.

"Nope, I gotcha now," Jamal said.

"What y'all doin'?" Jerry jabbered as we blasted through their storm door.

Before we even heard a response, Jamal turned his comical ire toward us. He took the long, serpentine water hose in the front yard and spritzed us, strengthening the pressure of the stream with an attachment. We yelled at him to stop as we ran off the porch to hide behind a big spiked-leaf bush. As Jerry and I huddled for cover, we heard Jamal's comeuppance when Joshua took a longer hose from the other side of the house and avenged us. As Jerry and I guffawed at Jamal's drenched school uniform, they teamed up and sprayed us. The cool water on our hot skin was refreshing but still elicited squeals. Then, a woman's voice halted our laughter.

"Why is the water on?" their aunt said, daring Jamal and Joshua to explain.

She crossed her sturdy arms and watched as the older boys hung their heads and scrambled to turn off the hoses.

"Look at y'all," she said before turning to me. "And you got this baby wet, too? Y'all go in the house and change now. And get him some clothes, too."

Mrs. Dobson smacked Jamal on the head and chastised him for being "the oldest with the least amount of sense." Joshua flinched, but she didn't repeat the punishment with him. Jerry and I just followed them to the back of the house, where all the bedrooms and the laundry room were located. "Y'all just put ya clothes near the dryer," their aunt said from the front, before returning to a phone call interrupted by our shenanigans. "I'm gon' wash and dry them in a minute." The boys thought nothing of stripping down to their bare bottoms, but nudity wasn't as common at my house. By now, when my parents ran my bath-water, they would leave the room and give me privacy. They trusted I knew how to wash up well, asking me if I'd hit all the crucial areas when they'd return. But here it was different. The boys seemed unfazed, so I followed suit. As I held on to the wall of their narrow hallway and pulled off my underwear, I resisted the urge to cover myself. Then, I followed them into their aunt and uncle's bedroom, realizing I had never been in that part of the house. We congregated in front of the large king-sized bed that reminded me of my parents'. Then, Jamal gathered a few dry tighty-whities from a pile of unfolded laundry and he threw them at his brothers before nudging a pair into my chest. I felt his warm hand linger and graze my nipple. He had a glint in his eyes that I had never seen. A different kind of noticing. I pulled on the new pair of underwear as the younger brothers ran to their aunt's vanity, making silly faces at one another through the mirror.

As I looked at my new bland underwear, I resisted frowning. I was used to colorful boxers with cartoon characters like the Teenage Mutant Ninja Turtles or Spider-Man. But Jamal interrupted my mind when he pulled me close and held my face before directing me to the floor beside him. There, he pressed against me and pecked me. "Ew," Joshua said, looking at us through the mirror. Jerry just watched. "Shut up," Jamal said as he turned back to me and held me close. The other boys went back to horsing around. We started hunchin', as older women in the South say. As our private areas pressed into each other, I didn't know what was happening, but some of me enjoyed it. Minutes later, we heard the swift pacing of their aunt as she approached our side of the house. Jamal snatched away and the moment vanished. Whatever had been going on, he must've known she would disapprove.

When my clothes were ready, their aunt directed Jamal to pull them of the dryer. He handed them to me, and I threw them on. I tried to avert eye contact with Jamal, seeing him in a way that warmed my cheeks now. Later, when my dad picked me up and walked me home, I wiped my mind of the encounter. I knew he wouldn't approve and that I could never say anything. After all, he'd chastised Momma for simply cuddling with me, and I knew he would ensure I never saw my friends again. So, I kept quiet while Jamal's advances continued over the next few years. We graduated to deeper explorations of each others' bodies, mimicking the adults in movie scenes. I didn't protest them but I did feel guilt after each encounter. With few words, I'd run to our upstairs bathroom and shove a translucent yellow bar of Dial soap in my mouth. As the astringent taste floated over my tongue, I'd think of older Southern folks' threat for when kids cursed. Perhaps I was punishing myself, yearning for a balm to save me from whatever sinfulness that was hurtling toward me. But I was never saved. In fact, I developed crushes on other boys in classes, wondering if they'd ever feel the same way about me as Jamal did. I knew this thing had to be a secret for as long as I could muster.

* * *

OVER THE NEXT few years, my inner world expanded, and I ran away from the masculine expectations of everyone around me. My peers became more beholden to the gender binary, while I secretly identified with an undefined space. A bubble burst and I gravitated even more toward girls. Other boys would comment on my nonconforming essence. They called me out for being too feminine and referred to me as "gay" or "just like a girl," fulfilling their role as some kind of alpha police. They sized me up as if they had some rulebook that I didn't. In time, I felt a similar distance grow between me and the Dobson brothers, who were on a similar track as our male peers. When a new boy, Harold, moved into our neighborhood, he fractured my friendship with Jerry. He'd bombard me with questions like "Why you talk like that?" and "Why you always rollin' your eyes like a girl?" in front of other kids to humiliate me. It ruffled me every time he spat out his assertions. He was relentless, and no one, not even Jerry, ever stuck up for me. All the inside jokes and memories became awkward silences whenever I saw any of them. I began to see friends, and all relationships, as fragile, as things that could easily be shattered once people saw too much of me. *Would my family turn on me if they knew my secret too?*

I carved out spaces of survival. I'd dress up in outlandish outfits cobbled from piles of my siblings' clothes, sometimes winding a towel around my head to simulate luscious Pantene commericial strands. In solitude, I'd sneak in and explore my mom's vanity, apply an expired concealer and a raspberry rouge on my face. My heart would accelerate, praying my parents wouldn't catch me in this pastime. I wanted the feeling of the soft kabuki brushes pressed into my cheeks, of being pretty despite being told by the world that it was impossible. Sometimes my mom saw me studying her makeup application technique, but she never reprimanded me. She just went about her business with an unspoken rule that my father couldn't see me like that. She'd give a look like, "You know I love you, but your dad is different."

The closest thing I'd have to a beauty ritual was going to the barbershop every two weeks. There, in air scented with the anti-septic smell of aftershave and the surveilling presence of masculinity, I hoped the boys and men wouldn't discover that I was an imposter. So, I hatched a plan, convincing my dad to let me grow out an afro, lying that I wanted to emulate seventies aesthetic from photos of his youth. I figured it would mean fewer visits to that dreaded place and was my route to having longer hair despite not being relaxed like all of the girls and women I knew. I could at least break the binary in my own way, differentiating myself from other Black boys who had the customary Caesar cuts.

Unknowingly, reclaiming my hair expanded beyond gender. That afro signaled something about Blackness and respectability too. I'd taken stock of what happened when my siblings unwittingly brushed up against those things as well. They came up in moments like when Grandma Inez commented on my brother's hair, claiming it was too unruly. She called it "Can'tcha don'tcha hair," meaning "Can't do nothin' with it and don't wanna try." My brother and I shared the same texture that beaded up without ample grease and coaxing by boar-bristled brushes. On another occasion, Grandma once drunkenly referred to my brother and me as her "white" grandkids because we were lighter skinned and my sister as her "Black" granddaughter because she was darker skinned. Of course, this was after I'd come to expect her to chastise me for being out in the sun too long during the summer. Witnessing my siblings endure these slights with no rebuttal made me certain that my seemingly untouchable position would eventually become threatened too.

I knew this thing that made me different, got me called "girly" and "gay," was essential and wasn't going anywhere. Some nights I tried to pray my queerness away. I'd lay in bed, staring at the cerulean ceiling. It was a hue chosen by Chet. I wondered if I'd ever be normal like him. As the family's athlete, my father adored that he excelled in football, tennis, and wrestling. But that wasn't my path. I wanted to know: *Why couldn't God just make me a girl? If I prayed enough, could I wake up to a world that made sense, a world that regarded me as who I knew myself to be? Or would I forever be a dormant sprout in a field of expectations?* My life felt like a dream sequence. I became certain that freedom lay far beyond the confines of Augusta, my neighborhood, my school, my house, and the four blue walls where everyone saw me as a boy.

2

My Interior World

The stray oily droplets of Luster's Pink Sheen Spray hitting my forehead usually annoyed me, but today I simply wiped them off. I couldn't help but beam as I shaped my voluminous 'fro in the mirror. By now it had become a part of my identity, and my parents and grandma had come around to it. I'd gotten my daily ritual down, so it'd be perfectly round for school. But despite all the labor I put in each morning, there was little love for my natural hair here in the early 2000s. "Black is beautiful" had all but died decades ago, giving way to the Jheri curl fever of the 1980s. Thank God I missed living through those years. Still, kinky coils were rarely given their glory, acceptable only if tamed by a strong chemical or some other hairstyle. But at Davidson Fine Arts Magnet School (DFA), I knew there were a few other boys who wore their hair a similar way and I hoped that signaled the acceptance I'd find at the school too.

After years of asking, Dad had finally let me attend DFA, which was known as the "gay, artsy" school. Of course, he didn't know why I wanted to go so badly. But its queerness was city-wide lore among students. So much so that at the end of the previous school year, a vile group of popular kids stole my yearbook from a friend and scrawled that they hoped I found "a lot of boyfriends at my new school." Honestly, I did too. But when I saw my secret in writing, I teared up. Reprieve came after I angrily crossed the comment out with a black Sharpie and refused to let anyone else sign it. I didn't need any more witnesses to my humiliation.

Eighth grade, however, was my chance for a fresh start, and I was determined to eliminate every blemish on my face and in how I performed masculinity. For some ridiculous reason, I thought my use of concealer wouldn't completely undermine this goal. So, after checking to see if Dad was downstairs, I gently dabbed the applicator on the collection of recent acne scars on my chin. *It wasn't gay to wear makeup if it was for a purpose, right?* And if any knowing girls asserted that my flawless skin resulted from anything but genetics, I'd denounce it swiftly. This was as far as I could push to feel beautiful.

By my preteen years, I knew my queerness wasn't going away. My sexuality and gender had collapsed into one general experience of otherness. I was waiting for something— anything—to straighten me out and make the differences click. Then, puberty struck during my thirteenth summer. My body became foreign when the women in my life acknowledged the transformation. "You 'round here smellin' like a man now," Grandma Inez said. She insisted that Tussy, her preferred roll-on deodorant, was the antidote to the new odor emanating from my body. Sometime around then, Momma gushed over how my once-high-pitched androgynous voice had grown deeper and how her "baby" was growing up. She looked at me with such pride while I tried to hide my disgust. I liked the idea of getting older, but the thought of becoming a man frightened me. I knew if I didn't feign excitement enough that I'd be scrutinized. So, I tried to take advantage of the changes. I sank into an even lower register to mask my gay twang and squared my shoulders more, hoping to appear what society told me was normal.

My parents were oblivious to the years of bullying I had experienced, which included such highlights as the first-grade debacle wherein boys ripped up my Sailor Moon drawings and in fourth grade when a colossal boy flipped over a desk and threatened to attack me for defending myself against his months-long taunting. All Momma and Dad knew was that I made solid grades in school and that I struggled to maintain a high conduct score. Teachers just chalked it up to my talkative nature, never mentioning the teasing I endured in classes. They had to have seen it happening, but the most they'd do was half-heartedly command my bullies to cut it out before going about their business.

After I tested well and made it into my first magnet school in fifth grade, my friendships with the neighborhood boys shriveled up. Harold planted the idea that I thought I was better than them because I went to a "smart" school, and the jokes about my "effeminate" nature continued. At the school, a group of boys mostly teased me from afar at recess. I endured it, never wanting to appear weak. If they sensed my emotions, they'd only double down on their efforts. I'd daydream about concocting the perfect comeback to shut them down for good, laying the foundation for a coping mechanism drenched in sarcasm. I wasn't completely ostracized, though. Being somewhat sociable allowed me to form short-lived connections with other students who were usually outcasts in their own way too. That was the only release I had because I refused to tell my parents about how difficult my life felt. I knew if my dad found out I was being bullied, he'd ask me what I'd done to draw attention to myself. Then, he'd try even harder to correct who I was becoming.

* * *

On my first day at DFA, I was determined to keep a low profile and try to blend in. It was going to be an uphill battle, though. Most students started attending the school in sixth grade and were accepted as a particular cohort grew older and marched toward high school graduation. That year I was one of eight new students in our grade. I learned from brief exchanges that everyone kept a running tab on the newbies. I was awestruck by the independence that middle schoolers enjoyed. It was the first time I'd had my own personalized class schedule, locker, and rotating rosters of fellow students. My first real conversations of the day came at lunch. I tried to settle in with a gang of boys who were in my class in the prior period. A few were trying to figure me out with narrowed eyes. I imagined them thinking, "Is that the gay nigga from CTW? Nah, he can't really be gay." They drowned themselves in oversized shirts and jeans that reminded me of the Ying Yang Twins. To fit in, I quickly untucked the leftover white polo from my old school's uniform. Style was never something I'd thought about before that moment. While I had a handle on my face and hair, Dad decided what I wore and how I wore it. That would have to change, but for now I observed my male peers. I saw how their conversations all seemed to hinge on one boy's words. Nelson was short, stocky, and darker-skinned, with cornrows, a slightly raspy voice for his age, and impeccably clean New Balances. Whenever he directed his group's attention to anything, be it a girl he found attractive or another student he saw as his entertainment, they followed the target like a pack of lions. And I did not want to be on the receiving end of their feasting eyes.

I spent most of my first few months trying to blend in with Nelson's court of jesters, determined to ride out the masculine script and survive until my high school graduation. Part actor, part anthropologist, I tried to pick up on their interests and speaking patterns (short answers, limited expressions, deep grunts). I feigned excitement when they spoke on the hallmarks of their lives: the current NBA season, exclusive sneakers, or the latest mixtape. But it all became exhausting after a time, and I grew quieter. Nelson noticed this and turned his cutting tongue on me during our lunch periods. But I wasn't alone. He hazed all the boys in the group and rarely did anyone return the energy. The others just hung their heads until he went on to his next target. I found the dynamic especially suffocating. It reminded me of all those boys who had teased me when I was younger, of Harold, of what I thought the Dobson brothers thought of me, of what my father and brother might think if they even suspected my secret.

It didn't take long to realize that changing schools hadn't resulted in the fresh start I'd anticipated. So, I found another outlet. At home on the clunky desktop computer my mom handed down to me, I read forums where teens plotted their "coming out" journeys. The Internet had been a regular fixture since I was young. I'd glue my eyes to Momma's every keystroke and mouse glide as she graded and edited her students' papers. With my siblings away at their respective colleges, I had embraced this hidden digital world where my identity wasn't so weird. I felt like a thirteen-year-old spy meeting faceless peers from around the world through my illuminated screen. A Yahoo! chat room labeled LGBT became a safe haven. I once met this boy named Tanner from Nebraska. He claimed to be a little older than me, and for months we confided in each other about our dreams and fears. He was bisexual, played baseball, and seemed conventional in ways that I was not. I imagined him having a smoother time coming out than I ever could. Eventually, we sent each other our latest school photos to verify what we looked like. He had a mop of dirty-blond hair and a big, toothy smile. He told me I looked sexy in mine, and I returned the compliment. I had never told a boy that before, but it felt right. I dreamed of hopping on a train in the middle of the night. With my makeshift handkerchief bag full of essentials hanging on a long stick like the wanderers in old *Looney Tunes* shorts, I'd make it to his town early in the morning. After meeting him and sharing a nineties rom-com embrace, I'd have my first real kiss in years. But soon, I was back in my bedroom, excited just to have this fractured fantasy.

These online experiences made up for not having queer community in real life. As I talked more to gay kids and read their stories, I stopped beating myself up over my queerness. It was the first time I'd considered myself a part of a larger LGBTQ+ community. Here I didn't have to worry about being judged and I could be more myself than at school. At any given time, there was an endless conversation about celebrity crushes. I'd throw mentions of Usher's and Nelly's abs into the mix while stanning Janet Jackson and Ashanti as epitomes of bold, sensual femininity. The desire to integrate this freedom of expression into my everyday life grew. But just as this certainty swelled within me, religion consumed my prospects.

* * *

IF CATHOLICISM HAD a menu for its essential sacraments, its standard three courses would include a baptism, a first Holy Communion, and a Confirmation. The latter is described as the process by which a "faithful" person becomes "fully sealed by the Holy Spirit." It can happen anytime between the ages of seven and sixteen. Within our diocese, that is the region overseen by our bishop, confirmation happened around fourteen. My parents, who jointly taught the preparation class for the process, said it was a prerequisite for adulthood and a grand commitment to adhere to Catholicism for the rest of my life. I knew what the Church thought of me and of the national debates brewing around "gay" marriage. While our home priest never discussed politics in a partisan way, we had a deacon and traveling pastors who did. As I shuffled in the front pew, they'd rail on about protecting the "sanctity of marriage" in their sermons, invoking the concerted conservative push to reserve the right solely for heterosexual couples. Even the liberal politicians, the ones I had learned were supposed to be on the side of progress, refused to acknowledge LGBTQ+ people as legitimate. Between religion and politics, I developed a healthy skepticism of institutions. Everyone claimed to be trying to save somebody like me, but their words and actions consistently showed me otherwise.

Around that time, I was obsessed with making sense of my identity. If I could just build the perfect argument, then maybe my parents, society, and the world would understand me. I rummaged through my dad's books, squaring in on the Catholic Church's catechism and psychology materials from his master's in education program. The former spelled out how homosexual acts were "contrary to natural law" and constituted depravity. It urged gay people to move closer to being "perfect Christians" by taking a vow of chastity. The latter tomes described homosexual attractions as natural, offering brief insights on their origins. They clarified for me that, much like masculinity and straightness, getting Catholicism "right" was impossible. But I wondered where my parents had settled their thoughts. They said nothing about gay people, so I didn't know how they would feel when I inevitably came out. If I ever wanted to tell them my truth, I couldn't escape Confirmation no matter how much my heart told me it was against my values. Imagine me as the sole student in my cohort to reject the process. My parents would have been mortified. So I put on my best poker face that semester, even helping them prepare the room for their Sunday morning classes.

A few weeks into the Confirmation schedule, a dark-haired, freckled boy named Barry and his family started attending our church. Momma urged his father to enroll him in time to still be eligible for the ceremony in spring. In class, Barry was the ultimate jokester but, otherwise, he heeded my parents' direction. I'd eavesdrop on my parents' conversations with his and they cast him as a bit of a troublemaker. In fact, they always escorted him from class to mass, keeping tabs on whether he paid attention and did the assignments. One day, when our parents were chatting, he started helping me put away the supplies of his own accord. I didn't expect this, given what I'd heard about him, but I found the gesture nice. And from then on, I paid more attention to his sly, gray eyes and charming smile.

Barry and I grew closer during these moments. Like me, he could be blunt as hell and we bonded over not being "super-religious" types like some of our peers. He ribbed me about having such holy parents and being the biggest heathen in the class. But I got my licks back because his parents had forced him to go to a private Christian school. I always wanted to know why his family had moved and restarted their lives, but I feared offending him. In time, he confided in me about his manic depression, swearing that if he was ever rude, he didn't mean it. I swatted away the suggestion, finding his authenticity and vulnerability refreshing. I wished I could embrace myself like he did.

Months into our friendship, Momma and some other church parents took a group of us to the National Catholic Youth Conference. It was the first time I'd ever heard of it, but apparently it was a big deal because it was being hosted in Atlanta. I tried to keep an open mind. Besides, I knew I'd have fun with Barry. By now, there were weeks when I couldn't wait to see him after our Confirmation class. He seemed excited to see me each time too. My crush only deepened on our trip because we spent the entire weekend attached at the hips. We'd throw knowing glances to each other in between the contemporary Christian performances and aimless sermons in the arena full of thousands of God-fearing youth and the adults in their lives. When the chaperones were out of sight, he'd joke about us being boyfriends because of our closeness. He'd try to hold my hand, making a whole bit of it in front of the other students. They all just laughed, like it was the most impossible thing for two boys to be into each other. I pretended to be annoyed by his overtures, but I wondered if he really did like me.

After the conference ended, he got in the car with my mom and me for the two-hour drive back to Augusta. The entire way home, I wondered what would happen if I tried to hold his hand without an audience. But I thought better of it, fearing Momma would catch us in the rearview mirror. Still, a desire to tell him, not unlike the one to come out, swelled inside me. What if I just told him I liked him? Would he stop being my friend if he was actually straight? What if he told everyone I'm gay? When we arrived at his house, just the glimmer of a porch light greeted us. I hopped out to help him with his bag as Momma waited.

"This was fun after all," I said.

"Yeah," he said.

"Well, I'll see you next Sunday," I stammered.

"Yeah, you will," he said, as he hiked his duffel bag up on his shoulder and slammed the trunk down.

This regretful scene replayed in my head for days. *Did I miss my chance to have an actual boyfriend? Should I have been braver and kissed him right on the spot?* After that trip came the holiday season, so we saw each other less and less. And, in typical teenage fashion, my crush energy moved on to some other boy.

*   *   *

WEEKS BEFORE OUR Confirmation ceremony, my parents hosted a day-long preparatory retreat for it. They gave us a break after a few hours of quizzing on questions the bishop might ask, like "What are the fruits of the Holy Spirit?" A group of us walked outside, hoping a few moments of sun and fresh air would make it feel like our Saturday hadn't been stolen from us. As we congregated on the stone benches in our windbreakers, I talked with one group of classmates while Barry talked to another. He'd grown closer to his Christian school friends, but I figured we were still cool. I caught him looking at me as he whispered to a few kids near him. They giggled, then a girl with frizzy auburn curls said, "Oh my God," then whipped her head around when she noticed me watching. The kids at my table looked in their direction, and he squared in on me. "What?" I asked, genuinely wanting to laugh too. "Oh, nothing," he responded, eyes narrowing. A wickedness dripped off the response. Before I could inquire again, my dad called us back to the classroom. As we all got up, he stared and sang, "Baa, baa, Black sheep, have you any wool?" and a chorus of laughter sprang from the crew around him. It stupefied me for a second, then I understood the "Black" part of the chant to be about my skin and "wool" to be about my hair. *Wait, this is racism*, I thought. *Great!* I had unlocked a new level of bullying. As we took our seats inside the church building, I seethed. *How could someone I'd seen as a friend, a crush even, treat me like that? Were all the white people I'd ever known capable of this?* It became clear that being gay wasn't the only thing that made me a target.

My Blackness had always been a given. I never struggled with it or wished I was some other ethnicity or race. Nor did I revel in any deep pride about it. I saw reflections of it in my family (nuclear and extended), friends, neighbors, and the wider community. But my Blackness often felt secondary to class, education, and even religion. My window to Black history started with the morsels that Grandma Inez shared about distant relatives who left the South to "pass for white" elsewhere (California or New York) or found new opportunities overseas (France) in the early twentieth century. Our family never saw some of them ever again, but they presented their departure with pride. It seemed noble that they dreamed of lives beyond the social constraints of the day. Beyond those stories, my parents and siblings imparted our Blackness through what we listened to and watched. Whether it was playing Stevie Wonder's "I Wish" and Prince's greatest hits or watching *Family Matters*, *Living Single*, and *Martin*, and religiously, there was a beautiful intergenerational immersion. But at this point in the 2000s, difficulties were framed as a thing of the distant past and the dream of multiculturalism had more or less been achieved.

In school, I learned a diluted version of history, and racism as something our society had moved past. I, of course, knew that my ancestors were enslaved Africans (and white slave owners too). But the complexity of that oppression and the lingering effects of white supremacy lay like a dusty, unopened book in an old library's basement. We never dove too deep into those pages. Teachers positioned the genocide of Indigenous peoples and the enslavement of Africans as necessary evils to build the great United States. Figures like Frederick Douglass, Rosa Parks, and Martin Luther King Jr. were honorable for their sacrifices, but they weren't main characters. The white American was the default, and racial injustice was just as much something for them to get through as people of color. Simply realizing some white people had been hateful was the victory, not my people's liberation. We didn't hear about the glory of slave rebellions or how people of color had resisted white supremacist authority rather than waiting for it to be transformed. We didn't learn about how these dynamics continued all around us in the nation's particular gumbo of redlining, gerrymandering, and voter suppression.

That year I took a Georgia Studies class, taught by a distant relative. I didn't know about our connection until weeks into the course. I felt dread when she had us read a chapter that featured a diagram of our state flag's evolution. The book showed the first version I ever knew, which featured a Confederate battle insignia. That was the official symbol of the state from 1956, the year of my mother's birth, until I was ten years old in 2001. How disgusting was it that a marker of Black subjugation had been so widespread that it was just acceptable for white people to emblazon stickers with it on their vehicles or hang it like cherished artwork? I also assumed there were reasons our neighborhood was predominantly Black; our family went to a mostly white Catholic church, and my parents wanted me to attend charter magnet schools that maintained racial quotas for their student populations. But most adults in my life talked about race only in passing. If something ridiculous happened at work or some restrictive legislation was passed, the most I could expect was a quip like, "You know how white people are." Well, if I didn't before, I did once Barry shredded our friendship. I felt like I had more of an idea of how whiteness and, to some extent, Christianity actually influenced how people treated one another.

All those questions I'd had about religion flooded back. I wondered why I didn't look like our God or the white man with the disheveled hair depicted on the crucifix and in paintings on our church walls. I remembered when I asked my dad, "What if we're wrong about our Bible being accurate?" and he retorted,

"Well, I'd rather be safe than sorry." Why was it that if I ever struggled, it was because I wasn't faithful enough? It wasn't like I hadn't tried. But God never answered my impossible prayer that I'd just wake up as a *normal* boy or girl. Either he didn't care to or he didn't exist. So, I buried my tortured epiphanies.

3

Revelations

A steady, chilly rain greeted Momma and me as we waved goodbye to the remaining Red Cross youth volunteers at the Gracewood campus of the East Central Regional Hospital. Each month, our collective held monthly celebrations for the patients with developmental disabilities, complete with snacks, oldies played on their sound system, group games, and decorations. By ninth grade I'd been attending the events, since my older siblings were in the group. I enjoyed volunteering, spending time with the patients, and generally being a part of the excitement. But I wondered what the patients' lives were like once they retreated down the hospitals' long corridors. Some of the caretakers and nurses were harsh, often chastising these grown adults as if they were troublesome toddlers. I assumed they knew best but wished they were treated with more respect. Those events served as major introductions to my own privileges as an able-bodied, seemingly neurotypical person. I knew our society treated folks of other abilities horribly. In public schools, disabled students were thoroughly segregated from the rest of the student population. I'd only see them if I peeked in their classrooms. But, perhaps, these firsthand experiences made me more empathetic, the rare kid who railed against peers who used the r-slur in a time when it was one of the most popular refrains. I'd wince even though it was rarely hurled in my direction and be called sensitive whenever I shot down its usage. Today's Gracewood party, however, quickly devolved into chaos because of another slur. A gaggle of girls ran over to the kitchen to tell my chaperoning mother that two boys had gotten into an argument resulting in one calling the other a *faggot*.

As I concentrated on not filling the Dixie cups too high at the drinks station, I tuned in to my mom's exchange with the girls. Apparently, a boy openly cornered another about his sexual orientation. Assuming a person was anything other than straight was already a violation, but the slur was more extreme than most of my peers would have pushed. I felt implicated because I'd certainly experienced that kind of treatment numerous times over the years. But, of course, Momma was none the wiser. Bullying like that wasn't typical among volunteers, which was probably why it was the rare space where I never worried about being called out. So I sat perched, waiting for her reaction. Momma's mouth folded in on itself in disgust and she promptly summoned the instigator.

"Ma'am," the boy said.

"What's this I hear about you saying filthy things to people?" she said, searching his face for answers.

"I just wanted to know why he was acting so weird," he said, looking down.

"Why is that your business?" she said. "We don't go around judging people and talking to them any ol' kind of way. We're here volunteering out of the goodness of our hearts. What sense does it make to ruin it with something like this?"

"I don't know."

"Well, I need you to go right on over there and apologize."

"Yes, ma'am," he whimpered.

Watching my mom come to the other boy's defense unlocked an urge to tell her my truth. And my fear that she'd reject me thawed. *If she could understand the plight of this random kid, then she had to understand me, right?* My heart pulsated throughout the rest of the event as I pledged to share my secret.

When we walked to her car, my mind ventured back to the coming out advice I'd read online: wait until you're ready; you're normal the way you are; make sure you have somewhere safe to go if your parents disown you. I didn't think my parents would go that far but it was unclear how they would respond. Momma and Dad, perhaps due to infrequent opportunities, never mentioned LGBTQ+ people. I'd been vigilant for years, waiting for some clue of their acceptance to turn up in conversation, but it never did. They were staunch Democrats, which I hoped meant they'd be supportive. Still, based on the way others talked about people like me, then I should expect the worst.

Media was my main teacher on the current sociopolitical moment. Though my family never watched television shows like *Will & Grace* or *Queer as Folk*, I knew they existed and that something was shifting for gay people culturally. On weekends at Grandma Inez's house, I'd secretly watch marathons of MTV's *The Real World*, absorbing the stories of queer castmates like Ruthie Alcaide and Karamo Brown in the Hawaii and Philadelphia seasons of the show. Though their openness inspired me, the former's bouts with alcoholism and the latter's encounter with police officers inserted a danger into my vision of a smooth future. Grandma's love affair with CNN didn't help, either. Her multiple televisions inundated me with sensationalized stories like the murder of Matthew Shepard, a young, white, cis gay boy killed in Laramie, Wyoming. We shared the same name, so it was impossible to look at the news report chyrons and not imagine what could happen if the world knew my secret. If he could experience such brutal violence, perhaps it was inevitable for me too.

Rain trickled down the window of Momma's car and I stared out of it for the mostly hushed drive. The silence was broken only by the evening radio announcer teasing Anita Baker's "Giving You the Best That I Got." Usually, I'd let the R&B goddess's sultry notes whisk me away, but now I was pensive. Every time I tried to speak, my jaw clenched down harder. *Maybe this wasn't the right time?* A few guides had advised against coming out while the other person is doing certain things (like driving). Just in case they overreacted. My smidge of faith told me that my mother would at least maintain her composure.

"Momma, I have something to tell you," I said while slowly averting my eyes. "But I don't want you to hate me because of it."

I choked on the last words, and tears soaked into my shirt. I didn't have any resolve to hide my emotion, so I surrendered to potentially looking weak.

"It's OK, baby. You know you can tell me anything," she responded, with emotional deftness.

I openly volleyed the pros and cons of telling her. And within minutes, she said, "Well, you seem to want to say something. I don't know why you're fighting it, Suga."

Suga. That pet name lived among a colony of others she'd draped over all her children throughout the years. It was just the spark of warmth I needed to take the plunge.

"OK . . . Well, I'm gay."

I hoped if I just blurted it out, I could circumvent my apprehension. But I didn't stop there. Soon, the explanations I'd silently crafted over the years flowed out. "It's not really something I'm confused about. I've known since I was young. I was just afraid to say anything because I didn't want you and Dad to be disappointed or hate me for it. It's not something I can help even though I've tried."

There was little more than a blink from her. She just kept her hands steady on the steering wheel. She calmly asked the typical questions like how did I know I was gay and why hadn't I told her sooner, and she listened to my responses. I mentioned the years of bullying, which I thought might elicit more of a reaction. But she just assured me she still loved me and that it was just new information. *How could she be so unfazed? How could she not know?* My parents should have known before anyone else had. But I figured our religion and their traditionalism had shielded them from seeing the truth. She did relay that she wondered why my dad worried about her "babying" me too much. And instantly, I was transported to those formative moments and how they encouraged me to see affection negatively. Even then, I wondered what I had done, whether he liked me or not.

The thought of Dad possibly knowing my secret invited dread. The feeling deepened upon seeing his candy-apple red Camaro on our sparse lawn. Perhaps Momma considered his reaction too, because she asked me to vow not to tell my dad until I had graduated from high school. The concern was that he would react badly and that it'd irreparably damage our relationship. It made sense. We both knew how necessary it was for me to live up to his expectations, at least until I left my childhood home. So, I agreed. Still, I wondered if she could really lock my queerness in a box until I was older. I'd always known them to be transparent about everything.

In the final moments of our chat, I took in the only house I'd ever lived in. The illuminated lights in some of the rooms revealed where Dad had ventured since leaving work. I looked at my darkened bedroom, knowing how he could easily find my secret in my computer search history or scribbled in one of the journals under my bed. *Was I shredding my parents' dreams for me? Would I become an embarrassment to them? What was the path forward? How could Momma and Dad prepare me for the life that I was on track for? What kind of life was that?* My queerness felt realer than ever. And maybe if Momma could love me regardless, Dad would too.

Months later, Momma enlisted a counselor to support us in processing my identity, and I took it as a good sign. She'd asked my pediatrician for a recommendation, and at the top of the list was a man who ran a practice rooted in the Christian faith. I was slightly skeptical at first, fearing that he'd be unsupportive, but I kept an open mind. After all, Momma had gone outside of our church, so I figured she'd found someone who possibly leaned more into his psychological training than into traditional Christian approaches. And somehow, she engineered bimonthly sessions without arousing my father's suspicion.

The counselor, Rick, was a thirty-something white guy who favored Kevin Richardson from the Backstreet Boys. He was cordial, but his true intentions felt undetectable. Each meeting, he would have a ten-minute session with my mom, then spend the rest of the hour with me. As I glanced at the covers of Christian magazines, I wondered if he was telling her different things than he told me. *Was he championing a mainstream biblical analysis of queerness in there? Was he deepening Momma's concerns about my fate or assuaging them?* After years of gathering information about my identity, I was certain I knew more about myself than either of them did. But I tried to trust the process.

Through the end of my freshman year and the beginning of my sophomore year of high school, Rick, my mom, and I went in circles over my identity. Luckily, somewhere in that period my peers matured a bit too. While some still hurled snide homophobic comments and jokes, many seemed genuinely curious about my sexual orientation. The inquiries felt less nefarious now that we were all older. When I'd deny that I was gay, I could feel the disbelief. They'd search my face, then half-surrender. I hated that reprehensible imposter feeling. After another peer asked me if I was "metrosexual" during rehearsals for a school musical, I realized I'd reached the point where I was no longer ashamed of telling the truth. Something just clicked. If I was going to be asked this for the rest of my life, things had to change.

One Sunday after church, I waited until Dad went outside to do yard work. Then, I cornered Momma while she was engrossed in some Lifetime movie. I told her I had thought more about coming out over the last year and that I couldn't hold off until graduation. "I told you I don't think that's a good idea," she said as she turned the television volume down. I tried to reason with her that if he responded badly, we'd be able to repair our relationship while I was still at home. Otherwise, I feared that if we waited and I went off to college, we could become estranged. She disagreed, repeating her concerns. But determination to break my yearslong silence with the person I was most afraid of disappointing coursed through me. As I searched her eyes, I realized that I was on my own to execute this switch-up in plans. But I thought if things got too heated, surely Momma would help smooth things over.

I paced the next room until Dad walked back into the house for a break. As he poured himself a cup of cooled coffee, I rehashed the same words I had used with Momma about a year before.

"Dad, I need to tell you something," I said with confidence as Momma sat feet away in our den. He agreed to hear me out, suspecting nothing of the conservation to come. It was now or never, so I took a deep breath. I told him I didn't want him to look at me differently, but I'd known for a long time that I was gay. With a pause, I looked at him squarely, expecting a disappointed expression. His immediate reaction was stoic as he walked over to take his signature chair at our dining table.

"What would make you think that?" he challenged, as he took a hard sip from his mug.

"I've always been this way," I said, sitting down near him. "I've always liked boys."

"I don't believe that. We all can have confusing feelings."

"Yeah, but like, this isn't going away," I said with determination.

"You really mean to tell me you want another man's penis in your ass," he said, half-joking. He raised his eyebrows, daring me to respond.

"Well, it's not about that. It's not just like a sex thing. It's more than that. I like boys, the way other boys like girls."

"It's just a phase," he said dismissively as he rose to pace the room. "You'll grow out of it."

"Oh, so you grew out of this phase at one point?" I said sarcastically. There went my smart mouth. I wasn't trying to piss him off. I just hated the insistence that I didn't know myself, that what I was saying was something of comedy and delusion, that I hadn't spent years processing all of this shit in silence, that what I thought, desired, and feared didn't matter.

"You think this is funny?"

"No," I said desperately. "I'm just trying to let you know the real me."

He curled his lips as he told me he didn't want to know about my sexual "preference." Then, he said my being gay wasn't real. Every bad response I'd read online seemed to flow out of his mouth: "You're trying to live a life of sin," "You're not really this way, you just read something," "You haven't even lived life to know something like that," and "How can you know if you've never even had sex with a woman?" His anger rose and his voice boomed throughout our house. I even saw a vein in his forehead pulsate that was halted only once Momma intervened.

"Chester, Chester. Calm down," she said, soothingly.

"I won't calm down," he uttered. "Do you hear what he's saying?"

"I do," she said, cutting her disappointed eyes at me.

I had spent most of my childhood fearing this moment, fearing his rejection. *What in the world was happening?* Both of my parents were highly educated people who should know better. Dad had studied freaking psychology in graduate school. *How could he truly think being gay was unnatural?* In any other conversation, he'd reasonably balance religion and science. *Why couldn't he now? And why wasn't Momma coming to my defense? Was she really going to pretend like she hadn't known and like his reaction was acceptable?* Her I-told-you-so look enraged me. *Had she really abandoned me after knowing for a year?* I could have outed her for keeping the secret, but that wouldn't have done me any good.

Through tears, I explained how sick I was of lying and the burden of being asked by peers all the time and having to lie out of shame. Then everything got out of hand once I said I was coming out at school. "The hell you are," Dad growled. Then, he picked up the heavy oak dining chair he had just been sitting in. With both hands, he hoisted it in the air. I flinched at his rage. This was a point much further than I'd ever seen him pushed before. And in that split second, I feared for my life. Maybe I didn't know my parents after all.

"Chester!" Momma yelled, trying to break his trance. But it

was no use. With all of his strength, he drove the chair straight into our linoleum floor and broke one of its armrests. Then he yelled a string of statements: "Just keep it to yourself; it's your business," "If you're not doing it for attention, then it's unnecessary," and finally, "You think it'll be easier after you proclaim this; well, it won't."

Momma seemed transformed by the action of it all, and Dad's negativity seemed to seep into her pores. I could feel how upset she was that I'd broken our vow to each other. There was nothing I could say as I watched my parents contemplate my identity and fate. I hadn't considered the impact of her nearly yearlong silence. Still, her plight didn't matter to me at that moment. Now, I just wanted the conversation I'd sparked to be over. My parents were now a team, unloading their fears on me. They speculated that their lack of strictness and my disinterest in religion were the causes of my queerness. *Oh, right. They were perceptive enough to come to these conclusions but never suspected my sexual orientation.* As they continued their scolding, I walked into our den and buried myself in the corner of our green-and-maroon floral-patterned sofa. Now, it was chaos and I wanted to disappear into nothingness. They called me abnormal, immature, and selfish. Momma's betrayal hit me as I glared at her. In her barrage of comments, she confessed that she'd known for a while and that she didn't want him to know out of preserving our relationship. Then new insights pierced my ears. She hinted at kicking me out to go live with Grandma Inez before uttering the ugliest words I'd ever heard: "Now I know why some people kill their children." And with that, I realized no one else was going to be a champion for me in this situation.

By the time my parents finished griping, it was dark outside and they simply directed me to get ready for bed. I had long grown out of being micromanaged around bedtime, but it was an obvious ploy to regain some sense of power. After a tearful shower, I retreated to my room, grateful for the solitude. My parents had recently let me repaint it. I wasn't brave enough to choose any new color, so I'd picked a darker blue than the one the walls had been before. It inspired nothing new for me, serving as a reminder of just how long it would be until I was actually free. In the scarlet notebook I hid under my bed, I penned everything they'd said to me. Journaling felt even more necessary as a release right now. I'd mostly written cheesy songs about crushes and feeling misunderstood. But on the page in front of me, I wrote a letter saying everything I didn't dare tell my parents. I accused them of not loving me unconditionally, of reacting violently, of not being the Christians they thought they were. "You don't love me, you love the dream you had for me," I wrote. Afterward, I got on my knees, praying to God to forgive them. *Maybe I could use religion in my favor now? What the fuck else did I have?* Then I flipped my light switch and softly closed my door. I wanted to lock it, but Dad might have gotten even angrier if he checked the knob and sensed my demand for privacy as defiance. Looking up at the dark ceiling, with the streetlight peeking through the blinds, I feared for my life. *Would they hurt me in my sleep? Would this really be the last night I slept in this house? Had I shattered our relationships forever? Would they ever love me the same way again?*

* * *

I GAVE MY parents the silent treatment for weeks after their blowup. It was my first protest. They needed to experience the soul-crushing silence they were demanding of me. Of course, complete voicelessness was impossible. But I knew consistently clipped answers would be just as biting. I didn't care so much about their anger as I did my exhaustion. Plus, I had nothing else to say, or at least I didn't know what to say. I'd shared my truth, and they'd spat in my face. It clarified what I'd secretly feared: I had to have my own back. I was determined to remain unshaken in my resolve.

During this time, Mrs. Laurel, a teacher who served as both my homeroom teacher and the advisor for our school's yearbook staff, which I'd joined that year, called me into her office. From the concern on her face, I could tell that she knew something was up.

"You're not your usual sparkling self," she said as she gently grabbed my shoulder.

"Well, I can tell you," I said, after a few minutes of trying to swallow my words. "But can you close the door?" Without hesitation, she gave us more privacy.

"Alright," she said.

"Well, I'm gay. I don't know if you know or assumed. Everyone else does. But I am," I explained. "And I told my parents that I wanted to come out, and my dad blew up and it's a whole mess."

Mrs. Laurel was a straight shooter. A fire blazed in her, and with her thick Southern accent, she apologized for their reaction.

"I don't understand what the big deal is," she said. "You're still their child."

She was convinced they'd come around but thanked me for my bravery. She offered to get me connected with our guidance counselor and assured me that her door was always open to talk about anything. She was the first adult to flat-out tell me that nothing was wrong with my identity, and I held on to her kind words for weeks until my dad addressed my silence.

He summoned me to our backyard as a ferocious February wind signaled the spring to come. With hesitance, I walked out into the dusk with my mouth clenched shut. *What did he want now?* He tilted his head to gaze at the evening's emerging stars with his back toward me. I strolled up beside him, assuming a similar pose.

"Look, son. The silence? I can handle it. But don't put your momma through that," he advised. "When you get on up there, you're older, and making a life for yourself and raising somebody, you're gonna do whatever you can to ensure they are on the right path."

I stolidly took in the full moon emerging through the clouds. *Was this a peace offering?* It wasn't clear yet, so I just listened. He told me about his fatherly duty, how he just wanted what's best for me. He knew some things were out of his grasp of understanding, but he claimed to call on our ancestors to understand. He spoke of Grandma Novella and her insistence on the importance of family. Apparently, she'd encouraged him to give grace to Grandma Inez for not being a typical mother. Once he invoked their names, I knew this wasn't just a ploy to get me to speak. As he opined, I cried, half-heartedly putting up an internal dam to hold in my emotions.

"I may not approve, but I'll always love you," he said.

This was as close to an apology for his initial reaction as I would get. Now, in full tears, I anticipated his typical refrain to "cut all that crying out," but he didn't. For the first time since I was a little kid, he just embraced me and held my head at heart level. My quiet tears soaked into his shirt, and I fought not to get all snotty.

"It's just so hard," I wept.

"I know, son. But you'll figure it out," he said with relief. "And ya momma and me, we'll be here."

After my father released me and walked back inside, I lingered in the stillness of our backyard. I looked at the bare patch in the lawn where Jerry and I had tried to dig to the other side of the Earth before Dad scolded us to fill it in. I thought about how unfair it was that our friendship had dissolved in part because of how my queerness made me a target. The memory illuminated my long-fought war against expectations and the resistance I'd had to build up against my father, peers, and society. Somehow, though, Dad's vulnerability inspired me to forgive. I had to figure out how to hold on to my parents while carving out a place for my queerness to be fostered. If they didn't know what it meant to raise a queer kid, maybe I'd have to handle that bit on my own. It wasn't fair, but it didn't mean that they couldn't be exemplary parents in all the other ways they had been before. Plus, I was determined to prove that being gay didn't mean I couldn't have a full life. So, I accepted this complex ceasefire and did what I needed to survive without their knowledge. I vowed to come out, but my own secret promise was I wouldn't tell the world before I told the rest of my family.

Jessica had always been the most open-minded person I knew. Deep down, I expected her to react more favorably than anyone. In fact, it made little sense that I hadn't come out to her first. But she had moved away years before, graduated from Purdue University in Indiana, and settled in Queens, New York. Our relationship was a bit out of sight, out of mind. I clandestinely told her on a spring break visit to NYC with Momma. It wasn't face-to-face, though, because we were always in mixed company. So, after a long day of events, I waited until Momma and I made it back to my great-aunt's Brooklyn brownstone, where we were staying, to tell Jessica. I scanned the floor, making sure no one was within earshot and gingerly closed the door to make the phone call. "I just thought you were eccentric," she said in surprise and intrigue. She exclaimed her support, as I expected. Then, I asked how she couldn't have known. Apparently, the first time she considered it was when her fiancé mentioned it after a Christmas gathering. This made me chuckle; and after the tumultuous experience with Momma and Dad, it filled a well of encouragement.

Weeks later, I took advantage of one of Chet's weekly calls home to share my secret. Just like Dad, Momma had been fearful of me coming out to him. Chet had only grown more tradition-ally masculine since our younger days, but I hoped his youth had gifted him a less ignorant perspective. Like Jessica, he'd been out of the house for a few years working on a degree at Valdosta State University. *Surely, he had to have encountered gay people during his time out of the house.* I never considered that the encounters might have been negative in his eyes. Still, at the desk in my bed-room, where I'd first learned about anything queer, I stared at my reflection in the blank computer screen as his playful voice came through. My grip on the phone grew sweaty as apprehen-sion took over me. But if I ever wanted to be free, my brother had to know my truth.

"So, bro. I need to tell you something," I said, sheepishly.

"What's up, Young Blood?" he joked.

Just like Momma, he had his own collection of nicknames for me. Somehow, though, they always sounded like hypothetical rapper names. I hoped he'd keep this comical energy throughout the conversation.

"Well, I've always been different, and it's because I'm gay," I said, clenching my eyes shut. A long pause met my ear.

"Man, I don't believe that," he said in a disappointed tone. "Man, why you think that?"

I shared with Chet what I had revealed only a handful of times before: my yearslong attraction to boys, the bullying, and that I was no longer ashamed of myself. Without a second thought, he made it clear that he didn't accept me. Then, he accused me of choosing a life that would lead to me dying of AIDS in a few years. *What the fuck? This is even worse than Dad's reaction. This couldn't be the same brother who had saved me from drowning twice when I was younger, or the one I'd shared a room with for most of my life. Had I shattered our relationship? Was all he had to offer chastising cuts at my character?* I left that exchange convinced that he'd never understand me.

Interestingly, Grandma Inez, with her acerbic wit, delivered a much chiller reaction. She didn't actually believe that I could be gay, but unlike Dad and Chet, she assured me she harbored no ill feelings toward people who were "that way." She never treated me any differently, but she shared now and then that she thought I'd grow out of my feelings. I took her unceremonious response as a win.

With my immediate family all in the loop, I'd done my due diligence. Extended family would be a task for another time. Now, I had to free myself at school. So, I confided in a few friends who expressed concern during those weeks surrounding my parents' blowup. And they didn't judge me or dismiss me or ask invasive questions; they just accepted it. In fact, we all grew closer, forming what we came to call "The Pentagon," as there were five of us. Two girls, Shelly and Nora, were white and Korean, respectively. Despite being devout Protestant Christians, they were always open-minded and supportive. But I formed the deepest relationships with Armand and Isabel. The former was an Antiguan immigrant who had moved to the United States in elementary school. We bonded over his deep philosophical musings on human nature, and debated the existence of true selflessness and unconditional love. We became even more inseparable once he came out as gay, too. Isabel was of Puerto Rican descent and could lighten any mood with her bright spirit and signature guava-and-cream-cheese empanadas. Our late-night calls, sleepovers, and Target visits enlivened the rest of my high school experience.

Ultimately, coming out proved to be one of the best things I could have done. It opened me up to new friendships in ways I hadn't been since I was a small child. I became a social butterfly, befriending other peers in my classes and extracurriculars. Anyone who was previously critical of my "effeminate" nature or gayness lost their advantage. And I cared less, taking more risks with self-expression. I cut my hair short for the first time in years, feeling like I didn't need that marker of nonconformity anymore. After all, everyone knew my truth. But I unapologetically embraced what little makeup I could get away with wearing, boldly buying my own. I took control of my style, nixing my dad's oversized, hand-me-down sweaters in favor of zesty polos and hip-hugging "girl jeans" as tight as I could muster. My favorite of the latter flared beautifully around my calves, showing off the slight curvature of my thighs.

I became more confident in my arts classes, especially acting. Once I opted for a gender-swapped role as a female detective in a student-directed one-act. With a straggly wig and business skirtsuit from our theater department prop closet, I wobbled in high heels up onstage in front of a small audience. I could hear the whispers. "Is that a boy under there?" I relished their confusion. Another moment of gender play came during our school's annual Spirit Week. I participated in the Powderpuff Games in which girls played flag football while the boys served as cheerleaders. Complete with matching skirt sets and pom-poms, our grade delivered on performances set to nineties mixes each year. As I was getting ready, some girls told me I was pretty, and the feeling it elicited stayed with me. I dreaded when the festivities ended, but I knew that whatever I was feeling had to be kept in check. I could be gay, but I couldn't be too stereotypical. I couldn't stray too far from masculinity.

While I enjoyed many extracurriculars, my yearbook staff

obligations took center stage. In fact, I worked my way up to becoming editor-in-chief during my senior year. By then, Ms. Laurel had moved on to another school, but I enjoyed the leadership opportunity and took it as a sign that I should study journalism in college, with the dream of one day becoming a magazine editor.

Though I'd taken some control of my life, coming out hadn't solved all my problems. Despite a few other students having come out, I still felt isolated from the LGBTQ+ community. College was primed to be the chance for me to rectify all of that. And I was hell-bent on moving to a more progressive location. So, I sought out journalism programs in the Northeast and Midwest. New York City was my top choice, partly inspired by visits to see Jessica over the years. It had been the setting of my escapist fantasies since I had been thirteen years old—dreams that intensified when I realized that unapologetically owning my queerness would be a necessary part of my future. The openness of metropolitan life intrigued me. It seemed like an accessible aspiration.

I knew so little about our family's economic situation. Of course, we weren't wealthy, but I figured my parents had some kind of plan for me to attend any college that accepted me. But they urged me to apply to in-state schools simply to "have more options." So, I applied to the University of Georgia (UGA), which I really only knew because of its size, as well as its famed football team. After I earned Georgia's lottery-funded HOPE (Helping Outstanding Pupils Educationally) scholarship, I agreed to attend UGA, despite fearing that I'd be just as isolated as I was throughout most of high school. I scoured the Internet for anything I could find about UGA's LGBTQ+ student resource center. Even though the website seemed like a GeoCities throwback, it made me hopeful that I'd meet others like me. On one of the queer forums I frequented, I searched for guys who went to college in Georgia. Few search results came back, but I found a UGA student named Jake. We exchanged messages, and he assured me that the school and its town, Athens, weren't as close-minded as I assumed. He shared that the environment was generally accepting and that he and his boyfriend rarely worried about public displays of affection. His advice and anecdotes made me reconsider the school.

* * *

AFTER MY GRADUATION, Momma and Dad threw a celebratory dinner at a local favorite restaurant, The Partridge Inn in downtown Augusta. Over fried green tomatoes, savory gumbo, and sweet tea that made my lips pucker, friends and family cloaked me in support. As Dad gave a stirring grace for the food and prayed for my continued success, I felt gratitude for all we had been through. The diploma wasn't the thing that made me feel most accomplished. Despite my fears, I hadn't retreated into myself; I'd become more of myself. Even though my family and I never discussed my identity openly after our dustups, I relished having shared my truth with flying colors, no regrets, and faith in authenticity.

4

The Playground of Gender

Sequins, high-heeled pumps, and even higher hair—I didn't quite know what to make of my first real brush with drag performers, but my little gay ass was mesmerized. Weeks before starting at UGA, I visited Jessica in New York for one last summer's hurrah. It was bittersweet taking in the city, knowing that I wouldn't be moving there after all. But I was delighted to spend time with my sister. Yet again, we were in different life stages. Jessica had been married for almost two years, so she was settling into her new role as a wife. However, she was determined to hold on to her status as cool, affirming big sister by taking me to a surprise dinner show experience at the famed Lucky Cheng's.

As a nineties baby, I was introduced to gender nonconformity via the world's most famous drag queen, RuPaul. I was enamored of her presence as I soaked up snippets of *The RuPaul Show* whenever its commercials appeared on VH1. I downloaded "Supermodel (You Better Work)" for my first iPod. By then, I saw myself in this drag queen's journey a bit more. The man behind the persona intrigued me as well. I wondered how RuPaul Charles had the gall to so fervently be himself. *How could he make a career out of dressing and performing as a woman?*

Beyond glorious blond locks, perfect cinnamon legs, and a beat mug, he invoked fabulosity to its greatest extent. I'd steal away to Momma's wall-to-wall vanity, lip-syncing and pirouetting with all the sassiness my thin, prepubescent body could muster. He gave me hope that one day I would find an atmosphere that fully valued me.

It wasn't just that I cherished RuPaul. There was a seemingly universal acceptance of what he did. Even Grandma Inez loved him. Once when we saw a news segment about the personality, she said, "I always thought she was one of the prettiest women I've ever seen." I responded with some variation of "Well, that's not actually a woman. He just dresses up for shows and TV." Then, she gazed at the screen, trying to make sense of it all. By then, I knew the difference. Dressing up as a woman for entertainment was more acceptable than thinking you were one. But most everyone I knew conflated gender expression, gender identity, and sexual orientation, and I didn't have the language to fully tease those things out. All I knew was that because I'd been scrutinized most of my life for my "effeminate" nature, I needed to rail against femininity to validate my gay male identity. So, as a high school senior, when *RuPaul's Drag Race* premiered in 2009, I refused to engage in conversations with the straight girls who gushed about the show. I refused to watch, not wanting to become a stereotype. But here, far away from Augusta, some of that pressure lifted.

* * *

QUEEN AFTER QUEEN took to the small stage and showered us with hilarity. They prodded the crowd with their wit, whimsically twirling around. It was like being under a spell, and the liberating atmosphere made me feel seen by my sister. While my queerness had affected how the rest of my family saw me at various points, she never stopped treating me with care and love. Soon, though, the scene playing out in front of us snatched a hold of me.

"Now, who wants to compete in our little contest?" Janis, a queen with a dark beehive-styled wig, asked.

A few hands shot up while other attendees nudged their tablemates to hop in the ring. With scrutinizing eyes, Janis chose a diverse lineup of three contestants before explaining that she needed one more. To my chagrin, Jessica frantically waved her hand and pointed at me. *What the hell was she doing?* We didn't even know what I would have to do in front of all these strangers. The prospect of hopping on stage made my cheeks flushed with heat, and I felt tiny sweat beads forming along my hairline.

"No, no, no," I said, half-heartedly shaking my head. But something in the universe inspired the queen to throw her pointer finger in my direction.

"You're perfect," she screeched.

I death-glared Jessica before breaking into the fakest smile imaginable. As I shuffled onto the stage with the other victims, I realized I was the youngest. *What did I do to deserve this?* Janis sized us up for a minute before telling us we would have to lip-sync to a song of her choice. And if we came out victorious, we'd win a special prize. I glanced at Jessica again, mouthing, "Why would you do this?" But she just swiped her hand at me.

"OK, so you all go on backstage and get something from our nifty prop box," Janis directed.

I obediently tipped through the curtains, waiting in line behind the other contestants. I hoped they wouldn't grab all the good stuff. Lo and behold, they didn't. I snatched a honey-blond synthetic wig and a bright pink feather boa. *If I have to do this shit, I'ma go for it.* I watched from backstage as, one by one, the other amateurs took to the stage. Janis pried into their lives, asking with whom they had attended the show and their sexual orientation before the DJ played their track. The two gay men, who kicked off the contest, swayed in one place, committing to the bit as much as they could. *Bless their little hearts!* As I heard the cheers from their respective tables, I figured I could do better. Next was a shy straight woman who gave a little more movement, but she directed her performance to her "proud" boyfriend. *Forget that man. She needed to give that attention to the crowd.*

"Alright, here's our last contestant." Janis smiled.

When I walked out into the lights, they seemed brighter than before. I dodged eye contact with anyone but the host as my heartbeat picked up speed.

"Now, where are you from? I hear a cute little accent," she asked, thrusting the microphone at me.

"Georgia," I muttered.

"Uh-huh. And who are you here with, honey?" she asked.

"My big sister," I said, pointing over to her.

"Your big sister? How sweet! I wish I had a big sister that was this supportive," she said. "And how old are you, sir?"

"Eighteen," I beamed, feeling the excitement of being *legal*.

"Eighteen," she growled as the crowd applauded. "Fresh!

"Well, audience. Give it up for our Southern belle," she said before scuttling to the side of the stage and motioning toward the DJ.

Instinctively I turned around into a starting pose for dramatic effect. I prayed it was a song I knew. Soon, I heard the rattling opening of "Bootylicious" by Destiny's Child. *Jackpot!* I shifted my nonexistent booty to the beat. Then, I spun, pointing toward one side of the audience on, "Kelly, can you handle this?" Then I pointed to the other side on "Michelle, can you handle this?" and looked dead center on "Beyoncé, can you handle this?" With the "wooo" after "I don't think they can handle this," I hopped down to strut in the crowd. I might not have gotten all the lyrics perfectly, but I pretended I was dancing in front of Momma's mirror back home. "You better work it," Janis chirped in my head. Then, the crowd erupted as I played with my boa, wrapping it around a young woman's neck up front before ending with my best attempt at twerking.

"Wow! Looks like I'm going to be out of a job soon," Janis joked. "You've done this before?" I shook my head *no* as I tried to catch my breath.

"Wasn't that awesome, everybody?" she said, and they cheered.

"Alright, let's get those other bums back," Janis said, and the contestants assembled for judging. She explained that whoever received the loudest applause would win. Then, she sauntered down the line, hovering her hand over our heads like a metal detector. My fellow competitors received varying degrees of praise, but Janis struck gold once she made it to me. Even though I couldn't partake of the prize (free shots), the moment was a taste of unbridled expression. By far, the gayest experience I'd had in my life to date. This was the kind of excitement I hoped awaited me in college.

* * *

I FELT READY for the independence when my parents dropped me off at college a few weeks later. It felt weird moving into a high-rise with so many strangers, after living in a house my whole life. I'd wanted to at least be on the same floor as Isabel, the only one of my close high school friends to attend UGA, but the floors were gendered. I longed for a roomie I knew. In fact, I tried scouring the matchmaking groups on Facebook for prospective students, but most of the conversations I had didn't go far. I figured many of them were averse to rooming with me because of how gay I seemed even online. This left me to room with a stranger who I hoped wouldn't be homophobic. I had heard little from him before moving in; all I knew was that he'd be moving in the day after me.

Either way, I held on to optimism. After all, Momma and Dad's pride was palpable from their cheery expressions and light demeanors. Their youngest child was leaving the nest, and they had few worries that I'd be able to chart my path. At least I thought they did. We never talked about my queerness and how that might impact my college experience. My last major conversation with Dad was during my senior year, when I told him he needed to stop mentioning a hypothetical future in which I married a woman. He took it in stride and followed suit, seeming to evolve on some level. Momma and I never discussed my identity either. For her, the main focus was the milestone of having sent all her children off to college.

"You sure you have everything you need, baby?" she said, scanning the room.

"Yes, Momma," I droned.

"Alright, Suga," she responded as she came in for a tight hug, rocking me from side to side. "I love you." Then she burrowed a firm kiss into my cheek. After years of pulling away like a typical angsty teen, I figured I might miss those. Then Dad walked over and swiped his hand out for a shake before pulling me in for a hearty embrace.

"Now, what about this box?" Momma asked, prolonging their departure.

"Marilyn, the boy is fine," Dad muttered before directing her out the door.

"Alright, alright," Momma said.

"You take care of yourself, boy. Be particular," Dad said as he squeezed my shoulders.

"I will," I said confidently.

"Alright," he said. "Take care, son."

After he closed the door, I looked at the bare white walls surrounding me. *This is it,* I thought to myself. *I'm on my own now.* I briefly felt an emptiness, but I had been waiting for this day for years. It was time to do my thing.

* * *

EVEN THOUGH ATHENS was even smaller than my hometown, I was determined to make the best of my experience. Those first few weeks felt like summer camp, like there was some indeterminate date when I'd go back home. It didn't take long for me to adjust to controlling my time, though. In general, I liked learning, so it wasn't difficult for me to make it to all my classes. The struggle for me was the culture.

Let's be clear, I was aware that I was attending a predominantly white institution, but there was no way to anticipate how quickly students would fall into disparate factions. Signifiers of white privilege seemed most noticeable in Greek life. Within days of moving onto campus, swarms of young white women, donning sundress uniforms, would tip through campus to "rush" sororities. Young white men performed often-embarrassing tasks at all times of night to join good ol' boy networks that would ensure smooth postgraduate lives. Among the outsiders of this experience, there seemed to be a sense of scorn at their desperation to join these institutions. In fact, there was an air that those who hadn't quite drank that Kool-Aid, or, let's be real, didn't even have a chance to, had more common sense. It seemed harder for those of us on the margins to find other like-minded students. I mostly observed Greek life through my roommate, Charles. He was a lanky guy from Savannah who loved camouflage-patterned clothing and whose words had a thicker coat of Southern than mine. He differed from most of the guys in my hall, as his closest friends were South Asian, and they encouraged him to join a fraternity centered on their cultural identity. I took this as a signal of his open-mindedness. After about a week, I came out to him one night after we'd both just hopped into our bunk beds and were staring at the dark ceiling. He assured me that he knew I was gay as soon as we met, but that it didn't bother him. His response put me at ease, but I sensed that the rest of our campus wouldn't be as affirming.

Beyond race, I couldn't quite articulate why dorm life was so disorienting. For one, I hated having to depart from my girlfriends upon entering the building. It just didn't make sense for gender to determine so much. I would rather be on their hall than surrounded by the mostly white, childish, straight guys on mine. A familiar feeling of discomfort, of being in such proximity to masculinity, returned. I was at home in my gay identity and had even made straight male friends in the years since my coming out. But this anxiety wasn't going away. *Why did I feel so vulnerable and different?* I isolated myself from my male peers. Whenever I had to use the communal restrooms, I waited until most of my hall mates were asleep, sometime past midnight. I'd make my way to the empty restroom after grabbing my portable shower caddy, slipping on my slides, and tipping down the hall past a room where two guys hung the Confederate flag like a decoration. *After all these years, why couldn't I just be like other boys, straight or queer?*

My first semester, I felt like I had to hone in on one aspect of my identity versus another. Either I would join a Black student group and connect with people over a shared racial background, or join Lambda Alliance, the LGBTQ+ student group, and make the latter my signifier. The former didn't seem like a viable option. I sensed the heteronormative nature of Black student circles on campus, how it often influenced Black queer students to hide their deeper truths to assimilate. It wasn't uncommon to see queer Black men longingly peer inside the LGBTQ+ Resource Center only to go on to a meeting for another group. And whenever I passed them in the corridors, they seemed to write me off for being so perceptibly queer. Perhaps they figured it would be social suicide to further marginalize their selves by being seen in queer circles. On the flip side, the LGBTQ+ groups were predominantly white. But it felt more important for me to be in a space where I didn't feel like I had to hide or that I was judged for my queerness. After all, I'd been deprived of that kind of community my entire life and that was what I yearned for most in high school. And there was no hiding my Blackness.

Weeks into starting college, I attempted to engage with Lambda Alliance members. I'd read about it online and nervously spoke with someone at a booth at my summer orientation. I welcomed the opportunity, figuring I'd meet some friends and maybe cute boys. The meetings were on Mondays, so after my last class of the day I made my way to Memorial Hall, the site of all the multicultural student organizations. As I made my way into the main social area, I saw a crowd of students spilling out of the LGBTQ+ Resource Center office. Most attendees were upper-class folks, sipping on sodas and holding Styrofoam plates with steaming pizza slices. I nodded at the friendly faces as I grabbed a bite and scanned the small library of LGBTQ+ books.

Soon, Lambda's executive director introduced their self and the rest of the leadership team. They explained the center as a retreat from regular campus life where we could truly be ourselves. Then, they directed us to join breakout groups, but I felt overwhelmed. Most attendees were returning students who already knew one another and had tight friendship circles. I was reminded of other points in my life when I felt like a newbie and an outsider. I felt relieved when the meeting was over.

I put my mission to find queer community on ice and focused on the friends I was making in classes. Then, as the end of the semester drew near, I finally met Jake, who I'd connected with before starting at UGA, and his boyfriend, Terrell. I admired how they navigated Athens as an openly gay couple. Jake was more soft-spoken and shorter with stringy blond hair. He was cute and appreciated his trusting eyes. Terrell was a year older than Jake and sported a distinctively dimpled chin. Even though Jake and Terrell lived off-campus, they sometimes opted to eat in the dining halls. That was where I got to know them both a little better. They'd ask me how my adjustment to freshman year was going. I shared my disappointment with my first queer student group experience. They empathized and invited me to a holiday party they were hosting, assuring me it'd include mostly other gay guys they knew. Outside of a few fraternity parties, including one in which an inebriated white straight guy called me a "faggot," I hadn't been to one off-campus social event. I was thrilled and took Terrell up on the offer.

In early December, I dressed in a vibrant magenta sweater vest and black skinnies. Terrell welcomed guests with a YouTube playlist, hitting all the divas of the day, Beyoncé, Lady Gaga, and Katy Perry. The party vibe was pretty wholesome, with modest snacks laid out over their dining room table and different stations for crafts. We tried to build a gingerbread house and made holiday stockings, and I chatted with a few people. Jake generously offered to pour me a drink, asking what I wanted of their selection. To appear more mature, I said red wine. Outside of Communion sips at mass, this was my first time drinking alcohol, so I had no concept of pacing myself. But as the dark liquid enveloped my unrefined tongue, I took a liking to the taste. And I liked how it made my head feel like it was being hugged and seemed to lessen my anxiety.

I listened intently to their friends' stories about dating and hookups, yearning for my own experiences. But, at some point, I cozied myself into the middle of their sofa, drunkenly dozing off. Soon, I awoke to a cleared-out party and Terrell pulling me upstairs to a bedroom. He whispered an offer to stay the night, and I accepted in my lushed-up stupor. In the room, Jake was lying shirtless on their wrinkled, off-white sheets. I stopped and stared at the slivers of light shining through the window blinds onto his abs. Then, Terrell slowly undressed and locked lips with his boyfriend before pulling me over to the bed. I obliged, fumbling in the dark until we fell asleep. We didn't "go all the way," but regret visited me in the morning. During the next week, I ran over the remnants of the events in my mind, wishing I had declined their advances. Yet again, I was whisked back to my childhood and that tainted feeling. I felt used. *Had sex been all they wanted the whole time? Did they take advantage of the fact that I was a freshman and inexperienced with alcohol? Could things have been worse?* I was cordial to Jake and Terrell whenever I saw them around, but I felt awkward about continuing our friendships. If I was going to shake off the moment, I needed to find queer friends that didn't seem to have ulterior motives.

* * *

Weeks later, I sauntered into a Lambda meeting, noticing a collection of desks shoved together into makeshift vanities. The bright orbs of light surrounding the mirror mesmerized me as I took a seat closer to the back. Like the rest of the audience, I couldn't look away from the reflection of two students, Kane and Liquor Cherry. Apparently, this meeting doubled as recruitment for that semester's drag fundraiser. At these massive events, the campus community would come out to watch student amateurs and professionals strut their stuff on stage. The dollars raised would support Lambda's meetings and campaigns, like one focused on expanding the antidiscrimination and harassment policy to include gender identity and establishing more gender-neutral restrooms on campus.

Kane and Cherry explained how they made names for themselves at previous campus shows. I'd observed Kane, who was four years older than me, at that first Lambda meeting earlier in the semester. He'd arrived late carrying an electric sense of urgency and could have easily passed for the cool skater kid from any teen movie. Kane's authoritative tone would've given my professors a run for their money. He just had a surety about him that mesmerized the group. He deftly explained how he contoured his face, enhancing the angles of his chin and making his forehead boxier. Then, as if he was a fine artist, he methodically formed a goatee with hair trimmings and stippled dark brown stubble onto his upper lip and chin. As he put the finishing touches on his aesthetic, which involved stuffing his ginger hair under a wide-brimmed cap, he explained that he was both a drag king and a transgender man. With a simple explanation to his mostly uninformed audience, he told us that drag was about the persona you became on stage and that being trans was about identifying with a different gender than you were assigned at birth in your everyday life. I hadn't considered whether he was trans or not before the meeting. I just assumed he was like every other cisgender queer guy at Lambda. Outside of possibly a few performers at Lucky Cheng's, I'd never met an openly trans person before. But his revelation didn't shock me. In fact, I found him admirable and the idea of somebody being trans as incredibly normal. It simply inspired me to ensure that I always respected him.

While Kane doled out advice, the clacking of Cherry setting up various pencil cases–turned–makeup containers filled the background. Her hasty movements inspired smirks on a couple of our faces. Cherry had a more elaborate setup than her drag king counterpart and once she seemed ready for her spiel, Kane handed over the meeting. With a flick of her Kabuki brush, a cloud of translucent powder dissipated in the air and I was a part of her captive audience. I noticed how she contoured differently than Kane, traveling around the edges of her forehead, nose, and jaw with quick presses. With few words, she gazed in her mirror, entrancing even herself. Then, Cherry broke away from the desks and scanned us, as if we were prey. Then, just before giving up on her quest, she doubled back to me. Here was her rare gem.

"Wait," she snapped.

"Huh?" I said, looking around nervously.

"Turn your face to the left," she commanded. "Uh-huh. Now, to the right."

I silently surrendered to her ritual.

"You have magnificent bone structure," she said with intrigue. "You'd be great for drag."

Astonished and flustered, I looked at the other attendees as Cherry darted off. I was just trying to make new friends, not be put on the spot like this. *What did they think of me at that moment? What had Cherry christened me as?* A few of them beamed at me, but I joggled my head, shooting down the suggestion. Honestly, though, I felt a pinch of pride. It felt nice to be seen as capable of embodying beauty. But I also felt the danger. It was one thing to be openly gay, quite another to be unabashedly feminine. Performing in drag would be a bit of a social death. I feared that other gay guys would write me off as undesirable because of how far I'd strayed from masculine ideals. It seemed that no one liked the stereotypical gay, not even other gays. Think

Will & Grace. Jack's name wasn't in the title for a fucking reason. I didn't want to be told that I wasn't a real man. *After all, that's what I should want, right? Who would respect me? What would my family think? What would my father think?*

As I retold the story of my Cherry encounter in the dining hall to non-Lambda friends, they felt the thrill of it all. They asked me if I would do it, waiting on the edge of their seats for an affirmative answer. *How could I? I didn't know shit about drag.* So, I said no but I figured I'd watch my first campus show and decide for next semester's show. Weeks later, I shuffled into the packed event, sitting on the floor in the front because they'd run out of seats. With my legs folded like a curious child, I leaned forward for every act. Kane; his drag father, Connell; and his drag son, Bryan, performed a medley of *NSYNC songs. It was clear they'd put in hours of practice because they nailed a perfect rendition of the intricate new millennium choreography, harnessing an energy that made their brotherhood come to life on stage.

A few numbers later, Cherry strolled to the front of the crowd wearing a black hoodie and cargo pants. Then, Timbaland's voice flowed through the percolating beat of "Bounce." Menacingly, Cherry tutted her arms out, unleashing hip-hop movements. And the spotlight squared in on her as she turned to face us. After a brief pause, her background dancers encircled her, mirroring the same moves. Then, she lip-synced all the parts of the song from Justin Timberlake's melodies to Missy Elliott's tongue-twisting rhymes. Tonight, she'd chosen gritty over pretty. Even more so than in the Lambda meeting, she drew the audience under her spell. I felt inspired by her, that she'd shown the crowd and me that drag was an art form worthy of awe and respect. If I wanted to be fierce and powerful, I needed to embody her spirit.

* * *

THE NEXT SEMESTER, I sat by Needra, a short biracial girl with caramel skin and straightened hair, at the first Lambda meeting. She was serving an aesthetic that we would have described as a cross between "emo" and "scene" in the late aughts. Needra prided herself on being alternative—that is, appreciating Japanese culture and rock music in a time when those were nonconventional interests for Black folks. It was refreshing to see a sista in the space and I yearned to connect with her. Once the meeting ended, we exchanged perspectives on the group so far. She shared similar sentiments about how impenetrable it felt. After that day, we grew inseparable, attending future meetings together, sharing dining hall meals, and trying to make sense of our queerness beyond the watchful eyes of our families.

When the promo for the next drag show began, Needra and I eagerly agreed to perform together. We figured that joint numbers would settle our nerves, giving us a chance to break out of our repressed shells. A tinge of shame washed over me as I wondered what would happen if my parents found out. It seemed like another potential instance of disappointment for them. Still, I reasoned that this was a part of my life that I didn't have to share. So, under Kane and Bryan's guidance, we decided to perform two songs each, playing each other's love interest. My picks? Rihanna's "Hard" and "Rude Boy." Needra chose Jason Derulo's "Whatcha Say" and "In My Head."

Over the next month, I studied as much as I could about drag. I binged the first season of *RuPaul's Drag Race*, regretting that I let my insecurities keep me away from the show for so long. I also scoured YouTube for makeup advice, favoring videos by two creators: Petrilude and Misty Eyez. But I didn't stop there. Based on recommendations, I ordered two books by legendary makeup artist Kevyn Aucoin to round out my education. Oh, I wasn't playin'. Needra and I knew we had to take this seriously, so we scheduled multiple weeks of practice. We'd sneak into an unoccupied study room in her dorm and record our routines to review later. Kane and Bryan even watched a few of our rehearsals and gave us pointers. They advised us to choose drag names sooner rather than later. I decided on Rebel, a nod to the war against expectations that I felt I was in. I also wanted to honor Momma, so I went with the original French spelling of the name Devoe. And there we had it. Rebel Deveaux was born, and I imagined the persona as embodying the femme fatale demeanor of Rihanna's *Rated R* era. I'd followed the Bajan superstar since her debut, admiring her sense of self. She'd been through tragedy but still conferred a sense of unapologetic confidence and strength. I desperately wanted that and to toss everything that I'd been told about my "effeminate" nature back onto the world. And I tried to take on what I thought I knew of femininity: graceful arms, sly glances, and confident neck rolls.

Since Kane and Bryan didn't know what my aesthetic should be, they enlisted Bryan's girlfriend, Diana, to help. She was amicable, offering her place for me to get ready when the show date rolled around. She drove me to a spot called Junkman's Daughter's Brother in downtown Athens. It was an eclectic store with collectibles, costumes, and other oddities. I was more excited than I expected, and Diana made me feel less anxious about buying women's clothing. She helped me choose the perfect shoulder-length synthetic black wig, fishnet stockings, a multicolored zebra-print top, a black leather jacket, denim Daisy Dukes, and a gold-sequined bra. The latter was a splurge, but I just felt like I needed it. We couldn't find the size-twelve pumps to complete the outfit, so Diana agreed to let me borrow a pair of her shoes. They'd be two sizes too small, but we figured I could make it work given her wider feet. After a final run to the dollar store for a small metallic eyeshadow palette and foundation, we felt confident that we had all the ingredients to make me a star.

On the day of the show, I couldn't contain my nerves in my classes. All of my friends, by now, knew that I'd be in the show and vowed to attend. With every person who we saw in passing, Isabel inquired about their attendance at the show. In fact, she had encouraged this fabulous side of me all year. Even before the start of my drag journey, we'd record music videos in empty study rooms on campus. We'd lip-sync and dance across tables, laying the drama on thick. Other girls in the dorms would join in on the fun and I felt more myself with them.

In the dorm showers, I methodically shaved my body for the first time. As I smoothed cocoa butter lotion all over myself, I marveled at my supple skin. But I wondered if my legs, covered in scars from my boyhood adventures, would be feminine enough. It was the first time I'd thought so deeply about my body since I'd started puberty. Back in my dorm room, I stared at my bewhiskered face, ready to continue my shaving routine. I'd let my mustache grow in during high school, hoping it would confer a masculine maturity. But now I had what felt like a legitimate reason to get rid of it. So, I gingerly guided the razor blades across my upper lip and chin to prepare for the more exciting part of the transformation.

Diana offered to do my makeup at her apartment, but I told her I'd need to do it myself. It felt like a rite of passage. So, I analyzed my multicolored animal-print top and tried to mimic it with the metallic eyeshadow. I packed on layers and layers of the crumbly makeup with a flimsy applicator. I contoured my face too lightly and tried to use translucent powder as a highlight. After I finished my mug, I walked outside of Diana's bathroom. She and her roommates showered me in compliments. If I looked clownish, they didn't let on. I knew I was no expert, but I felt beautiful.

Backstage at the show, Kane gathered all the performers together for a word of encouragement. He assured us that having fun onstage was all that mattered. As we broke from the circle of folks, my stomach was in knots. I'd made it this far and now I had to deliver. *What had I gotten myself into?* Before I could even think of a rebuttal, the show's announcer summoned Needra and me on stage. *I couldn't turn back now.* Walking out, I absorbed the faux-flirty howls and whistles in stride. Luckily, Needra's song was first, so I got to be a supporting character for a bit. I sat down in the lone chair downstage and gazed at Needra. As her song reverberated through the performance space, I tried to focus on the brim of the cap she'd borrowed from Kane, and not the cheering crowd. She focused, hitting every move as she danced and glided around the stage. Being serenaded made me feel sexy, even if it was just my friend lip-syncing. I didn't know if I was serving enough femininity, but I tried to commit to my role.

Needra chivalrously lifted my right hand and guided me up as she took to the chair for her lap dance. Then, I felt the pulsating bass of my track from the speakers just in front of us. The speakers were facing the audience, so our track sounded muffled from behind. But instead of panicking, I just listened and tried to remember when the words came in. I mouthed, "Come here, rude boy, boy," to Needra, and before I knew it, my body was on autopilot. I wasn't worried about my wobbly gait in the red-and-black heels that Diana had loaned me or whether my barely pinned wig would fly off. This was my moment. My ass gyrated and hips wined as much as they could like the "Bad Gal" herself. I glided off the stage, and I fixated on folks as I walked concert through the audience. People eagerly rose to hand me dollars as I passed each aisle. But I was in a spicy trance, focused on my lyrics and hitting my marks, and I ignored the tips. So people just started slipping the money in my shorts or launching them in the surrounding air.

I forgot half of the choreography, but I never stopped moving. Luckily, this little mama knew how to lip-sync well and engage the crowd. But while this was just a performance for Needra, I felt something more profound. I didn't feel that I was playing a character. More like I was showcasing an extension of myself. It was both frightening and exhilarating. As the song went into the breakdown, I crouched in front of Needra for my best twerk attempt and the crowd roared. After a brief stare down of the audience, I leapt back up for my final pose. Then, Needra and I collected the dollars closest to us, dropped them in the collection bucket, and headed backstage.

"Well, we did that," I said breathlessly.

"We did," she responded through her own deep breaths.

"You guys were great," Kane gushed, having watched us from the side.

"Really?" I asked.

"Yeah, the audience loved you," he said.

"Okay, good," I said.

His affirmation was just what Needra and I needed after our first performance. I felt certain that this wouldn't be the last time we'd be on a stage together. After the show, our other friends waited for us to revert back into our regular selves. I went to an empty men's restroom nearby. I felt a bit of fear, wondering what might happen if one of the guys from my dorm caught me looking like this. None of them were in attendance as far as I knew, which gave me a bit of relief. As I looked at myself, I smiled and savored what I saw. Minutes later, I pulled off the now-disheveled wig and stuffed it in my book bag, along with the heels that had my feet throbbing. I washed my face, rubbing my eyes a little too hard to remove the mascara residue from my eyelashes. It didn't all come off. *Damn, waterproof!* I lamented the return to masculinity. I'd felt eerily comfortable in the femme outfit that was now scattered on the floor, and there was an effortless quality to the persona who wore them. This couldn't be the last of Rebel.

5

An Ill-Fitting Frame

I couldn't remember the last time our family had gotten to-gether for a portrait. Apparently neither could Momma, but she was determined to make it happen this Christmas. So, she chose just after mass as the optimal time to capture our growing family. Jessica had recently given birth to her first child, a roly-poly infant with ever-watchful eyes. Chet had joyously married his high school sweetheart, and their wedding photos looked like something out of an early 2000s rom-com. Outside of the mile-stones, it was rare to see both of my siblings at once. Nowadays, they alternated visiting their partners' families on holidays, so this moment felt precious.

"Alright, everybody's here," Momma cheerfully told the photo-grapher.

"Sounds good," he said with a deadpan voice. *Who could blame his lack of enthusiasm? It was a Sunday after all.*

"You look sharp, son," Dad said as he straightened the collar of my button-up.

"Thanks," I responded, but I didn't agree.

I could feel the space between the contours of my body and the loose dress clothes. It felt like a disguise. *What was going on?* I had that familiar feeling of living a double life again, just like I had in high school. Back in Athens, I was a totally different person. I wore what I wanted, which usually included more formfitting clothes. What's more, I didn't have to stamp down my queerness. In fact, just days before, I had referred to myself as queer in conversation with Momma, and she'd reacted in horror because she only knew it as a slur. "Oh, don't call ya self that, baby," she said. Then, I unsuccessfully tried to explain how more and more people in the community had reclaimed the word. I worried I was becoming everything my parents had feared when I first came out to them. Despite Momma's weekly inquiries via phone, I didn't attend church. As far as I was concerned, there was little room for a queer person like me in Christianity, and I'd long wanted out of that obligation. At college, I commiserated with peers who knew what that felt like. In fact, many had it worse than me, per the stories they shared about visiting home, if they ever visited at all. I was lucky, privileged even. At least I was out to my family about my identity.

I wasn't, however, completely out about being a drag performer, which was weird considering how important it had become in my life. Naturally, Dad and Chet couldn't know. That was a bridge too far away from the version of manhood that they idealized. To them any kind of dressing as a woman in public, even in the name of entertainment, would be worse than just being gay. But I'd confided in Momma and Jessica about my performances, and they were supportive, perhaps thinking it was just like any other extracurricular. It, in fact, had become a sacred outlet to transcend my everyday life.

* * *

WEEKS AFTER THAT first Lambda show, Kane asked Needra, me, and a few other students to join his burgeoning drag troupe, Misters Not Sisters. I nearly shirked the request because of the name alone. It seemed like having a drag queen in the mix wasn't initially a part of Kane's imagination, or at the very least I'd mostly be seen as a femme accessory. Still, he offered to be our drag father, pitching this as a chance to become better stage performers and building a chosen family. It felt organic because he'd already supported the rest of us so much. He also promised those of us who were underage that we'd gain entry into the bars and clubs in which we performed. It wasn't a guarantee, but drag performers just seemed to have more leeway and less scrutiny when it came to gracing the local establishments that we would frequent. Now, this wouldn't be a lucrative hobby, especially starting out, but it would be fun and it would give me a chance to join a like-minded group. There just seemed to be an understanding among all of us that our queerness made us brilliant and special. We had an innate and radical power to fuck with society's restrictions.

It didn't take long for our troupe to become a regular fixture in Athens nightlife. Kane negotiated with more seasoned queens for spots in their shows. They jumped at bringing us on because we were fresh and attracted the collegiate audience. We also served as a balance to another popular drag king troupe in the area who were committed to a dark, rock flair in their artistry. Misters Not Sisters was unique and more mainstream in our approach. I appreciated that we prioritized having the audience identify with what they heard just as much as whatever narrative we layered onto our performances. We also prided ourselves on our racial and gender diversity and how novel it was for drag kings and queens to perform together. Culturally, drag kings were more obscure, often eclipsed by audiences' obsession with drag queens, who they saw as "men in dresses." But we confronted that dynamic and didn't treat our personas as parodies. At first, I wasn't the only queen; Kane had initially recruited two others, but

neither lived in Athens and didn't stick with the troupe long. I
didn't mind. I enjoyed being a standout, a girl among the bois.
Plus, my status helped me become popular in my own right as the
youngest of only a few Black queens in Athens.

By the end of the first semester of sophomore year, I had several major performances under my belt. First, there was a huge
Misters Not Sisters performance at our home bar, Little Kings
Shuffle Club, where we did a rendition of Michael Jackson's
"Thriller." Our troupe spent the night before at Kane's apartment
shredding clothes and smearing fake blood on them for a zom-
bie effect. When we arrived at the venue, I was sure the bouncer
would reject the driver's license I showed him. One of Kane's
friends had generously offered it to me for indefinite use. With
bated breath, I watched the tall man clad in black hold the ID
in his huge, gloved hand before handing it back to me with a
knowing look and motioning me inside. Being in drag served as
a shield. Thanks to the patriarchal fear of gender nonconformity,
he didn't want to engage with me too long.

Another of my bold performances came on National Coming
Out Day when I gyrated outside the student union in between
classes to recruit members for a student group focused on edu-
cating and empowering LGBTQ+ allies. Lady Gaga's "Born This
Way" had just came out, and I had folks captivated by daring to
perform it publicly. I mean, when else had we heard a song that
explicitly said, "transgender" or "don't be a drag, just be a queen"?
Never. I loved those moments, but increasingly the devolution
back to the young man I was supposed to be became uncomfortable. The more time I spent with the troupe, the more I wanted
that freedom of expression to be permanent. By now, most all
of my troupe mates were calling me Rebel in and out of drag. In
Athens, I'd found a chosen family and community that seemed to
accept me unconditionally.

* * *

"Man, what you listening to?" Chet said, nudging me as he sat down on the bench I'd stolen away to. While the photographer positioned Jessica's family for their portraits, we waited on the sidelines.

"Nothing," I said dismissively. Conversations during which he didn't roast me were rarer than seeing a meteor, so I resisted engaging his words.

"You know he goes to school with a lot of white kids, so it's probably something they listen to." Momma chortled. Every now and then, she'd reinforce his jokester ways, much to my chagrin.

"Actually, it's not," I said. (They weren't entirely wrong. It was "Paparazzi" by Lady Gaga.)

"Yeah, it's probably some Celine Dion," Chet said, as I dodged his reach to pull out my earphones.

"And how do you know who that is," I snarked, whipping my head toward him.

"I know some thangs, mane," he said, giving up on his tease-fest. He wasn't trying to be malicious, but I was in a sensitive space.

"I don't know why something has to be white music or not," I shot back. "I like a lot of things. And it's actually white supremacy to put things in a box like this."

They both ogled me in disbelief as if I was speaking another language. *Was something wrong with me?* Since I'd started taking women's studies classes and performing in drag it had become impossible not to see how the white supremacist patriarchy had infected everything in our society. All of these arbitrary expectations around who I should be as a Black queer person had become suffocating. This insistence that I couldn't have certain interests because of my race made me think of childhood, when

I was told that gender designated what I could enjoy as well. I hated that I had to play with certain toys or have particular interests. I loathed feeling like a failure for wanting to be surrounded by girls instead of boys. I'd always been skeptical of why boys and men had to be a certain way, why girls and women had to be another, and why there was no space for any of the rest of us who didn't neatly fit in either box. I'd first seen it in my parents' relationship. At a young age, I noticed that Momma almost always accepted the finality in Dad's tone, even when he was wrong. I felt like she should stick up for herself, and I once said as much to her. "Well, you have to choose your battles," she responded, but somehow it never seemed like there was an equilibrium to who won and who didn't.

There were always two voices in my mind: one that implored me to do what I *should* to conform, and the other, often stronger, pushing me to do the things I actually *wanted* to do. With my new friend group and studies, it was comforting to know that all the ways I'd felt sidelined for my femininity weren't off the mark, that I wasn't alone in feeling disoriented by it all. It was like realizing there had been a trap of oppressive lasers around me, like you'd see in a spy movie. I'd been contorting myself around them, trying to mitigate the harm. *How could I keep quiet now?*

Over this holiday break, I'd started to feel the distance growing between my family and me. I realized that I had never stopped feeling uncomfortable with how I needed to comport myself around them. Though they knew I was gay, I still felt like I had to soften the edges of my queerness. Broadening my shoulders and stamping down the flair in my voice was becoming harder. There was a recall happening on my pubescent mission to prove my masculinity. That urge was incongruent with whatever else was happening internally. I wanted to challenge everything I'd ever known. *What was I outgrowing?*

Soon, the photographer posed Momma and Dad for their couples portrait. We all marveled at their decades-long love. Momma prodded Dad to smile, something he typically resisted doing. There was an ongoing family joke that he always looked mean in photos. And it was true for many of them. But today was different. Momma had to do a little less to coax out the tenderness and joy. In fact, this moment beautifully reflected how he'd changed over the last few years. Where he'd often maintained a thick layer of stoicism and seriousness when I was younger, his demeanor was now lighter. He cracked more jokes, had more patience, and even seemed more open. As a result, our relationship had grown stronger. It wasn't perfect, but he seemed to accept my identity as much as he could. And I'd made peace with his opinions, though I still held out hope that I could transform most of them. He seemed more affectionate and hugged me tighter whenever I came home. He'd even started texting me more while I was away at school. Just to check in. These attempts at intimacy still felt unfamiliar, though. It was a softness that I couldn't fully accept because a greater part of me still felt unworthy of them.

There may have been chaos in my bones, but I appreciated my family. My parents' love had created something beautiful. I looked at my partnered siblings and couldn't help but be reminded that my path wouldn't resemble theirs at all. But I still hoped that I had time to eventually merge onto a track of normalcy. I was supposedly headed in that direction by many standards: keeping my head in my studies, being involved in a broader community, and finding my place in the world. Like my siblings, I'd soon tackle graduation, build a career, and somehow, as a queer person, craft my version of love. Maybe after all that, the portrait would be stunning and the frame would truly fit.

6

Letter to My Father

Dear Dad,

There was something different about that January morning. I could feel it in my broken sleep as my mind avoided sinking into a deeper cycle. When Chet jerked me awake, that usual moment of disorientation—as if I had just been beamed back to Earth—wasn't there. Just like you, he has never been a gentle creature. So the tense alertness that he inspired almost suffocated me. As I slowly lifted myself off the twin-sized childhood bed, I knew something had happened to you.

After I walked to Jessica's old bedroom, her beleaguered eyes darted toward me. As I searched her face, she gripped our clunky wireless landline phone. The one that was usually situated on your deep-cherry mahogany end table. I sat beside Jessica on the edge of her uncomfortably firm bed while Chet paced in and out of that lilac-colored room. I'd never seen his nerves take hold like that. Typically, he'd maintain a comical demeanor reminiscent of Will Smith from *The Fresh Prince of Bel-Air*. Of course, it didn't help that he even looked a bit like him. I wondered how he was feeling, what he was feeling.

As I leaned toward the phone, Momma's soothing Southern drawl flowed from the other end.

"Alright, Jessica, I'm gonna put the doctor on. He has more information for us," she said concernedly. I had stumbled into the middle of a conversation, but I couldn't tell how long they'd been talking. *How much did they know about your fate before waking me up? Why would we all need to be on the phone together? Couldn't they just tell Momma the information? Why were you still in the hospital in the first place?* Soon, the doctor's measured voice halted those swirling questions.

Within minutes, we learned that you'd suffered another stroke after the one you'd had days before. Apparently, this one was on the opposite side of your brain. *It didn't make any sense.* Just a day before, you'd been jovial and cognizant. It seemed like you were on the mend. *What the fuck was going on?* I waited for a sliver of hope from the doctor, but the dread in his voice never shifted. I looked at my siblings, searching for answers to allay the grief on their faces. Whatever final words flew out of the phone missed my eardrum. And, before I knew it, the call was over.

There was little time to be stunned; that's just not what our family did. We didn't process emotions; we simply acted practically. At least that's what I thought I had done days before your condition worsened. While Jessica had booked a flight from New York and Chet was driving from Nashville, I stayed in my dorm room, just two hours away. You and Momma had just dropped me off in Athens to start my second-semester classes, but a blizzard coated the northernmost parts of the Southeast. The next day, after I heard what happened to you, common sense guided me home. I didn't have a car at school because you and Momma didn't think I needed one. Remember, you said you didn't want me to be tempted to let anyone else drive it? I wouldn't have, but I didn't protest your opinion too much. Anyway, I hopped on a bus to Augusta, naively figuring that I'd be there simply as moral support. But after hearing about your fate, I noticed that Jessica's room seemed much smaller than it did minutes before, and life did as well.

Any other Sunday morning, our family would be getting ready for church: we'd be showering feverishly, ironing formal attire, and working patterned ties into Windsor knots. Today's agenda was strikingly uncertain. My body was on autopilot as I washed my weary face and brushed my teeth. I stared in the mirror as if looking through myself before noticing the steamy mist of water was far too hot for rinsing my mouth. As I waited for the stream to cool down, I inspected myself. My hair had recently been cut into a mohawk just after Christmas break. I'd hoped it made me look queerer. When you saw me, I expected you to hate it, to chastise me for it. But you reacted with a smile as if you had finally accepted my nonconformity. My coils had been a battleground where I waged war against society's expectations. Remember when I grew it out in fifth grade? That was a defiant act of queerness, maybe another little protest I picked up along the way. But I also wanted to spend the least amount of time anxiously navigating our neighborhood barbershop. Even at that age, I knew I didn't fit—and I always worried someone would scrutinize me in front of you. But you were so revered that no one would dare question my identity on your watch. Your presence protected me in ways you didn't even realize.

* * *

JESSICA, CHET, AND I drove to the hospital under an overcast sky. For the first time ever, my siblings opted not to have the radio on, and a gnawing silence filled the space between us. As familiar thoroughfares whirred past, I realized I might never see my hometown the same way again. My trips back had already grown fewer and further apart as I entered my sophomore year. I was evolving, feeling less obligated to step back into this environment. And, now, I felt guilty. *How many precious moments with you had I surrendered?* My trance ended when we walked into the intensive care unit waiting area. Momma, Auntie Robyn, and her husband, Uncle Garry, were gathered together with the same solemn expressions that Jessica and Chet had earlier. Either they had collected their emotions for our sake or else they were cloaked in denial. Momma was surprisingly calm, ever the voice of reason during otherwise freak-out-worthy moments. She never panicked whenever I hurt myself while pulling some ridiculous stunt as a kid. Remember when I somersaulted off a moving golf cart after a yellow jacket stung me and I shredded the flesh of my right middle finger on the pavement? She didn't even wince when the doctor injected a local anesthetic, smoothed my brown skin back over the digit, and sutured it. It almost made me wonder if she was worried at all. As I matured, I realized she buried her feelings to keep the rest of us at ease, in true matriarchal fashion. That's a Black mother for you—concerned with how everyone else felt, even though the love of her life was on his deathbed.

We all exchanged deep hugs with Auntie and Uncle. You know your sister. She's on the exact opposite end of the "keep it together" spectrum as Momma. It seemed like her face could crack at any moment, and a river of anguish and sadness would gush out. She had a reputation for not accepting death like most folks. Decades later, she would tear up at the slightest mention of Grandma No. Uncle was stoic as ever. The concern was there on his face, but he heeded the call of masculinity well, like Chet. You wouldn't see either of them crying in front of the rest of us if they allowed themselves to show emotion at all. Unlike Momma's selfless stoicism, theirs seemed more about self-preservation.

Soon, your children paced into the hospital room, where your body lay unresponsive. The respirator was methodically cycling air through your lungs. Jessica, ever fearless, led the way in greeting you. She kissed your forehead and caressed your face, longing for a response. My sister seemingly never stifled how she felt. I admired and envied the freedom she had to emote while I was expected to encase myself within a hardened exterior. As Chet took his turn, he just looked on, muting his shock. *Maybe it was because I was there looking on. Would it have been different for him without an audience?*

After Jessica and Chet left, I lingered. You were dying. I'd never seen you so helpless, silent, vulnerable, and weak. *How could I hold in the unfairness of all of this?* I couldn't adhere to your gender rules right now. You're my dad. During my grade-school years, you were the one who overcooked my dinner sometimes but made it out of love. I had no more gripes about your insistence on shaking my hand versus hugging me or how you listened to the radio so loud that my earphones never stood a chance at blocking out the sound. You did your best to raise me to survive, even though you didn't fully understand who I was destined to be. All those moments when we had disagreed mattered less as I held your left hand, analyzing it. Those long, slender brown fingers that had baited my hooks on fishing trips, pumped up flat tires on my bike, and fixed the collars on my dress shirts. Your hands looked so much like mine, albeit older and rougher. It was one of the few times I noticed your fingers. Usually, you had on some ornate ring, or at least your golden wedding band. Nurses had collected those things in a small plastic bag per hospital custom. All the things you adorned yourself with mattered much less now.

As your chest rose artificially and fell naturally, I imagined that you were just in an eerie, deep slumber. You were only fifty-seven and seemed spry and healthy. Even now, your face gracefully betrayed your age. It was the same complexion as mine, but bespeckled with moles of various sizes. Your visage was far from anything I would have expected at your death. Maybe you'd have a full head of gray hair, and your forehead would be more wrinkled. You'd definitely still have your signature scowl. It was something we shared with Grandma Inez. Y'all called it the "Willis face," but I've learned the rest of the world simply calls it "resting bitch face." I proudly claim my legacy.

Soon, our priest arrived to perform your last rites. With his skeletal frame and sunken eyes, I would have thought that he was more shocked by your sudden death than your loved ones if I didn't know him better. When he walked over, I shook his hand firmly and looked at him with direct eye contact, just like you had taught me. He'd raced to the hospital after the day's services to pay his respects. Then, after a glance at you, he summoned us—now a constellation, including distant relatives and family friends—to gather around your hospital bed and hold hands. Relaying a standard prayer in his thick Irish accent, the priest sprinkled in unique details about your life and presence in our community. Finally, he asked the room if anyone else would like to speak. A few people did, but Momma drew the tears out of us.

"I never would have imagined this," she exclaimed, gripping your hand. Then, she flailed as if all the energy was leaving her body, releasing the dreams y'all undoubtedly had together. You'd been married for over thirty-three years. *How could she anticipate your premature death?* In fact, it wasn't until you were in the hospital that I ever considered y'all's future and mortality. The assumption was that you'd both grow old together. As fifty-somethings, you were, it seemed, only halfway through your lives. Selfishly, I had only thought about your future in terms of my own milestones.

Grandma Inez's reaction pulled on my heartstrings as well. Just a few days before, she had sworn she wouldn't bury her child, but we learned that fate rarely acquiesces to those assertions. She couldn't handle seeing you on your deathbed and refused to be present. With few words, she listened to the prayer over the phone. I know y'all didn't always see eye to eye, and that your muted affection toward each other was mostly translated through laughter and wit. But your departure broke her.

After everyone said their goodbyes to your living presence, the doctor halted the ventilator. As your chest settled, the doctor looked at his watch, ready to record your time of death. I hoped for a miracle in those nanoseconds, like in all those movies I had seen growing up. Maybe you would pop up, open your eyes, and be with us again. As you took your last breath, your body jerked up violently, startling all of us. But it was inconsequential, the final jolt of energy from a body that had operated for over half a century. All it took was a few seconds for another human to seal the last moment of your life. I had felt your presence for so long that I instantly knew what it felt like to be without it.

Silent tears gave way to shame. I'd shed too much emotion already and needed out of that hospital, out of that town. The night before I had already planned to head back to school, since classes started the next day. I'd convinced myself that you would have wanted me to focus on my studies rather than sink into sorrow. After all, this visit was only to check on you. You were just supposed to need physical therapy or something. Your premature death wasn't supposed to be a part of our family's story.

I appealed to Momma about missing my first day back, leaning on our family's sensibility about education. Other people would have been looking for a way out of classes, but I was racing toward them. Chet half-offered to take me back home, probably judging my decision. But a neighbor chimed in and offered to take me to pick up my things so I wouldn't miss my bus. I jumped at the proposition, rushing through parting hugs. Before I knew it, I was sharing a car with an older man I barely knew. I didn't envy him having to small-talk with a nineteen-year-old who had just lost their father, but he was a minor casualty. I learned the numbness of leaving a hospital after someone dies. I had lost a few distant aunts and uncles, but your death was the first of anyone close to me. I felt stupid for not considering that you would never make it back home.

On the Greyhound to Athens, I tried to escape reality by napping. My thoughts remained unsettled. Looking out of the frosted bus window, I noticed a blackbird flying low. On a regular day, I never noticed birds in the sky. This wasn't any other day, though. The blackbird made me think of the collection of bird paintings you kept on our dining room wall. You took pride in them, consistently adding a new one when our family least expected it. I took this blackbird's presence as a sign that things would be alright.

When I returned to campus, I figured a few days of classes before the funeral would be my refuge, but I was destined to do serious reflection instead. The night I returned, it stormed. The media dubbed it Snowpocalypse because it was Georgia's first major blizzard in nearly a decade. Accidents ensued, flights were canceled, and my classes were postponed. There would be nothing to distract me from the grief. I had traveled back to Athens for nothing, knowing I had to return to Augusta for your funeral by the end of the week. I didn't have the energy to unpack my suitcases, so I pushed them aside and collapsed on my twin-sized bed. *Was it selfish to leave my family at a time like this?*

I was in and out of a hazy stupor for an indeterminate amount of time. Minutes and hours flooded together. I couldn't even trust

the sun because of the endless glow of the frost. It had to be day-
time when my friends texted me to come out and play in the snow.
I just lay still. Any other time I would have relished the rare treat of
winter weather in my home state, but none of that mattered now.
*Would I ever love snow again? Would joy ever take the place of this
void in my heart?* Now and then I'd scarf down some of the basil
tomato soup that Isabel's mother told her to share with me. It was
all I could do to keep it down along with the toast, heavily buttered
in true Southern fashion. Since the dining halls were closed due to
the weather, I appreciated the gesture of care.

I felt hopeless and alone, like something in me had died with
you. In between creating Facebook posts trying to commemo-
rate you, all I could do was reflect on how unbelievable it was
that I was fatherless. I was only nineteen. You hadn't seen me
accomplish anything. I envied Jessica and Chet. At least you'd
seen them become their own people. But what hurt most was
that deep down, I didn't know if I ever could have done enough
to prove my validity to you. I wasn't on track to have a neat, acceptable, palatable life.

In my dorm room, I spent a lot of time looking in the mirror,
searching for answers. I observed my prickly chin and volatile
acne. I may not have looked the way I wanted, but I was determined to get closer to my fantasy. I threw on a random playlist
featuring my current favorites, Nicki Minaj and Rihanna, but
also some I shared with you like Etta James and Prince. Then, I
soothed myself by playing in dollar store makeup: an oily foundation that was nowhere near my shade; bloody, easily smeared
lipstick; and grainy mascara. I accepted that this wasn't just a
therapeutic thing for me. While a part of me was trying to conceal the feelings of pain, loss, and anguish at that moment, another part was trying to carve out who I'd become in a world
where your approval mattered less. Slowly, those gendered ex-

pectations you instilled in me melted away, and the woman inside was bubbling to the surface. Your death saddened me, but it also freed me. I could love you and not fit your mold. I could love you and I didn't have to see myself as a failure for not being the epitome of Black masculinity. I could love you and I didn't have to surrender my brief, precious life to your dreams.

Sincerely,
The Child Formerly Known as Your Son

7

Death to Expectations

No matter how much I tried to busy myself and barrel through the rest of my sophomore year, there was no escaping my grief. Those months after my father's death, I wondered if the vignette filter on my life would ever completely lift. I tried my hand at therapy for the first time since that horrible homphobic experience during my teen years. But it still felt like a waste of time to talk to some random straight white man who seemingly had no concept of what I was going through. I wasn't in a place to truly make sense of the loss of my father. Plus, I'd handled my struggles on my own for so long that I didn't trust outside support. I was reticent with friends as well. I didn't want them to see me in a state of weakness. No, I had to be strong and level-headed. Death was a regular part of life and I just needed to accept it. Besides there was nothing they could do. It's not like they could bring my father back.

The rest of my family seemed to have a similar approach. We never had deep conversations about Dad's absence. There were small quips about what he might say at any given moment, but that was it. One solution came in the form of a short summer trip to Aruba as a remedy for such a difficult year. After binging on alcohol and beach time, we returned to our emotional silos. As far as I knew, my siblings had little space for contemplation as they tended to their own families. Since they lived miles away, I committed to visiting home every weekend. It felt necessary to see Momma as frequently as possible. She had fallen into a pit of despair, and it gutted me to think about her waking up every day to an empty house. She'd always cherished being the glue that held our family together, the catalyst for her loved ones to become better people. After years of praying for Dad to reach his potential, he'd done it. He'd gone to graduate school to become an educator of psychology, sociology, and the humanities. And he'd started matching Momma's involvement in church. They'd planned to ride their shared passions through to retirement and on through the rest of their lives. While Dad had made this major transformation, Momma maintained an air of invincibility. She was the one who urged us to consider our blessings and to never forget that there's a bright side to everything. My dad's death eclipsed that perspective, shattering her rose-colored glasses and disturbing even her thriving professional life. For someone who had always found fulfillment in her familial roles, Momma was in a fix. She took nearly a year off to grieve, finding solace only in a rekindled love for gospel music and a heightened obsession with physical health. It was painful to witness the breaking of the most optimistic person I knew.

Grandma Inez didn't fare any better. When I visited on the weekends, I'd drop by her house to watch *Judge Judy* reruns just like we always had. I'd plop down on the chair across from her bed as she lay in repose, focused on the television screen. I'd never know how her spirit was truly faring. In her world, it seemed like so little had changed while I dreamed of Dad knocking on her front door and interrupting our viewing sessions like he did once upon a time. Longevity had made her tough in her own way. She'd outlived all her younger siblings and now her oldest child. It was a harrowing experience. *Who could blame her for not wanting to make sense of Dad's absence?* So, we focused on superficial topics like my studies and the news. Sometimes I'd tell her about my involvement with the LGBTQ+ student group at UGA, and she'd affirm it. But now and then, whether sparked by something I mentioned or a television segment, she'd circle back around a few minutes later. "I just don't think you're gay," she'd confess, hoping I'd come to some new revelation. I brushed it away as wishful thinking, satisfied that we could talk about my identity on any level.

As summer drew near, Grandma's skin tightened around her petite frame, and she moved from needing a walker to a wheelchair or electric scooter whenever we went out in public. For the first time, she regularly requested me to drive when we ran errands. The role reversal was jarring initially, but I didn't think too deeply about it. I reckoned she was just getting older, and her independence was expectedly slipping away. Her continued exuberance shielded me from seeing the deterioration of her health. But soon, Auntie Robyn questioned her doctors and learned that Grandma had stage four colon cancer. The kicker? She had only several weeks to live. After an already hellish half-year, it jolted our family, and I immediately regretted the few times I hadn't made enough of an effort to see her during my weekend visits. Now, there was no gambling on my remaining time with her. Amid summer classes, I made it a habit to join her in hospice.

The hospital room's silence sparred with the boisterous Georgia summer. While my friends and classmates partied, only Grandma's weakened smile sparked my joy. I hoped she wasn't in pain, and Auntie and Momma assured me the morphine was doing the trick. She looked as comfortable as possible in the final bed, framed by an enormous mahogany headboard. If the beeping machines weren't there, I might have forgotten we were in a medical facility. The constantly muted television hovering high on the wall signaled her transition. We talked less as her infirmity grew and I dreaded the day she'd stop responding. I knew it could come at any moment like with Dad months before. So I held on to the few words she squeaked out, hoping to etch them in my mind forever.

While I had observed only glimpses of Dad's quick death, I was front row to Grandma Inez's gradual decline. There were days when she maintained a reassuring energy, charming the nurses with her electric spirit. On others, the gauntness of her sleeping face was all I could focus on. Fulfillment came in spurts like when I held her straw so she could drink water. *How was she really faring?* Once, while Momma and Auntie were there, she popped up in a stupor, calling out to her long-deceased siblings. Auntie saw it as evidence that our ancestors would receive her whenever her departure came. That sentiment comforted me. .

Just before Independence Day, Grandma lost the ability to speak. Her only communication was looking up every now and then to see who was in the room. I'd smile back, wondering if she could register the adoration on my face. Despite my loosened connection to religion, I found refuge in the hospice meditation room. With my legs crossed, I imagined what Auntie had forecasted: my dad and other relatives welcoming Grandma into a spiritual realm. That motif repeated in a vivid dream the night before her death. Lying on an uncomfortable cot, I saw three blackbirds perched outside Grandma's hospice window. *Was it a signal that everything would be alright?*

Before I knew it, I awakened to the screeching sounds of the vital signs monitor. Without hesitation, I hopped up and carefully grabbed her hand. Then, I glanced out the door, noticing two nurses rushing to the room. After a quick check of the machinery, they told me to spend my last moments with her, and that they'd alert the rest of my family. Just like with Dad, I analyzed her thin, pale hands as I held them. I noticed the red nail polish residue that the nurses must have hastily tried to remove when she was first admitted. No one could fully strip her of glamour, even at her most ill. With nervous fingers, I gently brushed back the dark hair she'd dyed blond for as long as I could remember. Feeling the moist forehead, I was transported to those moments when she asked me to help her coat the roots that she couldn't reach on her crown. Now, there were more silvery strands than she would have liked. They were beautiful signifiers of a long-fought-for life. One she'd lived on her own terms.

"It's OK, Grandma. You're OK. I'm here, Grandma No, your sisters, your brother, and Dad will meet you on the other side," I said, before kissing her forehead. Here I let the instincts of affection, of compassion, of softness take over me. She wasn't alone, I'd made sure. I relished not having to live with the guilt of not being present for her last moment.

When the nurses returned, I watched as they chronicled the details of Grandma's status. When Auntie Robyn arrived and we embraced, I thought about how different our family was a year before. She'd lost her mother and the only sibling she knew in the course of months. I'd lost two-thirds of the parental unit that had raised me. We shared a loss too immense to understand. *Had Grandma died from a broken heart as well? How the hell could such a tragedy happen twice in one year? How do we just accept that two of the most influential people in our lives were just gone?* The sliver of grace was that I didn't feel quite as cheated by her death. She'd lived a long life, unlike my father. There was a steadfastness to her unapologetic nature. She was beautiful, cherished, and loved, flaws and all. She'd defied expectations. Now, how would I?

8

Seen, Differently

There were no directions guiding me as I entered my junior year of college. Somehow, I kept a grip on what was necessary for my future as mourning glacially retreated from my life. The thawing was expedited by the joy and purpose sparked by my drag family and campus involvement.

Misters Not Sisters provided refuge, and our lives became deeply intertwined. Kane's and Bryan's authenticity in their transmasculine identities unlocked a desire in all of us to follow suit in our own ways. As we spent more time around one another, I saw more and more similarities in our journeys. Like me, they had been unwittingly gender-nonconforming children who defined their selves by their queer sexualities before learning more about the complexity of gender in college. I didn't quite think I was trans, but I knew I wasn't cis. Despite our close relationships, I was too intimidated to talk to Kane and Bryan about my feelings. Perhaps I was afraid they wouldn't understand from their post on a different side of the gender spectrum or perhaps I was afraid they'd understand too well. I found it easier to commiserate with Vic, another younger troupe member, who confided in me about questioning their own identity. They had been assigned female at birth and came from a traditional Filipine family. After a heartfelt conversation, we both confessed the potential we saw in identifying as "genderqueer." It seemed to help us better describe our experience within our community. I didn't think it'd be possible for me to consider myself a woman. After all, I was only in femme on stage, as my drag alter ego. Even though the troupe seemed to make little distinction between my everyday self and my doll self. Rebel Deveaux never had to go away within our troupe, even when the wigs were stripped off and the makeup seeped down the drain. For now, I found solace in the folks closest to me knowing the truth.

With a more expanded understanding of my gender, my self-consciousness wavered and I realized there was no victory in living my life on other people's terms. I had always been an outsider and trying to conform wouldn't make me less than one. I wondered what would happen if I just embraced the spectacle. Since my peers had always been intrigued on some level, well, shit, here's all of it. I cared less about how I was perceived and, for the first time, embraced my femininity, a quality I had been told to suppress. The line between my persona and my authentic self blurred. I found myself not wanting to take off my drag, feeling my beat face and the synthetic wigs become less of a costume. I pierced my ears and colored my natural coils a vibrant amaranth, inspired by Rihanna's *Loud* album era. And whenever anyone questioned whether I was really a girl, I played coy and mysterious, relishing the exhilaration.

That fortitude translated into the rest of my school life. I picked up a women's studies minor and queer and trans theory inserted extra dimensions to my life. I tried my best to absorb selections from *Gender Trouble* by Judith Butler, but it was Julia Serano's *Whipping Girl: A Transsexual Woman on Sexism and the Scapegoating of Femininity* that altered my understanding of my place on the gender spectrum. The term *transmisogyny* articulated what I'd known since childhood: femininity is demonized in our society, even in people assigned male at birth. Yet again, the internet became an indispensable resource. My cohort of young millennials were using social media like Tumblr to share snippets of political education and I began to feel less isolated by my fervor around social justice. At some point, nearly every queer and trans person I knew was using the platform to chronicle our fears, desires, and lives. It felt like some collective awakening was happening.

I deepened my involvement on campus by joining the leadership boards of the LGBTQ+ Resource Center, Lambda Alliance, and another student organization, Ally Outreach. My contributions largely drew on my course of study, and I led event marketing and promotions within these groups. Much of this programming enriched my intellectual growth, and I ravenously fed on the lectures of visiting trans figures. Kortney Ryan Ziegler, a Black trans director, screened his documentary, *STILL BLACK: A Portrait of Black Transmen*, and it served as a necessary articulation of the Black transmasculine experience. While there was a robust white transmasculine community in Athens, trans folks of color were seemingly nonexistent. I chalked that up to seemingly greater freedom white folks enjoyed to buck against gender norms. Their racial privilege served as a shield that Black trans folks like me couldn't wield. Nevertheless, these events and spaces were crucial in broadening my lens.

I may have been intimidated when I first attended Lambda Alliance, but by junior year I was a key leader in the organization. In fact, I was regularly assigned along with the other directors to lead weekly meetings. One time, I co-hosted one with Kane's girlfriend, Sabrina, about queer dating and safer sex. It mostly catered to freshmen, with hopes there would be nuggets of advice for all attendees. It felt like a cosmic joke for me to advise anyone on these topics considering my limited romantic and sexual experience. And I carried shame about it. I was twenty and had never had a serious romance, in contrast to many of my peers, especially the white cis queer women and trans men I knew. The stakes were higher for me. Of course, being Black made me acutely aware that I had a limited dating pool at a predominantly white institution. The Black gay guys I knew seemed to keep to themselves or, worse, stayed in the closet. And even if they didn't, they never approached me. I didn't think I was unattractive, but I knew I wasn't desirable in the context of Athens, Georgia. My nonconforming gender expression seemed to make me a tough sell because I'd throw almost any potential partner's identity and ability to fly under the radar into question.

I'd been on a total of one actual date. It was toward the end of my freshman year before drag consumed my life. This lanky Latino guy and I shared a friend group that congregated in the dining halls together. David had this alluring and infectious grin and I think he appreciated my sly eyes and signature snark. Finally, after months of crushing hard, we confessed our mutual attraction at a house party. As the celebration wound down, the inches between us disappeared. We danced close, and chatted with tipsy innocence under a dense gathering of trees. "I like you," I whispered in his ear. "I like you too," he responded. With the release of our secret, naive thoughts about having my first boyfriend flooded my mind. *I needed to jump at the opportunity, right?* After the party, he texted me to make sure I made it home safe and courageously suggested we go on a date. Nothing could stifle my anticipation.

Days later, he picked me up from my dorm in a low-sitting manual convertible. I was impressed as I had proudly driven my dad's Christian Louboutin–lacquered Camaro throughout most of high school. David won more points when he opened the door for me, doling out a chivalry I hadn't ever experienced. *Did this count as chivalry if we were the same gender?* At dinner, the awkward silences were broken only by our bites. We seemingly had so little to talk about without the rest of our friend group. *Maybe we were just nervous?* I figured a solid good-night kiss would be the ultimate clue whether we should see each other again. But when he leaned down and held me close, I wasn't transported to some dream sequence. All I felt was the scratchiness of his mustache and our shared moist breaths. I put on a satisfied front, but days later I shared my reservations with him. Luckily, we salvaged our friendship after a brief period of discomfort. But I left the experience wondering if another opportunity for a relationship would come my way.

During this Lambda meeting, I didn't relay my meager dating history. I let Sabrina spill her personal anecdotes while I led the discussion on consent and contraceptives. For much of the audience, this was probably the first time queer relationships and sex had ever been openly discussed. But Sabrina and I were an entertaining duo. She had a bubbly personality that complemented my wry sassiness. Eventually, Sabrina divulged her thoughts on her sexual orientation and how her partner's gender was inconsequential. She rejected placing too restrictive of labels on herself. Then, she put me on the spot, asking for my opinion. Honestly, I'd only been attracted to cis men until that point, but I figured I was attracted to masculinity, in general. After all, I knew that there were different kinds of men. My best friends, Kane and Bryan, were trans, so it didn't seem like too much of a stretch that I could be attracted to and respect a transmasculine partner. I communicated my open-mindedness with little thought about how my body and identity would factor into a relationship with this hypothetical beau.

I stressed to our audience that none of them should be

ashamed of what they had or hadn't experienced. That college was all about exploration and it was important for them to consider what they liked or needed in any kind of partner. Then, I said, "For instance, I need someone who isn't insecure about me being a drag queen. And yes, physical attraction is important. But, I'd like someone who can handle my sarcasm. Anybody who wants to be with me needs to have tough skin." A few students giggled at my earnestness, signaling that I had delivered in my facilitator role alongside Sabrina. After the session ended, I entertained follow-up questions and requests for free condoms and dental dams. Then Alessio, a curly, auburn-haired freshman coolly walked up and told me he liked what I'd said. He'd been to a few Misters Not Sisters shows and hung out with Kane and Bryan, but we had only spoken in passing. In fact, I had the faintest memory of making eye contact with him during one of my performances. Now, he looked at me with an intense curiosity that almost made me feel like I was on stage again. I shook it off and thanked him for his kindness, then I moved on to help stack chairs.

"Tough skin, huh?" he said, slickly.

As I muttered, "Yep," I felt a smirk form on my face. We locked eyes briefly before he caught up with his friends. I appreciated that he'd listened so intently to what I'd said during the meeting. Then I wondered if he was flirting with me.

Alessio and I circled each other a few more times before speaking at a house party weeks later. As I sipped and chatted with friends, every now and then we'd lock eyes. After a bit, I noticed an empty spot beside him and plopped down. By his mellow smile and lethargic movements, he seemed hella high. But somehow, he maintained what I was beginning to recognize as a signature charm. We chatted about his adjustment to UGA and his immersion into the Misters Not Sisters orbit. Soon, our brief exchange was interrupted when Kane and a few other friends made plans to go out to some downtown Athens bar. Alessio and I were a part of the underage minority of our friend group, and both of our wheels seemed to spin. I did have a fake ID, but I'd only ever used it when I was performing or at least in drag. I assumed if I tried to use it out of femme, the bouncers would be more likely to scrutinize my resemblance to the years-older and inches-taller guy who had bequeathed it to me. Bryan offered an alternative to the downtown escapade though. He and his girlfriend, Helen, were going to hang out at his place on the other side of the apartment complex. That surely wouldn't be as exciting, but I considered the option. Then, I looked at Alessio as he stole a moment to coolly swipe Blistex across his lips. I tried not to stare. Then, he glanced back with that same look that had made me wonder if he was flirting before.

"What are you going to do?" I asked.

"I don't know," he said. "I can't get in anywhere downtown anyway."

"Yeah," I said before a couple of friends asked if I was coming.

"Ummm, well, I think I'm just going to go to Bryan's," I said, answering them but directing the response to Alessio.

Excitement spread across his face as if he didn't want to part ways either, and the night was set. I tried to hide my own thrill as we followed Bryan's lead to his spot. Helen had a pep in her step once she realized we were coming. After all, she and Alessio were roommates, so I knew they were close. I worried if I'd even get much of a chance to talk one on one with him. After walking into Bryan's sparsely furnished home, he offered us shots of Fireball whisky. Bryan, Helen, and I downed the shot glasses like they were nothing, but Alessio's disgust was palpable.

"It's not that bad," I teased.

"The hell it's not," he laughed.

Soon after, Bryan insisted that Alessio and I make ourselves comfortable as he and Helen retreated to his bedroom. So, we did. Alessio took charge and threw a mound of pillows on the floor, so I followed suit. We stumbled into a cozy, unintentionally romantic vibe, complete with a dim lamp in the corner that desperately deserved an end table.

As we stared at the ceiling, I asked how college life was treating him so far. He revealed that he came out as trans just months prior and that his family, friends, and girlfriend had been accepting. When he mentioned the latter, a pang of disappointment flowed through my body, but I remained intrigued by his story. Apparently, Alessio had been perceived as a boy for years, so most people expected his coming out. I admired his certainty about his identity. *Who would I have been if I could've been a truer version of myself in high school?* Being gay was enough of a hurdle. I couldn't imagine anyone I knew understanding the complexity of gender back then. Even now, I wasn't out to most folks as genderqueer. I'd had a throwaway conversation with Momma recently about not feeling completely like a man or a woman, but it felt more philosophical than rooted in a desire to transform how I navigated the world. In between hard gulps of Pabst Blue Ribbon, I confided in Alessio about how drag made me reconsider my identity before sharing how it was the last thing I needed to worry about months after my dad's and grandma's deaths. By now, I expected condolences to flow out before I finished my next sentence, so his didn't surprise me. Still, I was stunned by how easy it was to talk to him. As he spoke, I couldn't help but look over periodically and stare as his plump, rosy lips parted. Throughout the night, our bodies inched closer and closer over the plush beige carpet. An uncontrollable urge to touch him appeared, and I suppose he felt the same. Soon, we were embracing under the same blanket, emblazoned with our school's bulldog logo.

"Wait, what's going on right now?" I said, popping up out of his arms.

"What do you mean?" he said innocently.

"I mean, this." I motioned in between us. "Like, you have a girlfriend."

"Yeah, I don't know," he stuttered, looking from me back up at the ceiling.

"Well, obviously nothing can happen."

"Yeah, no. I mean, I know."

"OK, well, let's just keep our distance," I said, scooting away from him but still sharing the blanket.

"Yeah," he said with disappointment. I felt it too.

Whatever had sparked between us seemed inevitable. And out of his arms, we might as well have been miles apart. But soon the moment's awkwardness evaporated, and we settled back into our heartfelt conversation. Alessio was candid about his lack of surety of what he wanted out of life. He hadn't been the best student but loved learning about animals, nature, and philosophy. I'm sure I seemed like I had it all together to him. I talked about my dueling dreams of being a magazine editor or building some grander career out of drag performance. The latter didn't seem all that impossible now that we were a few seasons into *RuPaul's Drag Race*. Eventually, the tide of our dialogue brought us back to the shore of each other. There was swiftness to our familiarity, like we'd divulged decades' worth of insights in one night. Whether the vices in our system had taken effect or we were in a dawn-induced stupor, his olive eyes met my chestnut ones and we pulled into each other again. We timidly pressed our wanting mouths together. Whatever I had been longing for seemed to sprout within my chest. Alessio seemed startled by how *right* it felt too. Our hands never left each others' faces and I sensed a mutual fear of the rest of our bodies. We had both spent years being attracted to people of similar sexes, so this was something totally different. But I let the thought leave my mind. I stayed present, dreading that the night would ever end. After forever, we dozed off, intertwined.

The following day, Bryan's voice jolted us awake. He offered to drop us back at our respective apartments. At some point, Alessio and I had migrated back to opposite ends of the couch. Sheepishly, we took Bryan up on the offer. Alessio's wispy strands were going in every direction, but still I admired him. On the ride, I wondered what would happen. Clearly, Alessio and I had a connection, but it felt taboo. He was still dating his high school girlfriend, despite her going to a different college. I tried to reason through the infidelity. *I mean, he painted it as if their relationship was running its course.* Then there were the identity issues. Even though I was identifying as genderqueer, I was still mostly perceived as a gay guy in our circles. Meanwhile, Alessio was accepted in his transmasculine identity and hailed from a lesbian experience. Lastly, both of us desperately wanted to resist introducing drama into our friend group. If anything serious happened between us, we might jeopardize our relationships with our chosen family. Our lives overlapped so much: Bryan's girlfriend was Alessio's roommate, Kane's girlfriend was my roommate, Bryan and I were drag siblings, and Kane was a drag father to all of us.

Weeks of silence ensued after that first night with Alessio. During that time, Kane centered on becoming his mentor and encouraging him to perform with our troupe. I wondered if we would ever discuss that night and make sense of what happened. I couldn't shake how special our closeness felt. Then, after a few awkward interactions, Alessio sent a long direct message about how he'd compromised his values by drunkenly cheating with me. He said he had been an experiment for straight cis girls and didn't want to put me in that position with him. I hated that reductive framing though. It made me feel powerless, like I was a victim in the situation. I told him the responsibility lay with both of us; we both had to get our shit together. But more weeks of lingering looks at one another continued to give our interest away to our friend group. When we were in a room together, we couldn't keep our eyes off each other. Even if we weren't talking to each other, I felt him. And I knew he felt me. I confided in Bryan about how complicated things were and he discouraged pursuing the connection. He thought we'd be a horrible fit together. *Did Alessio feel the same way? He couldn't, not with the way he looks at me.* I was committed to dropping the whole issue until he texted me after another party.

"So how was your night?" Alessio texted.

"It was good," I replied. "I met some new peeps."

"Yeah, I saw . . ."

"What's with the ellipses?"

"Yancey was all into you."

"Really?" I replied, feeling a stir in my body. Yancey was some other junior who was at the party. I'd focused on him during the party to keep my mind off Alessio, but I wasn't attracted to him in that way at all.

"It's obvious he likes you," Alessio continued.

"I don't think anyone noticed but you," I accused.

"I mean, he's just corny."

"What's your deal with him? Are you jealous?"

"I mean, I didn't like seeing you with him."

Then I felt that feeling of inevitability from our first night return. As the night wore on, we sorted through the awkwardness of the past few weeks. Alessio revealed that he had broken up with his girlfriend and also couldn't stop thinking about me. We pieced together a toxic game of telephone, deducing that both Bryan and Kane felt uncomfortable by our attraction to each other. Apparently, they didn't think it made sense for a trans man to transition and not date a cis woman. The idea of trans people with queer sexualities was fairly novel in our little group. We had this precedent because of Kane's and Bryan's experiences that trans folks should desire cishet-appearing relationships. It was problematic as fuck, countering the radical queerness they claimed to instill in our group. Not only had Kane and Bryan dissected Alessio's masculinity and made him feel less of a man because of his queerer sexuality, but they had reduced me to a male-bodied individual on some essentialist nonsense. It was dismissive of my gender identity. Sure, I wasn't necessarily trans, but I definitely was genderqueer. I felt insecure after learning that people I trusted had thrust in my face all the ways I already felt undesirable. Even worse, it felt like Kane and Bryan, who I'd been friends with longer than Alessio, had thrown me under the bus. Our whole lives we'd been saddled with one box of gendered expectations, and now our friends were hitting us with another. It was the first time I saw how the patriarchy would threaten even queer and trans relationships. Luckily, after hashing out the situation, Alessio and I felt empowered to give our *thing* a chance.

Perhaps due to our complicated start, our relationship never completely settled into a healthy groove. There were batches of days where things seemed fine, but whenever the slightest conflict arose, Alessio would retreat from me. He'd stop communicating and avoid me, not unlike those first weeks when he was confused about his attraction. It was a confusing routine that regularly disoriented me. My inner critic would deem me as unlovable time and time again. Then I'd send Alessio a dissertation on what he needed to do to be a better partner. We'd have a long conversation, and then somehow we'd remember why we liked each other again. The passion would sweep us up and refuel our connection.

Alessio and I never hurt for sitmulating conversation, but physical intimacy was a hurdle it seemed we'd never clear. His dysphoria became the third person in our relationship, and it hurt to feel his recoil. Sometimes when we simply hugged, I could feel the tortured tenseness in his body. In those moments, I couldn't help but steal a glance at the faded white binder, which flattened his breasts just under his shirt. Initially, I thought the sole trigger was how different my body was, the masculinity that I was forced to embody. It reminded me of the years I felt deprived of affection, when my father warned of me becoming soft. I never would have imagined my first romance would be accompanied by so many guardrails. It didn't make me feel any better to know that he'd seemingly had few intimacy issues with previous cis partners. I'd once felt too feminine for most cis gay guys and now I was too masculine for my trans boyfriend. *Would any of this ever make sense?*

I couldn't blame Alessio, though. I tried to imagine what sexual intimacy might be like for us. *Which categories applied here? Would he use a strap-on or would I be expected to top? How would we navigate gender comfortably then?* There were so many unknowns and there were no real outlets to discuss my concerns. Some of our friends already didn't understand why we were together and if there were resources for trans and gender-nonconforming partners, I didn't know where to find them. We might as well have been clueless, bumbling adolescents all over again. Despite all the swirling questions, we let our relationship unfold organically.

One night, Alessio came over to my apartment and we talked, as we always did, about classes, our friend group, and whatever else. As we lay on my teal-and-brown comforter, we stared at each other admiringly. Then we kissed and our bodies grew warmer. Slowly, we undressed, staring ravenously at each other. By then,

I had come to understand his binder as necessary armor. As we melded into each other, our fear and reservations seeped out of the room. He guided me as we deciphered his boundaries. Our eyes trustfully met each other's. I felt relieved that we had entered a new relationship phase. Our being together felt right, but not in this configuration. While I enjoyed our closeness, my disappearance inside of him felt wrong. A shiver of shame drowned out the ecstasy, and I met my own dysphoria. As he stared at me with pride over having broken through this barrier, I fixed the muscles in my face to mimic his expression. It'd taken us weeks to get to this level. There was no chance that I'd allow how much I detested my penis to color the moment. So, I nestled into a pillow beside him and allowed the fatigue to transport me away from my insecurities. Sometime after, as we said our goodbyes and he left, I sat on the edge of my bed, now swallowed by a large T-shirt, some tight briefs, and gym shorts. I looked at my reflection in the mirror across the room. I scanned my flat chest, angular frame, and the bulge just below my pelvis. Somewhere within the victory of that night, I yearned for a different body.

I thought it would be enough for Alessio to know the complexity of my gender. Before him, I knew I wasn't a man, but our relationship underscored it. His presence gave me the confidence to embrace a deeper truth, beyond the morsels of clarity that came from drag performance. Dreams of a life in which the world acknowledged my womanhood flooded back. I retraced my childhood, uncovering long-lost memories of praying that I would just wake up as a girl, feeling a natural distance from the men and boys in my life, and being unfulfilled after I came out as gay. I realized I had still committed to a role, trying to fit into acceptable expectations for someone assigned male at birth. Gay was the only language accessible to me. No one back in Augusta had articulated the complexity of gender to me. How could they? They had neither the language nor the tools that I had been exposed to in my women's studies courses, nor the friend group of trans people to clarify experiences, nor the space to explore the contours of their own identities. Now, I had to figure out what I was going to do with this truth that had been revealed to me.

One night, Alessio and I video chatted while I straightened up my ever-cluttered room. I'd just returned from a weekend trip to Washington, DC, with Kane and Sabrina for the Campus Progress Journalism Summit. We were invited for our work in trying to change the antiharassment and nondiscrimination policy to include gender identity at UGA. I'd enjoyed the experience but was depleted by having to introduce myself to so many people by my birth name and gender pronouns that no longer fit. As I chipped away at a mountain of fresh laundry, Alessio and I talked more about gender transitions, and his plans to start hormones. Then, my life forever changed.

"You know, if I could just be a woman all the time in my everyday life, I would," I said absentmindedly as I placed some jeans in a dresser. I'd texted those words to Alessio before but saying them out loud felt heavier. My body stiffened.

"Wait," I stuttered, looking at Alessio's expectant smirk. "I think I'm a woman."

"I'm a woman," I repeated as tears of joyful revelation slowly streamed down my face.

"You are," he said back.

"I am," I repeated, looking around my room as if I was in a new world. "Wow.

"I wish you were here right now," I said, looking back at him.

"I wish I was too," he said. "I should be."

I never appreciated him more than in that moment, aiding me in my epiphany. It was affirming to have a trans boyfriend in this early era of my gender transition. He sweetly asked if he should call me his girlfriend from now on, and I told him we'd try it out to see if it felt right. And it did. He became even more of a haven for me. Our relationship showed me that desire and love could still be possible as I inched closer to Black trans womanhood.

Despite my revelation, Alessio and I couldn't seem to fully organize the chaos of our relationship. Now, whenever he retreated, I feared I'd lose the only person in whom I could confide. I couldn't allow him to be my only release. So over Christmas break, I cornered my mom as she sat on the same couch that I had buried myself in when I'd come out to Dad years before. I was less afraid to tell her now than I had been when I was a teenager. She'd seen bits and pieces of this newer part of my journey. After Dad died, I shared more with her about the performance aspect of my life. She'd even given me her old clothes at various points to repurpose into new costumes for Rebel and excitedly watched. With her legs curled under her, Momma listened intently. I asked her if she remembered one time when I told her I didn't feel like I was specifically "male or female," and she did. Then, I shared that I'd figured out more about myself and that I really needed to figure out my transition. I told her I planned to see a gender therapist in the new year to figure out what my options were in terms of transition.

She assured me that my transness made a lot of sense. Then, she hugged me, and encouraged me to keep her updated about my journey. I told her I didn't know where my transition would lead me, but that I was determined to figure it out. There was something so impossible about uttering to my mom that I was a woman. It felt like a door that I'd have to leave ajar for the moment. *Besides, how could I claim that identity in the body I had now?* I also felt guilty for being relieved that I didn't have to come out to my father again. He might have officially disowned me if he'd lived long enough to see me completely turn my back on the manhood and masculinity he'd tried to instill in me. It would have been one of the worst outcomes for his son. I thought about the chair Dad had broken years before, how its unrepaired remnants sat in a closet just feet away.

9

Chrysalis

Weeks after starting gender therapy sessions, I dreamed that I encountered myself as an infant. This version of me resembled an image that Grandma Inez had hung proudly on her living room wall throughout my childhood. Encased in an ivory frame, it was visible to anyone who walked through her front door. With my large observant eyes, I'm gazing up and my pillowy cheeks are hugging an almost smile. My wiry, dark brown hair hasn't been cut yet and I'm dressed in a white, lacy outfit. In the dream, I'm flying across the sky alongside the baby version of me. The cherubic figure has determination, but the adult me is terrified that we're going to plummet into the abyss. So, I pull baby me into my arms, muttering affirmations that things are going to be alright, and they trustfully look up to adult me before the image fades out.

When I woke up, a mix of loss, yearning, and catharsis stayed with me. In this last half of my junior year, my transition had become like a whole 'nother course of study for me. Each week my therapist and I waded through my transition concerns. I was convinced that the woman in me was clawing to the surface, that my old self had to die for the new one to live, that the caterpillar had to surrender to the chrysalis. It seemed like the most pressing decision revolved around starting hormone replacement therapy (HRT). I'd done as much research as I could about it online. Most of my forecasting was fueled by anecdotes from long-running forums of mostly middle-aged white trans women's experiences. The conventional wisdom was that the later you began shifting your hormone levels, the fewer physical changes you could expect. I'd just turned twenty-one, and I lamented not being able to start sooner. But having my external appearance align in a traditional way with my internal sense of gender felt necessary, even though I worried that it might lead to me never having biological children. Restricting my testosterone for an indeterminate amount of time would mean that I might never again produce viable sperm to create a child. *Should I sperm-bank? That would be a tremendous yearslong cost, plus who knew when I'd meet someone, and we'd be ready to make that kind of commitment. Or would I embrace adoption as the only option?* Being a parent was still a part of my life plan, though I worried what a future might look like for children raised by a queer or trans parent in a society that didn't want our family to exist. At twenty-one I felt so young considering my child-bearing options, even though there were plenty of cishet folks who became parents at an even younger age.

My journal became a space to muse about my lifelong relationship to my gender and sex. I'd always had dysphoria around my genitalia, but I couldn't say I always knew I wanted a vagina. That wasn't a possibility in my little mind. Vivid memories of growing up and being perplexed by the appendage between the top and bottom halves of my body during bathtime returned, as I pondered. When my parents left the room, I'd splay a washcloth over the area. As if performing a magic trick, I pretended my penis didn't exist. Afterward, as I stared at myself in the mirror, I'd pull it in between my legs and squeeze my thighs together, imagining my body without it. I didn't hate it; I didn't know I could. But there was a wrongness to it. A similar strangeness engulfed me on beach trips where I longed for a feminine bathing suit, to cover my bare chest and whenever puberty's curse of spontaneous erections sprang up. Eventually, I opted to wear the tightest underwear imaginable to conceal any hint of a bulge, even in the ocean. By the end of my teen years, the intrusive thought of grabbing scissors or a knife and eliminating my penis ran through my mind on more than one occasion. A tiny reprieve came with discovering the art of tucking. Coaxing my testicles into my inguinal canals became a way of life even outside of drag. But it wasn't a perfect cure. There was still the chaffing, the pinches, the constant fear of spilling out beyond the rudimentary gaff. *How had I not realized sooner that most boys and men don't feel that way? How had I not realized that I had already long crafted a life that maneuvered around my maleness?*

I didn't wait to make some easier changes, though. I shifted my wardrobe to a more gender-neutral style. I collected earth-toned deep V-necks, grew out my hair just as I had in elementary school, and began going by Rebel full time with my school friends and advisors. Something must have been in the air, though, because I also learned about two other trans women on campus. One was a professor who bravely embarked on a social transition over a Christmas break and came back to campus as her true self this semester. The other was another student, Heather, who I saw a few times in the dining hall. One day, as she piled food on her plate, I sidled up to her and welcomed her to sit with my friends and me. She had a short bob, no doubt growing her hair out, too. Within months, she became an indispensable resource, sharing all the tips she'd accrued. For her, transition was just a series of steps, and I thought if I followed them correctly, then I'd have a chance at a happy life. Sometimes her advice grazed my self-esteem like when she told me I needed to quit performing in drag because it betrayed my budding womanhood. And another time, after divulging the surgeries she planned on getting, she candidly remarked, "You might not need that much work done," as she observed my face. Instinctively, I brushed my hand across my chin as if verifying her assessment. According to her, what had worked for me on stage wouldn't work off it. I hated how rigid and prescriptive she was sometimes, but I coveted her surety.

Heather loaned me my first trans memoir, Caroline Cossey's *My Story*. I rapaciously devoured its pages in days. Even though I wouldn't ever be a world-class model like Cossey, better known as Tula, the volume gave me hope I could build a life for myself. Of course, I'd have to consider the consequences of being open about my identity for the rest of my life. I didn't want to get myself in a bind where my trans identity became even more of a liability and I had to fear being sensationally exposed. Heather was determined to bury any evidence of being assigned male at birth lest she eventually be outed like Cossey. She had a seemingly airtight plan to live stealth, reject the radical qualities of unapologetic transness, and fully assimilate into a cishet world. She told me she'd find the man of her dreams and never share that she was trans. If her infertility came up, she would tell her husband that it resulted from a congenital birth defect. The idea seemed extreme to me, but I understood. Love was uncertain for girls like us. That was a fact I knew all too well considering the off and on nature of my relationship with Alessio.

I wasn't swayed by Heather's plan to be stealth though. Plus I'd already become so visible locally as Rebel. I'd also been an outspoken student leader for years. For Christ's sake, I'd been elected the executive director of Lambda Alliance and continued my obligations with other LGBTQ+ student groups on campus. Being open about my experiences was crucial. I didn't want a life where I was yearning for acceptance from people who didn't cherish the real me. There was no hiding my identity now, so I searched for alternative ways to navigate my future. I revisited examples of trans women living openly, like the story of Isis King, the Black trans model who made history as the first on *America's Next Top Model*. On a viewing marathon, I observed the confusion of the other women on the show and how some of them ostracized her. I'd felt pride in seeing her pursue her dream despite the odds. In high school, a part of me appreciated the fact that I was *just gay* and didn't have to contend with extra gender hurdles when I first encountered her story. Now, rewatching old episodes online, I was certainly eating crow.

I realized I'd seen more harmful or shallow depictions of trans experiences than authentic or complex ones. As a kid, I saw trans women sharing their identities with lovers on tabloid shows like *Jerry Springer*, but they were often depicted as creatures of deception and depravity, deserving whatever rejection that came their way. There were also rare moments when trans folks were guests on relatively more respectful shows like *Oprah* or *Sally*, but I still didn't consider them as more than an oddity. In my teen years, I saw trans characters (mostly played by cis actors) in shows like *Nip/Tuck, Ugly Betty,* and *The L Word*. Our stories always had an element of tragedy to them, as in movies like *Boys Don't Cry* and *A Girl Like Me: The Gwen Araujo Story*. These real-life instances of anti-trans murders stuck with me and were never balanced with positivity in the years after.

In the sole class with an LGBTQ+-centered curriculum for my women's studies minor, I watched *Paris Is Burning*. In place of texts about the experiences of trans women of color, this was our window into the experience. Our syllabus mostly focused on readings from books and excerpts by white LGBTQ+ writers, so hearing the stories of Octavia St. Laurent, Dorian Corey, Pepper LaBeija, and Carmen and Venus Xtravaganza inspired me profoundly. So much so that the next time I went home, I ambushed my mom as she was getting ready for bed and convinced her to watch the movie. I told her I'd never seen myself so much in a film, and she seemed to understand. I could taste Octavia's and Venus's desire to be beautiful, to be "somebody," in the world. Of course, the latter's untimely death only added to the long arc of grisly trans narratives.

Not long after, I discovered *TransGriot*, a blog run by a Black trans elder named Monica Roberts from Houston. Her site was constantly turning up in search engine results about Black trans people. I sifted through her posts on history-making figures like Sir Lady Java and Tracey Africa Norman, appreciating their legendary strides. I yearned for other Black trans people in my life who would end the drought of connection I felt in Athens. Finding Monica's work broke open new possibilities of blending my interests in journalism and social justice post-graduation. She also made me curious if there were other Black trans writers out there.

Lo and behold, I found a *Marie Claire* article about a Black trans journalist in New York. The introductory paragraph read: "Janet Mock has an enviable career, a supportive man, and a fabulous head of hair. But she's also got a remarkable secret that she's kept from almost everyone she knows. Now, she breaks her silence." To say I was intrigued would be a woeful disservice of the moment. The first thing I thought was how gorgeous she was and how I'd be lucky if my transition was half as glorious as hers. Paragraphs later, I felt like I'd stumbled upon a mirror. I said to myself, "This is me." It was the first time I'd ever read about another Black trans woman who started her transition in her youth. Beyond Cossey, most other narratives I'd read were about older white trans women who came out later in life. Even further, many had lived cishet lives, married women, and raised children. Janet's story was so revelatory and she became a North Star that made me feel like I didn't have to fumble through my post-collegiate life.

Though I didn't have Black trans folks surrounding me, I did at least seek out friends who were closer in experience. After a short-lived fling with Kane, a girl named Deidre and I bonded over the tokenism we often experienced at UGA, our Black feminist inclinations, and our love for the rapper Azealia Banks. Whenever Alessio pissed me off, I'd drive over to Deidre's home, an old converted church, and glom onto her for refuge. Not long after, we met Roblé in our Critical Feminist Readings class. They were also from Augusta and seemed to be similarly yearning for a space to be their full Black queer selves and complain about the patriarchy. Our inseparable trio found biblical guidance in tomes like *Black Feminist Thought* by Patricia Hills Collins and *Feminist Theory: From Margin to Center* by bell hooks. They were the first required readings I hadn't mostly skimmed in years. Our unofficial consciousness-raising group felt like a treasure trove for understanding ourselves and the world. We could talk for hours about society's hierarchies, drafted by people who didn't have the needs and dreams of people of color, women, LGBTQ+ folks, and others on the margins in mind. Then, we could lose ourselves in whatever magnificent distraction Beyoncé gifted the world.

* * *

THE MORE I delved into what womanhood might look like for me, my gender dysphoria became an invisible villainous force, controlling the levers of my body, affecting how I moved and sounded. It became increasingly unbearable, and I saw my life's bifurcated path clearly. Down one branch, I could attempt to live as a feminine queer man continuing on the insufficiently fulfilling journey I'd embarked on in high school. I'd bury my truth, letting this era of exploration fade from my life's story. I might find romance and craft a family, but it would be formed on a false foundation. Then there would always be a chance later in life that I could try to reorient my life around the truth, having lost crucial time. On the other path, I could attempt a gender transition and try to get the people in my life to understand my complex identity. I might never look the way I desired; I might lose family, friends, and take on more complicated difficulties of finding love. But I'd become the woman I knew myself to be, braving the fierce storm of authenticity. Neither journey would be easy, but a life of not being seen and respected seemed like the worst thing that could happen—and I had to ward that off as much as possible.

My mind prepared an altar for the old me. I succumbed to the woman inside me, relinquishing that longstanding belief that my femininity was some kind of disease. As I retraced my experience, I felt like I'd been cheated out of freedom for so long. *Who would I have been without those day-one boxes of gender, if I was less consumed by what others thought of me, if I could have been the driver of my own destiny?* It felt like the old me had to die. I no longer accepted this perpetual division between who I wanted to be and who the world wanted me to be. I felt a terrifying thrill in relinquishing the future I thought I would live.

I decided that pursuing a medical transition would be my only chance at an enjoyable life. I no longer cared about the risks. Sure, I hated that I had to sacrifice my fertility for a more promising future, but it seemed necessary. If I were ever to be a parent, I would love my adopted children as deeply as I would've loved any biological ones. Besides, if I didn't transition, I'd never be able to even be a great parent or a person, period. I'd be living in constant regret and resentment. Passability mattered less, too.

If I were never regarded fully in my womanhood, at least I knew I was living with dignity on my own terms. And I hoped the people in my life could adapt and understand me.

So, on a weekend visit, I told my mother that I had reached a conclusion about my gender after months of therapy. She seemed to anticipate my revelation. "You've lived all your life trying to live up to other people's ideas of who you should be. It's time for you to live your life for you," she said. That encouragement soothed me, and I assured her I'd let her know when I was ready to start HRT and that I'd figure out how to tell my siblings. For now, I was focused on my studies and my first major international trip.

* * *

IN MAY 2012, I traveled to Milan, Italy, for a six-week fashion marketing internship. I'd learned about the program from an informational session on campus, applied, and was accepted. Our internship group was about twelve deep and we all came from countries as disparate as Canada, Argentina, and Turkey. Once again, I found myself as the only Black person and the only one assigned male at birth. The young women in my cohort were cordial and welcomed me. Apparently, my obvious queerness disarmed them. So, I didn't feel awkward sharing a room with them and navigating the space. I appreciated their open-mindedness and even confided in two women about my gender. They received it well and tried their best to be affirming, understanding my decision to revert back to using my birth name and masculine pronouns because of the language barrier.

I emailed Jessica first, hoping to gain some more confidence. I had to hold off on sharing with my brother. He and his wife would be birthing their first child at any day, and I worried about putting extra stress on them. *How wild was it that my truth was potentially that unsettling?* Besides I'd learned from my first coming-out experience that I could only control so much in how people responded and that I had to have a steel resolve if I was going to make it through this process in one piece.

It was an excruciating few days' wait, but eventually Jessica replied. She empathized with how low my self-worth had fallen and the difficulties I had faced silently for so long. Then, she probed with thoughtful questions about how long I'd known, what a physical transition might look like, and whether I'd thought about the delineation between general insecurities and actual gender dysphoria. Then, she urged me to have "the patience of Job" with our family. I somewhat balked at the assertion. I felt like I'd done that my entire life, and I wanted to move forward now that I'd found some solutions that could make up for lost time.

In my final internship days, our group made a final sprint through the Italian towns (Pisa, Rome, Verona, and Venice) we hadn't seen throughout our trip. Hostels came in clutch as we woke up at the crack of dawn to catch early trains and mapped out hours-long excursions. While in Rome, we ventured to the Vatican. Though I was fully agnostic by now, I stared up at the imposing walls with reverence, thinking of my late father. *What would he think of the transformation that awaited me when I returned?* I imagined his disappointment but thought he might respect my tenacity on some level. Then, on one of my final train rides in Italy, I saw a trans woman on a train. At least I thought she was one of the dolls. She towered over most folks in her worn heels. Her long, glorious dark locks, big shades, and hastily applied red lipstick made me ready to return home. I wanted to make eye contact to let her know I saw her, that I appreciated her, that I was like her. Then, I remembered that it'd be no use because I wasn't presenting as my true self. I wasn't quite in the sisterhood yet. Still, I took her presence as a sign that I was on the right path.

When I returned to the States, I set up an appointment at an endocrinology clinic in Atlanta. All the trans people I knew in Athens had to travel nearly an hour and a half for competent, gender-affirming care. Kane, Bryan, and I made a solidarity pact to start HRT on the same day. My excitement stalled when my brother responded cruelly to the email I sent once I made it back home. He typed a long response about having been embarrassed by me for years and how, no matter what I did, "whether I grew my hair long, cut my balls off, or grew knockers," I'd never be a woman. His reaction stung, but it wasn't shocking. By now, I had little hope that he would ever come around and resigned myself to caring as little as possible. My mother's and my sister's support more than made up for the absence of his.

Undeterred, my friends and I traveled to our appointments and got our first prescriptions. After returning to Athens, one by one we bared our butts to one another as we assisted in giving our first injections. Kane proudly punctured my skin, and my medical transition began. So much in those early days involved crossing my fingers, hoping for any slight change. Within months, my skin grew softer, and my acne diminished. I welcomed the idea of growing breast tissue, never having erections again, and producing less body hair. Still, there was no certainty of what changes would occur. In 2012, there was never enough research accessible to me about what to expect, but I held on close to anecdotes from Internet strangers and excerpts from the World Professional Association for Transgender Health standards of care. This would hold me over for now.

10

For Women Who Had a Boyhood

M y senior year of college felt like a race against time. The moment when I'd be ejected into the real world was hurtling toward me. Beyond the medical shifts I wanted to see, I pressed on with the social aspects of my transition. I emailed all of my professors, explaining my identity and my use of a different name and pronouns than provided on my student records. I couldn't officially update them without a legal name change, but they all obliged with just a few mistakes and hiccups along the way. I was most soothed by the responses from Valerie Boyd and Cynthia Tucker, noted Black women writers who taught upper-level courses at UGA's Grady College. Boyd was a decorated biographer who had written extensively about Zora Neale Hurston. She was never short on inspiration. Tucker also regularly checked in with me, understanding the Herculean task of transitioning during my senior year. They never doubted my ability to find my journalistic voice and have a career post-graduation, but I still worried about whether potential employers would be affirming.

Early in the semester, I chose National Coming Out Day to share my transness on social media. It seemed like the smoothest way to let a large swath of people know all at once without having to have a million short conversations—though I still anticipated clarifying questions. In preparation, I gave in to the desire to shred as much of my past self as possible. I digitally tucked the evidence away, hoping that one day I'd be able to go through photos without grimacing. When the annual observance came, I drafted and shared a short post about my gender journey. Within hours of hitting *publish*, I received messages of solidarity from friends and even some strangers who praised my bravery. It felt like a necessary step to clarify who I was, and alert folks of my new name and pronouns. I'd settled on Raquel after weeks of thinking my name over. It wasn't super common and it allowed me to more easily hold on to Rebel as a nickname. I wanted folks to know how to address and respect me from now on. I thought little about coming out to anyone else directly after that, assuming they'd heard through the grapevine. That sentiment would come back to bite me on the ass.

Days later, Auntie Joanie, one of Momma's younger sisters, passed away. I had plenty of memories of her infectious chuckle, sense of adventure, and hedonism. She always had the best bootlegged DVDs (particularly Madea plays) and a never-satiated sweet tooth. I loved our trips to get some Baskin-Robbins pistachio-almond ice cream. But while I was upset by her death, I was also unsure of whether I should attend a major family event this early in my transition. When I'd come out to my immediate family, I had given little thought to connecting with extended relatives. I didn't know how I would discuss my identity with my elders. In fact, I hadn't considered what it'd be like for them to witness my gender transition or whether they could accept me. For so long, I'd assumed there would be a day where I'd have to stop going to family reunions and other gatherings. After all, I didn't know of any openly queer family members. My complicated identity just seemed incompatible with their—what I considered to be—country and Southern sensibilities. As a whole, my relatives were highly religious, and were pastors and leaders in their churches. I never imagined they would accept me like Momma had. As Chet claimed, she was different and would support me through whatever. That didn't mean they or the rest of the world would.

I was also still figuring out how to navigate everyday life as a woman. In fact, I had just started having strangers respect and see my essence, like when I was ma'amed while running errands. But most of my adult experiences had occurred on a predominantly white liberal college campus. I worried about what it would be like to be surrounded by people who'd known me since birth, who expected a particular type of Southern Black womanhood. *What evidence did I have that they understood the gender binary and sexual essentialism?* I mutually followed some relatives on social media, so I knew at least a few were aware of my identity. When I expressed my condolences and concerns to Momma, she assured me that the rest of our family could understand, adding the caveat that if anyone gave me a rough time, she'd handle it. That didn't completely quiet my reservations, but I knew it would mean the world for my mother to have all her children present for her sister's funeral.

After my last class of the week, I packed up my car and made the nearly seven-hour drive to my mom's hometown, Jacksonville, Florida. Auntie Joanie's funeral would be there while the burial would take place in Live Oak, Florida, where my maternal grandma's family had cemetery plots. As I pulled up to my mom's childhood home, I noticed a few cars in the driveway and on the ever-lush lawn. I panicked instantly, preparing myself for being deadnamed, misgendered, and potentially ostracized by whoever was in the house. I rang Momma on her cell, hoping she would escort me inside lest I gamble an awkward interaction. She didn't answer. *Really? This is when I really need you to build me up.* Anyway, I mustered the courage to make it across the walkway to the small house.

The white wooden door was wide open, but its accompanying screen door was locked. When I was a kid, I never understood how Grandma Ida could ignore the swooshing cars on the thoroughfare. Apparently, nothing could tear her away from the drama of her stories—that is, her soap operas. Oh yes, she was an avid fan of all of them, but especially *The Bold and the Beautiful, Passions,* and *The Young and the Restless.* The rest of the family would gather around her and wait to chat during the commercials. Peeking through the screen door, I saw that the living room walls were still the same carnation pink I remembered, and the furniture hadn't changed either. The only thing missing was the people, so I timidly pushed the doorbell. As it dinged, I heard Momma's shuffling. "Comin," she yelled. *Thank God,* I thought. I quickly assessed whether I looked OK, worrying that my family would think my appearance was weird or judge what I was wearing. But I had put a little thought into it. I'd kept things simple with my new favorite black shirt that had a panel of leather fabric across the bodice and some blue skinnies. These were items Momma and I had picked out on a back-to-classes shopping spree weeks prior. She'd insisted on helping me find a new, more gender-affirming wardrobe. To top off the look, I'd dusted on some light makeup and a rosy lipstick. At that time, rarely did any of the women in my family shy away from a bold color. As Momma approached the door, I could see the excitement in her step. After she opened it, she beamed and yanked me into a hug.

"Momma, I called you," I complained.

"Well, I was in the back, Suga," she replied as she embraced me. "You look good, baby!"

"You sure?"

"Yes," she said, as she locked the screen door behind me.

When I stepped inside the house, the nostalgia almost flushed out my anxiety about my relatives' reactions. I asked Momma who all was there, and she told me her older sister, Auntie Thelma, was just around the corner. I grew a tad nervous as this auntie had been known to serve some problematic views on LGBTQ+ folks, so I expected a little resistance. But she wasn't the only offender. When I was younger, while watching some television show featuring gay characters, I'd heard Grandma and Auntie Joanie talk about how disgusting the idea of two men together was. So I shuddered at our inevitable interaction. Perhaps Momma could see my apprehension, so she accompanied me to Grandma's bedroom. As we made our way down the hallway, Auntie Thelma stepped out of a bedroom and gave me a quick up-and-down, trying to absorb this newer version of me. Then she pulled me in for a hug and told me I looked beautiful before darting to the kitchen. That tiny moment went better than I expected. Just after, I followed Momma into Grandma Ida's bedroom.

"Momma," my mother overarticulated. "This is Raquel, your youngest grandbaby."

Grandma had been sitting on the edge of her bed watching TV. She joyfully looked up and her eyes switched from Momma to me. She'd been diagnosed with dementia, so I had no idea how she might react or whether she'd recognize me. Momma led me over to her and I bent down to hug her tightly. She just looked at me and said, "You look pretty, like me" in wonderment. I let out a relieved sigh, then sat beside her on the bed. The claiming, the validation, was just what I needed after so much self-doubt. I could tell that she knew she knew me, but I doubt that the complexity of her grandchild transitioning genders made sense. It was enough just to have her hold my hand as I leaned into her warm body. Somehow, through the fog of her mind, she saw me, and I hoped the rest of our family would too.

After bringing my suitcase inside, I basked in the minor victories of the day. I figured I could easily make it through the weekend if everyone reacted like my aunt and grandma. But soon, I heard Auntie Thelma tell Momma that a few of my guy cousins were coming over. The two oldest were about the same age as my older siblings and one had a son who was a high schooler. The last thing I needed to wade through was judgment from cishet men, especially considering my brother's response to my identity. Still, I said a silent prayer that the rest of the evening would prove inconsequential.

When my cousins arrived, they doled out hellos to everyone. Unfortunately, they birthnamed me and I prepared to respond the way I typically would have pretransition. I had this generic, faux masculine, "Not much, man" sort of response. But then I realized I didn't have to do that bullshit anymore. As I returned to a higher register, I croaked out, "Hey, y'all," and they responded in kind. They bypassed me to hug the other women in my family. I could tell they didn't quite know how to interact with me now. I understood the conundrum, but I couldn't help but feel like my transness was a deadly contagion they didn't want to rub off on them.

Soon after, Momma plopped down near my cousins at the dining room table and saccharinely said, "Now y'all are gon' have to get used to my baby's new name. It's Raquel." They didn't seem too shocked, so I figured Auntie Thelma had given them a heads-up. My oldest cousin repeated the name to confirm and joked about me possibly having a new nickname by the end of the weekend because they hadn't quite gotten the pronunciation down. I was learning that the damned q in my name was going to regularly trip people up. Anyway, they all smiled supportively and seemed to understand. I wasn't quite ready for this impromptu reintroduction, but I felt blessed to have a mother who loved me this much, who could do this heavy lifting, who believed in radical transformation. Hopefully, we'd survive the weekend unscathed.

Soon Jessica and her family arrived. I was excited to spend more time with my nibbling (a gender-neutral word to refer to my siblings' children), who Momma described as growing like a weed. His cheeks were so huge that it looked like it hurt when he smiled. Now, at about two years old, I relished the fact that he recognized me on sight. The only hiccup was that he now had to tease out how I was related to him. He made us laugh because he apparently had only two female family names to reference: Mommy and Grandma. So he seemed to ask whether my name was the former twice before figuring that I must just be another grandma. It took us a while to get him to say "Auntie," but eventually he got the hang of it. His loving squeaky voice gendering me correctly was fulfilling.

Just before bed, Momma and Jessica pulled me aside to discuss what we'd be wearing. Of course, I knew I needed to wear black, but I still had a limited wardrobe. I showed them two options, and they awkwardly agreed that one of them would work out fine. They clearly weren't thrilled about my meager pickings, but it was late and there wouldn't be time to get other clothes. So this was what we had. In the morning, I noticed the lacy black gloves all the women had and stared at my bare hands. It was a reminder that I still had so much to learn about navigating this new set of Southern Black womanly customs.

When we made it to the church, I clung to Momma as much as possible. Her presence was like a shield, and I felt like a kid relearning how to interact with everyone. Soon, Chet and his wife strolled up to the crowd we were in. We exchanged hugs but said very little. As we coalesced in front of the church, I learned that there would be a procession of the family through the congregation. *Great; the last thing I needed was more eyes on me.* I tried to avoid any eye contact with relatives, though I saw a few weird looks in my periphery. Soon, the pastor welcomed us all to be seated as the organ player's tune touched our ears. He spoke of "Sister Joan" and her commitment to her faith and family. Then there was another selection, and we joined the recessional.

As my family walked down the aisle, I saw Auntie Robyn and my uncle standing in a pew. They both had a mortified look as we passed them. My heart jolted. I hadn't seen either of them since Dad's death, nor had I expected my dad's sister and her husband to attend the funeral of my mother's sister. As we walked outside, I lay low, trying to avoid as many people as I could. Soon, Momma said she needed to go to the restroom and, seeing my fear of being left alone, she beckoned me along with her. I decided to wait outside the bathroom so as not to cause any unnecessary awkwardness. I hadn't been clocked in a restroom in a while, but I didn't want to take any chances with so many relatives. As I sat on a bench, I relished the lack of traffic. After a few older women left the restroom, Auntie Thelma burst into the area using my birth name while asking about Momma's whereabouts. My temporary solace was destroyed, and embarrassment replaced the comfort I'd been seeking. I looked at her stupefied, then the older ladies stopped and looked around for this hypothetical man. But it didn't take long for them to "get" what was going on. One of them looked at me and nervously said, "God bless you!" then shuffled away awkwardly. *I was blessed, alright.* I wanted to correct my auntie at the moment, but I had to excuse it and let the moment pass.

When Momma and I headed back out of the church into a small crowd, one of my distant cousins came up and said, "Well,

I haven't seen you in a while." *Yeah, clearly*, I thought to myself. Instead of crumpling, I came up with a plan for anyone with a bewildered look. Before they could even mention my obvious transformation, I pivoted to discussing my upcoming college graduation. It was the perfect distraction. Just like Momma, the rest of my family cherished an educational accomplishment.

Shortly after, Momma and I followed a line of cars for the hour-and-a-half drive to Live Oak, Florida, for the burial. This is the longtime home of Grandma Ida's ancestors. And there's a site that has for generations served as the final resting place for the family. When Momma and I arrived at the graveside, I saw Auntie Robyn on the phone in her car. I could sense the tension. As the pastor gave the final eulogy and the casket was lowered, I realized that my aunt had missed this part of the ceremony. I wondered what was going on, as it seemed weird that she would come all the way from Atlanta and miss such a crucial part of the ceremony. *Maybe something happened? Maybe it's a work thing?*

At the repast, I lingered in the car for a bit, trying to focus on my breath and catch my bearings. As soon as I finally regained the energy to return to the gathering, Jessica darted toward me and snapped, "We need to talk right now!" *What's going on?* I thought. But I simply followed her over to a patch of grass where her husband, who also looked perturbed, was standing.

"Auntie Robyn is upset with you," Jessica said.

"Wait . . . why?" I responded.

"How could you not tell her about your transition?" she asked.

"What do you mean?"

"How could you not tell your auntie about this life-changing event?"

"Why would I have? The only folks I was concerned about was immediate family," I explained.

"That's selfish," she said. "You need to fix it."

My brother-in-law nodded along with my sister's words. I was dumbfounded by their anger as I searched their faces for clarity. *What the hell was I supposed to do?* I didn't even understand the source of the problem. I wanted to set the record straight in the moment that I didn't owe anyone any explanation and that I'd faced many hurdles that day. But I didn't have the energy, plus I wasn't interested in setting them off more. I was already facing a mountain of scrutiny. So, I thought for a second, assured them I'd figure things out, then headed over toward Momma to divulge this new information.

My first instinct was to get Momma's perspective. When I approached her, she was talking to a few women and introduced me as her youngest child before nervously stuttering on my name, referring to me as Roxanna. Two of the ladies smiled, but the third had a confused look on her face. "Marilyn, I thought you only had one daughter," she said. *Oh, so now we have a detective on our hands?* Well, Momma froze up and blurted out, "We'll talk later." As we tipped away, I explained Jessica's and Auntie Robyn's reaction to her. She reassured me it didn't matter what anyone else thought and advised me not to be discouraged. Then we agreed to go try to talk to my aunt. But when we approached her, she said with exasperation, "I can't talk right now. I just can't." Then she sat back in her car for a long while before I glimpsed Jessica talking to her again, perhaps trying to smooth things over.

In the meantime, I got my plate at the repast. It was typical and glorious Southern fare: fried chicken, mac and cheese, potato salad, collard greens, and cornbread. While I stuffed my face with my brother and his wife, one of our great-aunts came up to me and shared that she knew a young man who was going through the same thing as me. For a second, I wondered whether she was conflating a cis gay male experience with a trans woman experience, but then she revealed that he "hasn't even changed his name yet." I appreciated her understanding.

"I know this is complicated for the family," I said with a hint of shame.

"Well, it's not complicated, just new," she assured me. "Everyone will get used to it."

Our conversation had finally smoothed out until another aunt strolled up and asked the supportive aunt, "Do you know who this is? This is Chet's brother." I looked at her, trying to conceal my aggravation. I just directed my attention to the aunt who had given me the kind words while the other kept gazing at me. Luckily, the event didn't last too much longer after that exchange.

Back at Grandma Ida's house, Jessica's family prepared to leave, and I asked her about her follow-up discussion with Auntie Robyn. She said she'd just tell me tomorrow. *Wait, so just like that this pressing issue was now a non-starter?* I was frustrated, especially after how urgently she had wanted me to "fix" the situation just hours earlier.

Apparently, Momma was perturbed as well, and her words shredded Jessica's plan to postpone the conversation.

"I don't know why she acted that way," Momma said as she rinsed some dishes off at the sink.

"Yeah, I don't know why she acted like she was the fucking victim," I said, shocked by my inability to hold my anger in and, of course, swearing in front of Momma. But I couldn't stop. "I'm the fucking victim here."

"No, she was upset because you hadn't told her beforehand. She's your aunt. She should have known about something this big before this," Jessica said, her voice rising. "We talked about this a month ago, and you said you were going to tell her. So it's on you for not telling her and you need to call her and fix this. She was really hurt."

"This was a fluke event. It's a funeral," I explained. "How was I supposed to know someone was going to die before I had time to talk to her about it? Besides, I didn't expect my father's sister to be at a funeral for my mother's sister. And I don't see why people feel like I owe them something. It's nice for folks to know, but I don't owe anybody any explanation."

"See, you're just being selfish," Jessica said. "This is something that affects all of us."

"Maybe I am being selfish. Just like people who have been selfish my entire life telling me how to look, how to act, and what I'm supposed to do," I said, now on the verge of tears. "Besides, this is someone who is of the mindset of 'If you're gay, take it to the grave.'"

"See, you're putting stereotypes on people," Jessica shot back. "You couldn't even pick up the phone and call your aunt! How could you not do that?"

My sister had a point. I didn't actually know what Auntie Robyn thought of LGBTQ+ folks. She had always been refreshingly open-minded and sophisticated. And she wasn't some distant relative; she was a crucial person in my childhood. In fact, we saw her and my uncle on almost every major holiday. When my parents reacted negatively to my plan to come out as a teenager, I wrote off telling my extended relatives. But in this moment, I couldn't see all of that nuance. I was at a sensitive point in my transition where nearly any critique felt like a slight against me. I didn't take my aunt's or my sister's concerns seriously. It all just felt like transphobic rejection.

"Do you know how much is on my plate? How am I horrible for forgetting to tell one person? I just don't understand why people act like they have more room to be hurt than I do," I yelled. "Do you know what I go through daily and all I have to think about? And then I come here and get that same treatment. So I'm sorry, but I'm not *that* sorry."

"You should have told her and handled this," Jessica said, having the big-sister last word.

Eventually, we both calmed down and hugged it out. Of course we loved each other through it all. But there wasn't any resolution to the weekend's events. I wasn't moved to contact my aunt nor follow up with Jessica afterward. Our family just simply didn't handle conflict well, so I didn't fathom the situation as more than a lost cause. All I knew was that this fiery resolve would be necessary to make it through this stage in my life. This event served as a signal that my transition would reconfigure my relationships in unforeseen ways.

Just two weeks shy of the reelection of Barack Obama to the U.S. presidency, I experienced another situation that would illuminate the distance between my understanding of my identity and that of the people around me. Alessio, Kane, and I were having a much-cherished munchie meal at Waffle House. Both of them had grown closer, eventually becoming roommates. I should've been ecstatic about their friendship, but it was complicated. Since Kane was older and saw himself as a mentor, it often felt like he meddled in Alessio's and my jagged romance. Often when Alessio and I argued nowadays, he seemed to parrot a self-absorbed perspective that I'd expect from Kane. I imagined him in his ear, like a little proverbial devil, stoking flames of discontent or encouraging him to ditch his commitments to me. Tonight was one of those nights when, if I wanted to see Alessio, I had to step into their world. As I scarfed down a smoked bacon omelet and they sopped up syrupy golden waffles, Kane complained about a post I'd shared on Tumblr.

"What do you mean it's not a real thing?" I said incredulously, glancing at Alessio to see if he was similarly outraged. But his mouth spread into an agreeing smirk as he cleared his teeth with a hard flick of his tongue.

"*Transmisogyny* is just a word people came up with to put trans men down," Kane said, preparing his next bite. "It's just used when people want to say that trans men are toxic."

"That's not what it is at all. It actually has very little to do with trans men." I snickered. *He couldn't be serious.*

"Oh, so what is it?" Kane responded, daring me to correct him.

"Well, it's about the specific oppression that trans women and transfeminine people face in a world that has told us almost since birth that we shouldn't be who we are. That we shouldn't be feminine," I said with clarity, albeit with a few stutters peppered in.

"Nah, I only hear it when people want to trash trans men," Kane said, on guard. "Besides, we're the ones assigned female at birth. What oppression do trans women have over trans men? It's all the same."

"It's actually not. Femininity is so demonized in our society. How can you even say that?" I scoffed. "You may have been assigned female at birth, but anyone embodying and even identifying with masculinity is experiencing a privilege that others don't."

"We have it hard, too," Kane shot back. "Why does everyone think trans men have it easy?"

"No one is saying that you don't," I said, looking at Alessio for some backup, but he averted his eyes. "But compared to trans women, it's a different story."

"I mean, I've seen the same thing," Alessio chimed in. "Transmisogyny is used a lot to say trans men aren't going through struggles."

"But it's not, though. Have y'all even read Julia Serano's book?" I said, surprised that my boyfriend was cosigning this fucked-up argument. Serano had been top of mind as our LGBTQ+ Resource Center had recently announced her as a guest speaker for the next semester.

"I don't need to," Kane responded. "I know how it's used to keep us down."

"Oh, okay," I said, with a deflated tone. There was no correcting "the father" of our friend group of his ignorance. He was incorrigible and infallible. We'd exalted him in that role for years, and it felt like he'd conditioned us to just accept anything he said. I had no problem acknowledging that trans men experienced oppression, considering I had been surrounded by several of them for quite a while. Kane, specifically, had a troubled upbringing with parents who disowned him as a teenager for his queerness. Along the way, his educational status had been threatened by financial barriers. Still, it hurt that he'd twisted a social media post into a contest about whether trans men or trans women had it worse in our society.

As I settled into Alessio's bed that night, he had the audacity to ask why I was *so* bothered by that discussion. *Oh, he could tell?* I'd retreated from conversation, and our wordless drive must have signaled it. I couldn't calm myself. I just stared at the winding Athens road in front of us. We said our muted good nights to Kane and headed upstairs. Now, here in Alessio's bedroom, there was no escaping the tension.

"I just don't understand how y'all can say trans women don't experience our own particular type of oppression," I said. "And for you to sit up there and agree with his privileged ass is ridiculous."

"Oh, here we go," he said, as he washed his face. "Look, Kane has been through things. He's not privileged."

"He's white and masculine," I said. "What do you mean? He sure as hell doesn't experience racism."

"And you're light-skinned, attractive, and come from a middle-class family. What do you even know about racism, anyway? It's just something you've read about. You have all the words but haven't actually had a hard life. You've never been told you were unloved," Alessio said in a rapid-fire retort. He'd been splashing his face with water. But now, without even wiping, he just stared at me, daring me to respond.

"What do you mean I don't know what racism is?" I said. "I'm a Black trans woman. Racism isn't just burning crosses on lawns; it happens every fucking day. I'm surrounded by mostly white people in all of my classes. Even in our friend group, I'm the only Black person and the only trans woman. And just because you think I'm light-skinned or attractive doesn't change that."

I wondered who this stranger was that I had been laid up with for the past year. Our relationship had always been complex, but I never questioned whether we were on the same page about privilege, especially the kind granted to him because of his whiteness. In his so-called laying out of my identities, he'd given me a glimpse into the unspoken ways that he justified his attraction to me. He laid my desire capital on front street without any qualms. I went back and forth on this. *Maybe he's just pissed. Wait, but what right did he have to be pissed? He should have been on my side.* I'd always been relieved that he came from a liberal family, especially at a university where that political orientation wasn't a given. But now, that sense of security had dissipated. The venom he'd spoken settled into every memory of us. *Had he been waiting to assert that I was a pseudo-feminist, or worse, a paranoid Black girl?*

There was nothing I could say, so I just turned over and stared at his dark red walls. *Who paints their room such an evil fucking color, anyway?* I thought to myself. Soon after, he silently hopped in the bed. *These uncomfortable thin sheets. And why, after all this time, did I have only one designated pillow?* I nudged myself as far away from him as I could. My skin felt like it might ignite if I touched him. By the time I woke up, our minds might as well have been light-years away. I played as nice as possible when I said goodbye. This time, though, I was ready to claim my space away from him and Kane. That squabble made me more grateful for my friendships with Deidre and Roblé.

After a celebration party for Obama's reelection, I finally stopped dodging Alessio's texts after a little over a week. Perhaps it was liquid courage or the swelling pride of having a Black president staying in the White House, but I demanded an apology from Alessio and Kane. But Alessio refused to understand how much he had hurt me, so I left him on read. He seemingly didn't understand that the policing of my body, experience, and gender didn't start as soon as I transitioned. Just like him, I had been policed my whole life. *What did he know about being a woman who had a boyhood, who couldn't stretch beyond the box of expectations that had been set by society? What did he know about my particular brand of stunted intimacy and lack of freedom?* His whiteness had afforded him more space to explore gender nonconformity as a child. Not to mention, his parents had recently allowed him to take time off from school to support his mental health. It was beautiful that he'd had that kind of grace in his life, but I never would have been extended that by my traditional Southern Black family. Sure, we both came from middle-class families, but he certainly had more access than me. I had been raised with the expectation to grind myself to the bone, to endure by any means necessary. Even when my father passed, I hadn't even taken time off to mourn because I was consumed with making it through college, with achieving until I could fill the void left. It felt insulting for him to know all of this and still throw this idea of privilege in my face.

I might not have had as much experience as he did being perceived as a woman, but I was facing my own crash course on beauty myths and misogynoir. Seriously, I was coming into my womanhood on a campus where damn near every other girl in my classes seemed to be petite, cisgender, straight, and white with a sorority flair. They were the desirable standard, and there was no way he didn't know that. Plus, it was in his apartment weeks after I started HRT when Kane and his new girlfriend started openly commenting on my budding breasts. They'd joked about my nipples being too visible and how it was time for me to wear a sports bra. Sure, they painted it as helping me "understand" womanhood, but it was embarrassing.

And I wanted to talk about how I felt that he treated me in ways that he would have never treated his previous white, cis girlfriends. While he had met my mom and even visited Augusta with me, I felt like I was hidden from his parents, who lived just miles away. They knew I existed, but I met his mom on campus in passing, not by Alessio's engineering. She was a pleasant woman, but after I thought more about our encounter, I wondered if my Black trans womanhood had kept him from officially introducing me. He didn't know the battle of self-worth that I faced on a nearly daily basis simply from being his girlfriend. After Alessio badgered me for a response to his text, I simply responded, "You mad. Stay mad," at the urging of Deidre. Then I settled in the silence. I loved him, but I couldn't wait to be out of his orbit.

By the second half of my senior year, I was restlessly focused on life beyond graduation and a reignited dream to move away from Georgia. In between classes, I applied to as many journalism and marketing jobs in the New York area as possible and focused more on my transition. I opted for my first gender-affirming surgery, a tracheal shave (or chondrolaryngoplasty), in which they remove a bit of the cartilage from a prominent Adam's apple.

Mine had been prominent since puberty. I'd press it in so much, trying to imagine myself without it, that I'd made it sore. I also needed to be rid of it so I could use the surgery as the required evidence that I was truly embarking on a gender journey and acquire some new identity documents.

I was worried that I'd be turned away when I submitted the legal paperwork for my name and gender change. The standard in most places, particularly the South, was that you had to have bottom surgery before being deemed a woman by the government. But per advice from trans folks online, I placed my bets that the system wasn't sophisticated enough to understand the difference between various gender-affirming surgeries, and I guessed right. When I went in for my driver's license, the Danny DeVito–looking man behind the counter gave me a once-over and told me I was too pretty to have the wrong information on my ID. Somehow the patriarchy helped me out with that one, but it set a promising precedent. In the last few months of college, I updated records like social security and ones for school. Unfortunately, I'd have to wait to change the gender on my birth certificate and passport until I had bottom surgery.

As I entered these deeper parts of my transition, my relationship with drag shifted. It felt less authentic for me. I hated the insistence that I was impersonating a woman. No, honey, I *was* a woman. But it was a brutal battle to be seen and fully understood in a landscape where most drag queens were cis men. I worried, on some level, about how much I was internalizing what it meant to be the "right kind of woman." Sometimes it felt like I'd replaced one set of masculine expectations with another of the feminine variety. Still, with every transition milestone, I tried to assess whether I was deciding more for myself or to fit into society. The answer often seemed to be some mixture of the two, but I knew I needed to prioritize whatever made me feel more comfortable in my skin. It felt like there were two choices for my life post-graduation: either surrender to being stealth or continue to be open about my transness with the risk of being seen as some rudimentary facsimile of cisgender womanhood.

Toward the end of my senior year, trans acceptance seemed like it was rising. More and more students were openly identifying as trans and increasingly finding resonance in a growing identifier, *nonbinary (NB),* at the onset of their college experiences. In fact, most of the Lambda directors identified as trans, NB, or gender nonconforming by the time I exited leadership, which wasn't the case when I was a freshperson. Nationally, shifts were happening too. Vice President Joseph Biden publicly claimed that trans discrimination was the "civil rights issue of our time."[1] The *New York Times* reported that nearly half of the states in our country had adopted or considered regulations that would allow trans students to compete on teams that corresponded with their gender.[2] And, after strides with the Affordable Care Act, major LGBTQ+ organizations were publicly demanding Medicare coverage of gender-affirming care.[3]

At UGA, other journalism students became more interested in interviewing Misters Not Sisters troupe members about our experiences with gender. We were requested as subjects for a short student-directed documentary that won a few awards. Then, Bryan and I were profiled for the cover story of a campus magazine on the same topic. For the photoshoot I wore a bright red, studded skater dress with a matching lipstick and styled my hair with some curly extensions. The selected cover image was a close-up of me suggestively devouring a lollipop.

During this time, Alessio, Kane, and I made up after working on a project together for Lambda Alliance. By then, I could better articulate to them my disappointment in their unwillingness to see my perspective. They seemed to genuinely apologize, and we resumed our relationships. Alessio and I even rekindled our romance, but I maintained a perpetual side-eye, wondering if his problematic side would ever make a return. We figured that, because I had only a few more months left before my college journey ended, it'd be more enjoyable to experience those months as a couple.

In April, I sprinted through my last hurrahs. I was chosen as the student speaker for our Lavender Graduation, the special ceremony for LGBTQ+ students on campus. I encountered folks I had never seen before in the audience and I was fascinated that there had been so many more queer students on campus than I imagined. In my speech, as I looked out to friends who had touched my life, I thanked the center and my friends for providing a safe haven and all the encouragement for this Black trans girl from Augusta to leave her mark.

Weeks later, at a journalism school ceremony, I nervously waited for my name to be called as I sat on stage with other students. As soon as "Raquel Devoe Willis" flowed through the air, I walked across the stage, proud that I had fought for my name, body, identity, and life so fiercely. In fact, all those things were a greater gift than the diploma. As I looked out, I saw Momma, Alessio, and a few relatives cheering me on, knowing how powerful that accomplishment was for me. Though my siblings weren't present, I relayed my experience over the phone. And days later, on my birthday, Chet surprised me with a video message of him holding his son as he said "Happy birthday, Raquel!" which stunned me. It was the first time he'd used my name. I took it as a signal of his evolution, and it seemed to make up for those moments when he was incapable of understanding my journey.

Throughout my four years in college, I'd witnessed death, embarked on a public gender transition, made a small name for myself as a drag performer, experienced my first love, and entrenched myself in our campus LGBTQ+ community, all while continuing my studies. I marveled at the life I was crafting for myself, but I felt grief and uncertainty. I wondered what Dad and Grandma Inez would have thought, whether they would recognize me or be proud of me. My life felt unprecedented and full of potential because of my investment in my Blackness, queerness, transness, and womanhood. I was no longer a dormant sprout. My roots were firmly planted with a sense of surety.

PART II

Budding

11

Destiny's Detour

S ome kind of hell was happening inside my too-small black
pumps as I made my way to the top floor of a Wall Street
skyscraper. I didn't have time to consider how unglamorous my
New York experience had been so far. To be clear, I didn't have
a job yet. The plan was to "fake it till I make it," or at least not
crumple because I'd graduated from college with no career prospects and the looming threat of moving back to my childhood
home. Thanks to Momma's orchestration, I'd been able to visit
for a week, staying with one of her friends in the area. I would've
stayed with Jessica and her family, but they were packing for a
move back to Georgia. *Go figure!* But I'd made it and all I had to
do was charm at least one interviewer so I could stay for the long
haul. So, I replaced fear and uncertainty with a confident smile
as I stepped off the elevator.

This morning's interview came to me courtesy of Craigslist.
Don't laugh. The details were murky, and the website featured
poorly photoshopped images, but I'd found the one-paragraph
job description promising. It wouldn't be some highfalutin magazine role, but it was supposed to be something in the space of
communications and marketing. *Listen, your girl was desperate.*

Most companies I'd applied to never got back to me, or, if they did show interest, crushed my dreams when they realized I wasn't yet based in the NYC area. So, I placed hope in almost any opportunity that came my way. And beyond those dynamics, I was uncertain if any place would hire me if they even suspected that I was trans.

At the front desk in the waiting area, a blond woman was helping a tall, thin, nervous-looking guy. He must've been a recent graduate too. I glanced around and saw a few other people about my age sitting around, clutching clipboards. *If all these people are here, maybe the job posting isn't a scam.* Soon, the woman at the desk asked for my name with no "hello" or anything. Then, she typed away at her keyboard while barely looking up. I tried not to take it personally, but New York already felt like another beast. It was so uncomfortable forcing myself to avert eye contact with every stranger I encountered. Generally, in the South, you don't do the whole glossed-over autopilot demeanor. You acknowledge folks with some sense of decency and a smile. Here, that kind of politeness certainly wasn't the rule.

As I filled out my forms, a wave of people left a conference room together. *Group interviews? Great.* I hoped I wouldn't have to speak much in front of a large group like that. I feared that my voice would out me, betraying my gender. Soon, a young, bald guy called a selection of surnames from a list, including my own, and summoned us into a room with a windowed wall. As my group sat around the massive conference table, I stared at a questionnaire in front of me. Immediately, I noticed its vague questions and even a few laden with typos. "What's your dream position?" one read. I scribbled down a few answers as our interviewer, who was apparently the CEO, clicked through a brief presentation. He dashed through his words as if he'd had a really great cup of coffee that morning. The CEO claimed that his company had recently expanded to the Asian and Latin American markets and showed us random photos of his travels. He positioned them as perks of the job. But by the time he asked if we had any questions, I noticed that he hadn't said one thing about a specific job title or duties. I was too afraid to ask, and no one else did either. I think we all realized he was full of shit. As our cohort walked out wordlessly, the guy who had called our names collected our questionnaires. I said a light, customary "Thank you" and made my way to the elevator. *What a waste of time!* Dejected, I left the building in the desaturated hues of Manhattan.

* * *

LATER THAT DAY, Alessio called to check in after I'd finished another failed interview. Our relationship was running its course, but we planned to ride it out until the end of the summer, when I would inevitably move away to start a new life. I dreaded the end of our relationship because I figured it'd be a long time before I dated again. I was still in the mindset of living in a white college environment, where there was a seemingly nonexistent dating pool for a Black trans woman. We always had friends who were flirtatious with Alessio, though he played oblivious to it. In fact, I suspected that as soon as we were done, he would jump on to dating this alternative, almost gothic, girl we both knew. But I soothed myself with the idea that I wouldn't be around to witness him move on. For now, we grasped at our fading moments of connection.

"Hey," he said, his voice perking up. "Have you watched this new show, *Orange Is the New Black*?"

"Nah, I haven't had a chance. Is it good? I saw stuff about it on Tumblr."

"Yeah. I mean, I like it. And there's a trans character in it," he said, half in excitement and shock.

"Oh, right," I said. "Well, maybe I'll check it out."

"You should," he said. "I think you'll like it."

I didn't think much of the recommendation. But after I showered and scrolled through job posts online, I settled into bed to watch the new Netflix show. I'd definitely seen press photos about *OITNB* on social media, but I was turned off when I initially skimmed the premise. There was a sizable cast of women of color, but the protagonist was a privileged blond, white woman who "took a trip on the dark side" and went to prison. I knew how this would go. The main character would vaguely confront her privilege, and a sliver of screen time would be allotted to everyone else. Then, eventually, she would make it out unscathed while everyone else continued to suffer. But, within just a few episodes, the character Sophia Burset emerged, played by Black, openly trans actress Laverne Cox. I'd caught her on a few episodes of *I Want to Work for Diddy* in high school. But I hadn't registered the importance of her transness then. Something new stirred within me after watching *OITNB*'s first season and seeing a woman like me navigating discrimination, love, prison, a passion for hairstyling, and her gender transition. This portrayal, and more particularly by someone with a similar identity, was transformative and jolted me with a signal of progress at a time when I was uncertain about my career trajectory.

Days before my unsuccessful return to Georgia, another pivotal moment expanded how I viewed the world. While I was waiting for a bus, a CNN news alert about the George Zimmerman trial appeared on my phone. It resurfaced the pang I'd felt when I first heard about the killing of seventeen-year-old Trayvon Martin. Like so many other young Black folks online, I was outraged that twenty-eight-year-old Zimmerman had been protected from arrest because of Florida's stand-your-ground law, that he was allowed to use deadly force simply for feeling threatened. *How was this killing anything less than the extermination of another Black child?* Zimmerman's self-defense claim immediately seemed dubious as hell. In one of my earliest journalism classes, we'd discussed how the media impacted the general public's perception of groups on the margins, the disproportionate amount of coverage about Black people depicted as criminals in comparison to the broader white population. I was well aware that our media landscape was ill-equipped to consider Martin's humanity and how anti-Blackness had fueled this tragedy.

Zimmerman's being acquitted of all charges reopened that initial wound. When a new hashtag, #BlackLivesMatter, started trending on social media, I realized that I wasn't alone in my mourning. I didn't know the details, that it was birthed by the brilliance of Alicia Garza, innovated by Patrisse Khan-Cullors, and strategized by Opal Tometi, three radical Black women organizers. All I knew was that every post featuring the tag resonated with me. There was an ironic comfort in knowing that scores of Black people felt distraught over the fact that decades after the harrowing murder of Emmett Till, young Black boys could still be killed without recourse.

I saw myself in Trayvon. I was once a little Black boy who walked to the convenience store with my friends to grab Airheads and Sun Chips. We roamed freely in our quiet cul-de-sac until it got dark. In the summer, our absentminded parents would basically have to drag us inside as we said our goodbyes to each other and the moon. That a random man on the street could just gun me down would have never crossed my mind. *So, what could I make of Trayvon's fate? And what would I make of my own?* I was no longer navigating the world as a Black boy nor as a Black man, but as another threat entirely. As a Black trans woman, my existence was a protest against white supremacy and the cisheteropatriarchy.

Weeks later, I returned to these musings as I read about the murder of a young Black trans woman. Islan Nettles[1] was twenty-one years old—a year younger than me—and had been brutally murdered by James Dixon, who approached her on a Harlem street. It was reported that the young man had been flirting before realizing she was trans and attacking her. Apparently, he was set off after his friends clowned him about his attraction. Dixon claimed in various interviews that they tussled before he delivered a punch that knocked her to the ground. Authorities later shared that his story changed several times. But the ending was clear. As she pleaded, he pounded her head repeatedly on the pavement, knocking her unconscious. After being "battered beyond recognition," she spent a week in a coma and on life support before succumbing to her injuries.[2]

Islan's murder was the first death of a trans woman of color that I saw covered extensively in the media. It was disturbing to think that she lost her life because of the insecurities that some stranger had in his masculinity. A recent graduate, Islan was said to have come out recently about her identity to a family and community that cherished her. She was a young professional with a fashion design dream who presumably had a bright future. Even after checking off so many boxes that should've insulated her, being trans made her a target.[3] *If this could happen in New York, which I had long assumed was more progressive, what could happen to me in Georgia?* I might have received weird looks, been misgendered, or deadnamed, but I could count on my hands the number of times I felt genuinely unsafe. I even walked alone at night a few times, recklessly click-clacking in and out of bars. *Where could a Black trans woman go to ensure safety?*

Islan's story drew to mind the case of CeCe McDonald,[4] a Black trans woman who was arrested after using deadly force to protect herself from Dean Schmitz, who was in a group that attacked her and her friends as they were passing a bar. In the altercation, bigoted epithets were hurled, and McDonald was struck in the face with a bar glass. After the ordeal, she eventually accepted a plea bargain with a sentencing of forty-one months, despite some witnesses claiming she wasn't even the one to deliver the fatal blow to the assailant. So, it seemed not only did Black trans women have to fear being attacked for looking suspicious to non-Black vigilantes, but also for being attractive to insecure Black cishet men. Then, even if we defended ourselves, we could be criminalized. I felt ill-equipped to comprehend these experiences, having spent the last few years navigating an educational institution and social circles that, while predominantly white, were heavily insulated. In some ways, I'd been stymied in figuring out my social position as queer and trans within the context of the larger Black community. While Diedre, Roblé, and I often broadly discussed the implications of our identities in society writ large, we didn't quite get into the nitty-gritty of it all. They were assigned female at birth, so there was a distance between our experiences. Many of us knew about, as bell hooks described, the white supremacist capitalist patriarchy, but we had few tools to actually resist it. CeCe, Islan, and Trayvon's experiences made me consider my privileges around class, education, and respectability that, in some ways, shielded me from over-policing—whether through law enforcement or by residents in our communities.

Islan's murder made discrimination and violence seem so much more certain, but the images of the local rallies held in her honor strengthened my soul. Figures like Laverne Cox, Janet Mock, and others who were a part of the Trans Women of Color Collective, a group of local activists created in the aftermath of

Islan Nettles's death, underscored the importance of Black trans resistance. I dreamed of having that kind of community, something that seemed only possible outside of Georgia. As I contemplated my future, I felt less confident that I'd be able to forge a career and life as openly as I had in college.

12

Plausible Deniability

The smoky, verdant scent of weed wafted from Kane's bong before he entered the bedroom. Surely he saw me staring at the off-white popcorn ceiling with a curious mix of confidence, desperation, and trepidation. I ignored his presence as I reluctantly lifted my body off his uncomfortable wire futon bed. Good thing I'm a deep sleeper because there was nothing humane about that bed and the unbearably thin mattress that sat on top of it. Even worse, under those negative thread-count sheets was a plastic covering to protect it. *Was it that precious? Was it worth me enduring what sounded like Saran Wrap every time I took too deep a breath?* If Kane wasn't perpetually freezing and best friends with the highest degrees of his thermostat, the worn blankets I used wouldn't have been enough.

"You ready for your interview?" he asked as he glided across the worn, light-brown carpet, firmly holding the smoking device as if it was an extension of his being.

"Yeah, I think so. I just hope I get this job, so I can get out of your hair," I responded in between his violent Sativa-infused coughs.

I didn't want to be ungrateful for his hospitality, but I felt hopeless as fuck. Almost as soon as I returned from New York, Alessio and I finally broke up. It seemed to hurt me more during our final moonlit kiss. While I fought back tears, he half-soothed me with encouraging words about my bright, successful future. Up until the last minute, I naively hoped he might plead for us to stay together. There was a great chance that the fear of being alone would sweep me up and I would take him up on the offer. But no, our bodies tore out of the embrace, and he didn't hesitate to drive off. The next morning, Bryan helped me pack up a U-Haul between sobs and drive back to Augusta. But before I settled in, Kane generously offered the spare futon in his bedroom until I got on my feet. So, I jumped at the chance and found some quick freelance gigs to stay afloat. But after a month and a half, anxiety had taken hold of me.

"I hope I get this job," I told Kane as I played with the ruffles on my slate-colored blouse. I wondered if it was too much for this morning's interview with the editor of *The Monroe Chronicle* in Monroe, Georgia. It was a nearby town that was even smaller than Athens, but their vacant full-time news reporter role seemed promising.

Kane delivered platitudes as I tried to silence my dysphoria in front of his mirror. At just over a year into my transition, *clockability*, or the potential to be perceived as trans, seemed closely tied to how I adhered to traditional femininity. I tried to mask every feature that I deemed too masculine: contour in the hollows of my face, highlight the bridge of my nose, and accentuate my lips with the brightest shade of fuchsia in my collection. I took a page out of my mother's playbook and feverishly curled my hair into oblivion, praying to the goddesses that I wouldn't burn my forehead. I didn't have the confidence in my abilities that might come later with the years of practice. Still, I tried to appear more mature despite feeling like a teenager cosplaying as an adult. *Would I stand out? Would they think I was an extra from* To Wong Foo, Thanks for Everything!? Julie Newmar? I stared at my flat chest, trying to gauge the right amount of stuffing, so there'd be no questioning my womanhood.

I told myself I wasn't going to actively hide my identity. I'd been wearing my queerness on my sleeve for as long as I could remember. Plus, I wasn't even sure I could pass as cishet enough to fly under strangers' radars. Sure, it had been a while since I was misgendered, but that didn't mean people didn't assume I was trans. This job would be a test of sorts, of my ability to be *stealth*. It's like the idea of *passing* or moving through the world with an assumed cisgender identity. But while passing can simply be a momentary phenomenon, stealthiness requires a deeper sustained commitment. I saw these concepts as off-shoots of serving *realness*, understandings I absorbed while watching *Paris Is Burning* in college. In the documentary, Pepper LaBeija, a house mother, discusses the "realness" categories that competitors walk in during balls. She goes on to describe serving realness as a behavior modification—particularly as a way that Black folk can claim all of the things that white supremacist capitalism tries to steal from us (and indoctrinates us to desire).

"*This is white America. . . . We have had everything taken away from us, and yet we have all learned how to survive. . . . If you have captured the great white way of living, or looking, or dressing, or speaking—you is a marvel.*"

It's not all gravy, though. Realness, passing, and stealthiness often also serve as capitulations, compromises on authenticity. But with few models of Black trans women who were thriving, and virtually none who were also living in the South, there was little debate on my best chance at navigating this environment. Though I believed that being absolutely true to myself was noble, I also found it alluring to experience being a woman with a few less qualifiers, who could blend in. Besides, we'd have to see if I even made it through the interview.

At 9:00 A.M., I maneuvered my golden 2006 Toyota Echo into a slanted parking spot just in front of the *Chronicle*. The one-floor brick building was on the town's main thoroughfare. So far, Monroe looked like any small town you might see in a Hallmark movie. On the same block there was a local pizza spot, a hair and tanning salon, a small boutique, a generations-old supply store, and a recently built town hall in the distance. I nervously walked up to the glass-paned front of the building and pulled on the gold handle of the full-length wood-and-glass door. I timidly approached the front desk, where an older white woman with short gray-blond hair acknowledged me.

"Hi," I said in a cloying register that I reserved mainly for cis white women.

"Hi. You must be here for the interview?" she half-asked.

"Yes, ma'am."

"Yep. I'll go let Curtis know. It should just be a minute. Have a seat," she said as she darted down a short hallway.

I nodded and took one of the wooden chairs in the lobby. A stack of several editions of *The Monroe Chronicle* stared back at me. I'd read a few articles online from the week before, but I felt like I got the gist of what they covered. It was local news. Nothing that seemed beyond my J-school training.

"And here's Miss Willis," the woman said as Curtis followed her into the room. "Is it Rachel or Raquel?" Her smile seemed wider now that a man was present.

"It's Raquel. Thank you," I said, burying my aggravation. I momentarily lamented the name I had chosen for myself just a few years ago. Too often, people seemed incapable of discerning the difference between those two names. When does a *Q* make a *ch* sound? I wondered if it sounded "ghetto" to them. To disarm that assertion, I always had my Rachel Welch reference in my back pocket for older white people.

"Well, I'm Nancy," she said, stepping back to her desk. "Let me know if you need anything."

"Hi, Raquel, I'm Curtis. Let's head this way," he said, leading me down a hallway.

"Sure," I responded as coolly as possible, grateful he pronounced my name right.

Curtis was an average-height white guy, about mid-thirties with a head of short dusty-brown hair, a matching stubbly mustache, and a close-cut beard. As we sat around his desk, he lamented that the newspaper was selling the section of offices that we were sitting in. The plan was to merge the editorial team space with the marketing team in the front portion of the property that I'd entered through. I sensed his frustration, but it wasn't surprising that the *Chronicle* was downsizing. Throughout my time in college, there had been constant chatter about dwindling budgets, revenue, and staffs in the newspaper industry.[1] Some part of me hoped that if I focused on digital outlets and magazines, there would be more cushion and opportunities for employment. Yet here I was throwing my bid in for a small-town paper. As I patiently waited for Curtis to find my résumé on his desk, cluttered with papers and envelopes, I scanned his office. I felt like he'd transported me through some time warp. The paneled walls probably hadn't been updated since Jimmy Carter was president.

"Alright, so thanks for applying," he said, flipping through the pages. "I see you went to UGA. Impressive. So tell me about yourself, where you're from, and all that."

"Well, I'm from Augusta. I've been in Georgia my whole life," I replied, hoping I'd earn some points.

Beyond magazine publication and photojournalism courses, I dropped that I minored in women's studies, hoping it'd ward off any questions about my identity. Even though my leadership involvement in LGBTQ+ student activism was on my résumé, I skirted around it. *Maybe he'd think I was just an ally.* I charmed like only a Southern doll could, laying my accent on real thick. I may have seemed confident and calm, but I was dissecting everything about myself. *Could he tell I was trans? Was he just being nice? Would he laugh as soon as I walked out the door?* Before I knew it, he revealed that I was the most qualified for the position out of all the résumés he'd received and that I seemed the most intriguing. Plus, he saw potential in me.

"I assume you'll be commuting from Athens," Curtis said.

"Yes, sir. The commute wasn't so bad this morning," I replied.

"Well, if you're OK with the rate I sent over, all we'll need is a drug test, and you could start as early as next week if you're interested."

"Oh, yes. How exciting," I said, hoping he didn't detect my sarcasm. I'd had my share of weed over the last month at Kane's, but he'd assured me that he had just the trick to pass a drug screening. So, Curtis and I shook hands, and he gave me a brief tour of the building. Just outside lay an open office space where the other staff writer, Samuel, and the sports editor, Ken, sat. Apparently, both were out on assignment. But Curtis pointed to an unadorned desk that would serve as my designated spot. On it sat an outdated-looking PC and an old-school physical Rolodex. It wasn't some impressive magazine job or in New York, but it was something. When I passed the drug test, I got the job, and my fate and silence were sealed.

* * *

WITHIN WEEKS AT the *Chronicle*, I settled into a new professional persona to keep my white counterparts at ease. I fixed my mouth to speak as standard as possible, dropping any queer or Black slang. Every few weeks, I touched up my hair relaxer or opted for a Brazilian blowout to the detriment of my hair ends. While other coworkers shared the ins and outs of their latest country music interests, my love of R&B and hip-hop had to stay under wraps. And I simply had to endure the microaggressions from older white colleagues about my being articulate. No matter how much I comported myself by those standards, though, I was undeniably different.

While other departments at the newspaper were made up of women of varying races, I was the only person of color and woman on the editorial staff. Samuel turned out to be pleasant and respectful despite the traditionalism that he emanated. He reminded me of Dwight Schrute from *The Office*, with the same glasses, straw-like brown hair, and a similar uniform of light-colored button-ups and khakis. Curtis treated him like a sidekick and sneered about him having never left Monroe. It was biting and cringy, but Samuel always took it on the chin.

Then there was Ken, our resident white-haired sexagenarian who came into the office sparingly. Often when other staffers asked where he was, Curtis would throw up his hands with indignation. It was like he wanted to fire him, but he never did. I got to know Ken pretty well after being assigned to record his weekly YouTube series about local football coverage. In general, we were cool, but I could never forget when, just a few weeks in, he made a joke about "trannies" while we edited the latest edition of the newspaper. I never confronted him about it. I just let it wash off my back. If I drew attention to it, I might be implicated.

Working at the *Chronicle* quickly gave me a sense of purpose. I appreciated the power we had to elevate the status of small business owners and local initiatives. But I most enjoyed my weekly column. Each staffer was allotted a day each week to write an op-ed on whatever we wanted. Despite not being open about my identity, I used my Wednesday assignment to champion my social justice values and tackle larger cultural stories.

Since most of our regular columnists were well-to-do conservative white men who often espoused Fox News talking points, I expected my sentiments to ruffle more than a few feathers. When I urged our readers to reassess Christopher Columbus Day in favor of elevating Indigenous people, naysayers said I was being "a little harsh." In another piece, I opined about the importance of passing the Employment Non-Discrimination Act to ensure that LGBTQ+ Americans are afforded necessary protections. Then, a reader submitted a letter to the editor saying he was "weary of being lectured on diversity and tolerance" by someone like me, who didn't "live according to a set of moral values based in religion." I took that feedback as evidence that my writing was having an effect.

It wasn't uncommon to have my views critiqued as naive or something that only a liberal college education could instill. It was nonsensical to the vocal, conservative white male readership that anybody could truly be LGBTQ+ affirming, a feminist, or unsatisfied with their traditionalism. Sharing my beliefs was a risk, especially in conservative Georgia, where the veneer of Obama's "post-racial" era was often painted as more of a threat than an achievement.

There was some support along the way, though. When I covered an anti-violence youth event, a young teacher pulled me aside and thanked me for writing about feminism. And though it was hella premature, Curtis saw enough in me to send me to speak at a career day at a local elementary school. These instances were encouraging, but I made sure to dilute my message just enough not to completely alienate the average reader. Plus,

I had to continue to present these thoughts without implicating myself too much, especially when discussing gender and queerness.

Outside of my op-ed column, I was relegated mostly to the "lifestyle" beat. While I enjoyed this corner of journalism that focuses on supposedly "softer" coverage, like art, culture, entertainment, and human interest, it felt like there was a gendered element to this assignment. This section's stories were seen as less hard-hitting than the political and economic pieces that my cishet white male counterparts produced. I convinced myself that Curtis saw a level of empathy in me that would make me the best fit of our team. Perhaps that was why, one day, Curtis dropped a flyer on my desk about an upcoming drag show. As I slowly turned to my computer, scanning the assignment, my heart raced. *Did he know my secret? Was this a silent jab at my queerness and transness? How do I pull this off? Am I just being paranoid?*

I wondered if I had slipped up somewhere. It wasn't like I'd done too much to hide the rest of my life. After all, I had social media, and Athens wasn't far away. Plus, while I might have graduated, I hadn't completely left the collegiate bubble, as Diedre, Roblé, Kane, and many of my other friends were still in classes. In fact, I still attended campus events every now and then. At one, I met Nati, a tanned, multiracial queer student. Afterward, we added each other on social media and messaged endlessly about our lives and dreams. I felt similar feelings toward Nati as I had when I first met Alessio. One major difference was that they identified as a fairly gender-nonconforming woman at the time. Though I'd never dated a woman, I was pansexual and open to the experience. Plus, Nati was serving all types of gender nonconformity that resonated with my journey.

I was hesitant to date them at first, though. They were three years younger and in a totally different place in their life. But we bonded over similar thoughts on queerness and social justice. Nati was fascinated by how I'd transitioned in college, graduated, and started a career so seemingly seamlessly. I admired their authenticity and vulnerability and they just seemed to understand intersectionality; that is, the multiple layers of discrimination that we faced because of all of our identities, not just one. After my arguments with Alessio, this comforted me. They were also open about their complex relationship with gender and what marginalization felt like beyond queerness. Our budding relationship became a tether to my queer and trans identity and life outside of work. But it felt inevitable that these two parts of my life would coincide.

When I told Nati about covering the drag show, they jumped at the chance to attend with me. To them, it felt like the perfect chance to blend all these aspects of my life that I'd felt torn between for months. I didn't have the heart to tell them they couldn't come. There was no way I'd reject their insistence on joining me. I never wanted to make a partner feel like I was ashamed of our relationship. I mean, I'd dealt with some of that in my previous one. I did caution Nati that we'd have to be careful of public displays of affection. Despite understanding their self as more transmasculine now, we'd be read outwardly as a lesbian couple. They reassured me they understood, but I wondered what all of these boundaries I was putting up meant. *How strong were my values if a part of me desired the safety of being in a perceived cis, straight couple? What was the line? How far could I ethically go to keep my life sectioned off like this?*

On the night of the show, my heart throbbed as soon as Nati and I arrived. I breathed an audible sigh of relief after scanning the bar for any of my coworkers' faces. *Yeah, why would they be here?* Soon we made it to the show's green room where the queens were getting ready. One queen was diligently painting on her face while another was ironing a part of her outfit. Then I saw Bonnie, an older queen I had seen perform a few times in Athens. She was spraying her wig of the night, a huge auburn thing, crafted out of several smaller units.

"Oh, I didn't realize it was going to be you," Bonnie said, smiling. "You've grown up."

"So, you work out here now?" Sofia, another queen I knew, chimed in.

"Yeah, but I'm not out here, though," I said with a hint of guilt. "Just trying to keep my experience under wraps."

"I get it, girl. You gotta do what you must do," Sofia said.

It had been a while since I performed regularly and a part of me missed the days before I was ejected into such an "honest" profession. Sofia was also an OG queen from Athens, one of few trans women. It was rare that we performed on the same night, but I knew she was beloved. There was a sage essence about her, a maternal instinct that some more seasoned queens seemed to embody effortlessly. It might make it less awkward when they inevitably jammed your head into their bosom during a performance. In Sofia's response about my stealthiness, I heard a tinge of familiarity. Nearly every drag performer I'd encountered had to sacrifice something for the stage. That something could be a more respectable career trajectory, an unsupportive loved one or partner, and/or a different social standing. No doubt, Bonnie and Sofia had seen girls like me leave the drag world for a chance at "normalcy."

After putting my awkward feelings on the back burner, I was able to press on with my interviews. I felt like Clark Kent even though everyone knew my secret. It felt weird to position myself as an impartial observer as if I was on the outside of my community. Even with Nati there, maybe especially with Nati there, my guilt never completely disappeared. I wondered if they saw my desire to blend in as disappointing. After all, they were a little younger and able to live within the fictive freedom of the college experience where you wore all your convictions on your sleeve. I convinced myself it just wasn't like that in the real world.

The next morning at the *Chronicle*, my drag show review caused a stir before it was even published. First, Curtis called me to his office with a sense of urgency as he edited it. *Uh-oh, what's going on?* I thought. As I scurried through his open door, I put on a hopeful smile. But he had this confused look on his face as he cocked his head to the side and stared at his screen.

"I'm not sure you're supposed to call them 'she,' even if you're referring to their persona," he said, half-asking.

"Oh?" I said, somewhat relieved. "I'm pretty sure you use the pronoun that corresponds with their persona. If I was quoting them as their true selves, it might depend."

I tried to feign a lack of familiarity that seemed to do the trick. We went back and forth, but I didn't mind that he wouldn't surrender. In fact, I appreciated that he cared enough to inquire, and he even followed up with a contact at GLAAD, the leading national LGBTQ+ media monitoring organization to verify my claim. He cared about pronoun usage, even if it was more about adhering to a style guide versus respecting the performers, and that meant something. It made me briefly consider coming out right then and there. It would've been a natural time to assert my lived experience, that I knew what I was talking about.

I continued to think about the prospect as I returned to my desk and continued editing the photos from the night. While I was amping up the exposure on an image of Sofia as she applied a bubblegum-pink gloss to her lips, Catherine, a boisterous woman in the advertisement sales department, squealed in excitement behind me. When I looked back, she moved forward, bent her body a little lower, and peered over the top of her glasses.

"Oh, wow," she said. "Are these from the show?"

"Yep, I think they turned out pretty good," I said, trying to ignore her invasion of my personal space.

"Girls, come look at these photos Raquel took from the drag show," she screamed as she volunteered my screen to a gaggle of our female coworkers in the next room.

Before I knew it, four more women were missing out on the first few minutes of their lunch break to get a gander at a story I was trying to keep under wraps. I couldn't shoo them away lest I draw suspicion, so I let the moment ride.

"That one doesn't even look like a man," Catherine exclaimed as I begrudgingly clicked through the images.

I resisted rolling my eyes and scolding her for speaking so disrespectfully about Sofia. *Of course she'd have half the office around my desk for my most sensitive story.* Catherine always said exactly what was on her mind, unfiltered, and didn't mind asking a few too many questions about her colleagues' personal lives. I knew she probably didn't know that trans women and drag queens weren't necessarily one and the same, but I feared if I started to correct her, I wouldn't be able to stop. I knew if I divulged all that I knew, they'd look at me differently. After all, one of the things that can make you clockable by association is how people size up your support of the LGBTQ+ community. And if anyone would out me as trans at the *Chronicle*, she seemed like a prime suspect.

Some of the other women chuckled as they stared at the queens. "I bet you had a fabulous time," one lady said. They oohed and aahed at the immaculately applied makeup on the performers, stunned that an event of this kind would grace their county. I wished I could tell them that I knew this world inside and out.

I wished I could have been bolder, but I didn't have it in me. A moment of intrigue from these cis, straight women wouldn't be worth foregoing the commitment I had made to myself—that I'd survive, even if it meant diminishing my truth for now.

By my one-year mark at the *Chronicle*, I had settled into a bit of a groove. Curtis trusted me to deliver solid articles and meet my deadlines. I'd become familiar with local officials who I quoted at city council meetings and even met a few friends like Yazmine, who'd become my regular lunch buddy. She was several years older than me but never made me feel young or naive like my older coworkers often did. Her tempered, chill demeanor approach was cathartic to be around in an otherwise hectic office. Whereas all the other women, including myself, served up a traditional feminine presentation, Yazmine did her own thing. She always wore a bare face without a lip color, her hair slicked in a neat topknot, and a nondescript outfit. She was simply refreshing and our lunch chats were often the highlight of my day.

When her birthday rolled around, I dropped by her office to celebrate and inquire about her plans. To my surprise, she mysteriously shared that she'd be spending time with her "person." *Why did she phrase it that way? Why was she being so guarded?* I searched her face for clarity before gingerly shutting her office door. I shot straight. "Your person? Is your person a woman?" She responded affirmatively. Then, after a moment of apprehension, the secrecy I'd pent up over the last year softened. I shared that I was like her except that my boyfriend was transgender. I doled that bit of information out, testing the waters for sharing the full truth later. Nonplussed, she smiled warmly. But before she could ask too much, I sprinted out of the door, promising that I'd discuss more at lunch.

When our break came, she drove us to one of our regular soul food spots. She ordered her signature well-done hamburger steak entrée, and I enjoyed a scrumptious fried pork chop sandwich. As I sipped sweet tea, she shared that she was bisexual and never found coming out to be necessary. I could understand, especially since she'd lived in Monroe her entire life. I revealed that I was trans, just like my boyfriend. She gushed about never suspecting, saying the customary "I wouldn't have ever known" and "You're so gorgeous" refrains. When we got back to the office, I hated that our conversation had to end. But I was grateful that I'd broken the seal.

Not long after, an older white colleague, Mrs. Kerry, became another source of relief in the office. She'd regularly read and inquired about my columns. One day, in casual conversation, she said that her daughter was in the LGBTQ+ community. I hesitated to share, but I'd long sensed her progressive values in our conversations. So, I considered her a safe bet, and she became an unexpected confidant too. She never hesitated to ask for my advice and perspective on how she could best support her child, who was just a few years younger than me.

While my connections with Yazmine and Mrs. Kerry sustained me, they couldn't make up for the moments when I felt like the buffer between my personal and work lives was breached. For instance, one day, a newspaper reader, Josh, emailed about a column I'd written. He revealed that we'd met at a community event, but I didn't remember it and just took his word for it. I just appreciated that my words had prompted him to think more critically. Well, Josh and I emailed back and forth sporadically over a few months. He was a thirty-something white man who owned a local plumbing service. He was married with two young children and he often asked my perspective on how to be a more open-minded parent. I didn't have any kids, just nibblings, so I felt ill-equipped to support in that endeavor. Still, I imparted what I thought about topics like empathy, feminism, grief, and progressivism. He seemed well aware that navigating the conservative social climate of Walton County, as a young Black woman fresh out of the liberal corridors of college, was challenging. So, he was easy to talk to and it was almost like having a pen pal. But one email, months into our exchange, struck me differently.

My heart lurched as I read, "Hey Rebel Deveaux," from him for the first time. *No one in Walton County should know that name. Had he seen me onstage before? Did he know I was trans?* I tried my hardest to concentrate on the rest of the email, which was about the ongoing feud between one of our regular op-ed contributors and me, but I couldn't. *What do I say? Should I continue the conversation or just stop responding? But what if he gets angry and retaliates?* I played things as cool as I could in my response, focusing mostly on his inquiry. He didn't need to know how much he'd startled me, so I simply slipped in one line, asking why he called me "Rebel." As the alarms went off in my head, I wondered who else might know beyond him. *Should I have simply not discussed LGBTQ+ issues at all? Did everyone know I was queer and trans and was just playing along?*

Within an hour, Josh shot back, saying he'd known about my secret for a while. He didn't specify how much he knew, but, at the very least, knew I was a drag performer. He swore he would tell no one about my experience, but I maintained more of a distance with him after that. I didn't completely ignore his emails, but I definitely had to be more careful in future exchanges. Months later, as I was leaving an event, he called my name from a distance, walked over, and identified himself. We made small talk, and I tried to hide my discomfort. I thought I'd settled my fears about what he could reveal about me to the community, but seeing him face-to-face made me feel uncomfortably vulnerable. I knew I had to plot my exit.

During my last months at the *Chronicle*, I gave my all in my work. I explored even more hard-hitting issues in my columns, from rape culture to domestic abuse to gun control. Still, the limited space on the page and the nagging fear of appearing too radical to our more conservative readership became even more draining. Just as I was about to give up hope of making a mark on Walton County, Curtis and our publisher concocted the idea for a seasonal women's-interest magazine produced by the *Chronicle*. They appointed me as the lead for the project, pitching it as an opportunity to center empowerment. I welcomed the chance to curate the first issue, wanting to focus on the themes of career life, expansive healthcare, intersectional feminism, and building healthy families. At breakneck speed, I compiled a list of women writers and subjects from the community. I even placed a casting call for the first cover, hoping to draw women of different ages, body types, cultures, races, and spiritualities. But just days before the shoot, our newspaper was bought out. This formidable guy who had the means to tan regularly took the helm as both owner and publisher and scrapped the women's magazine to beef up the sports coverage. His good ol' boy ethos was clear. Whatever appealed to the male gaze and lens was of the utmost importance. Just when I'd found my most fulfilling opportunity to blend journalism and social justice, the patriarchy came in swiftly to shut it down.

One of the final moments in my tenure at the *Chronicle* came when Curtis assigned me to cover a local Republican rally. He'd always positioned it as customary for the newest person on staff to get some of the shittiest jobs. I watched as he and Samuel laughed heartily about the prospect of me being surrounded by the GOP. It seemed callous to throw a young, outspoken progressive Black woman to the wolves of small-town white conservatives as some kind of hazing opportunity. We were entering the last half of Obama's second term, and it wasn't uncommon to hear even more white supremacist gripes about his name and race in the media. This was also a post–Sarah Palin era, when the schtick of hokey ignorance reigned supreme and the veil of political correctness was dissolving. The month that I covered this event, the Republican House Majority Leader Eric Cantor[2] was defeated by Dave Brat, the first primary challenger to defeat a sitting house majority leader since the position's inception in 1899. Though Brat was never officially identified as a Tea Partier, he gave credit to various groups who carried the moniker for supporting him in his election. To political insiders, this moment signaled a GOP shift toward deeper conservative values, even at the expense of economic considerations. I wanted to scream at Curtis and Samuel that there was nothing comical about the terror conservatives struck in the lives of people on the margins, but I couldn't. Fear muzzled me, as it had many times in that role.

My departure from the *Chronicle* was a slow burn. Before finding a new role and apartment, I moved in with a gracious aunt just south of Atlanta. Nati and I parted ways, understanding that we were in different spaces of adulthood. Our short-lived romance had kept me true to my values and I appreciated them for that. I maintained my friendships with Deidre and Roblé, who were still finishing up their final UGA courses. They eventually moved near Atlanta as well and we would keep up our femmes' nights out. But when I shed Athens for good, I felt like I needed to do that with Misters Not Sisters as well. I'd experienced so much during my college years and turning the page felt necessary.

By the fall of 2014, I'd said my goodbyes to Yazmine, Mrs. Kerry, and my other colleagues. That last time driving from the winding interstate toward Atlanta, I beamed with joy. Somehow, I had endured my first real job and never completely lost myself or my identity. I'd even been able to do some meaningful work at the *Chronicle*. I'd covered city council meetings in which Black residents piled into city hall demanding accountability for extreme hikes in utility prices from local companies, the threat of a library closure in one of the smallest towns in the county, and rising HIV infections rates. I'd appreciated playing some minor role in elevating the voices of Waltonians who had been struggling, but I was ready to experience something new.

13

The Labyrinth of Desire

D amon's invitation made me feel special, at least for the night. When he pinged over his address, our days of inconsistent flirtation moved from the hypothetical to real. I hopped up to get ready as danger and excitement swirled in my body. I ripped off my work attire, swapping my sensible black slacks for a miniskirt of the same color. And I grazed my hand across my legs searching for any stray hairs. *We're good*, I thought. So I smoothed on some cocoa butter lotion, paying extra attention to childhood scars. I might not have had flawless skin like the models in Skintimate commercials, but I thanked the estrogen goddesses anyway. Hormone replacement therapy had softened my muscle tone, carving divots into my waistline. I'd admire them whenever I caught a glimpse of my figure, marveling at how unmistakable my womanhood appeared to me now. "This will have to do," I said to myself. I felt beautiful, sexy even, but after years of hormones, I certainly wasn't like any of the women I saw on TV. In fact, I didn't know what kind of woman I was, what kind of woman men saw me as. The Internet had been my only source of regular media featuring trans women, and the options seemed limited for us. There were those who strived to be top-tier actresses, those who were living out their editorial fashion dreams, and even the dolls who racked up social media engagement and moonlighted as escorts. Almost all of them fit a particular beauty standard: thin or toned, curvaceous, and utterly imperceptible. *What if I wasn't those things? Was that OK? Would Damon think I was OK?*

I forced a smile as I looked in the mirror, then slammed my favorite crop top over my head. It had this multicolored galaxy print. *Out of this world, hunny!* I touched up my makeup, refusing to put on a whole new beat for some random boy. I'd learned to wear less cosmetics during my stealth days at the *Chronicle*. If it was good enough to help me fly under the radar in my professional life, it'd work now. Plus, I didn't want to risk overdoing it, jeopardizing the realness factor. This was when it really mattered. I hurriedly spritzed the ends of my hair with a heat protector, then ran the flat iron over them. The little sizzle on the strands was gratifying whether it was a signal of heat damage or not. I made sure to part my hair in such a way that my slicked-down undercut was hidden. It was a haircut that felt necessary when I was dating Nati, like assurance that I hadn't fully turned my back on my queerness. Now, it didn't serve me as I vied for the interest of cishet men.

Loneliness had brought me to meeting random guys on dating, or rather hook-up, apps. Each one was different. There was one man, a tall, slender thing, who fancied himself a poet. He kept me up all night with philosophical musings as we popped molly and indulged in each other. Then, there was the Ivy Leaguer who was utterly self-absorbed. He spent hours boring me about his dilemma of the day—that he didn't know which European country he wanted his parents to send him to for his next break. Then there was the thirty-something business professional who spent most of his free time in the gym. I'll give it to him that his body was impressive, and I didn't mind that he always wanted to cud-dle. But he was always apprehensive to do anything more, like I was a mythical creature that he had to keep at bay. One of the last times I saw him, he bluntly told me that girls like me were fine in secret, but he'd never be able to seriously date me. Somehow, despite the disrespect and ignorance that he and so many of these men threw my way, their slivers of validation filled a void.

I didn't have many expectations for Damon. For now, he was just a fantasy. Judging by his profile pictures, he was a "pretty boy," even though his tight, neat cornrows signaled an edge. He was also an MMA fighter, a fact underscored by an image fea-turing his muscular shirtless torso drenched in sweat, gloved hands akimbo in front of his waist, and a mouth guard peeking through his lips. *How kissable?* His body inspired a million un-mentionable sensations, but I'd be pleased with just making out. It seemed like a necessary compromise with cishet men these days. It gave them just enough satisfaction without either of us ever having to engage with the rest of my body. They'd yearn to be inside me while I just wanted to be touched.

Damon made sure to amplify his Dominican heritage in his bio and seemed to care more about my ethnicity than even I did. Like most of the cis men I'd talked to lately, he'd insisted that I had to be multiracial. As if that gave him more permission to be attracted to me. When I responded that I was "just Black," their disappointment was palpable. Sometimes they'd argue me down in disbelief, making me wonder if I should have given them the whole spiel about white slaveowners who had raped their way into my DNA or the Native American ancestors that older rela-tives had long assured me existed. But no, I didn't want to be that girl, feeding the narrative that my Blackness wasn't gloriously beautiful without qualifiers. In fact, I'd wanted to lecture them on colorism and their problematic desires. But baby, I had enough to worry about. *How would Damon respond when I told him I was trans? Would he know what being trans meant? Would he care that I didn't have a vagina? Would he love my penis too much?*

I'd have to clear many a hurdle because of my gender, but being a thin, lighter-skinned Black woman who was often read as racially unplaceable and considered "pretty" often worked in my favor. It felt OK to cherish these privileged qualities because they seemed to compensate for the other identities that made me undesirable. Before my stint at living stealth, it felt like cishet men weren't even an option to date. In Athens, most of the supposed pool was white, so even if they were attracted to me, my Blackness gave them pause before they considered my transness. In fact, it felt like my race worked against my potential appeal in the mostly white queer spaces I'd assumed were the pinnacle of progressive values. Sure, I'd be bombarded with compliments when I was dolled up in drag, but it always felt more like people just saw me as exotic more than anything else. And I wasn't alone. The few Black queer folks I knew often faced more barriers in romance and sex while our white counterparts barreled forward with extensive love lives. I saw my relationships with Alessio and Nati as flukes, imagining myself as a placeholder for the white cis woman they'd rather date. *Was this mindset really colored by my environment or insecurity or both?*

Since I'd had two transmasculine partners, an insatiable urge to date cishet men arose. I was curious if the feelings of inadequacy I'd had in those relationships were because we were assigned different sexes at birth. *Would my dysphoria plague me the same way? Would it be easier to feel more at home in my womanhood? Would their bodies be less of a trigger? But most of all, had I officially crossed a threshold wherein I was so desirable my transness didn't matter?* With each cis man I encountered, I imagined an invisible switchboard and each having his own curious mixture of green and red indicators. Often, my transness and "pre-operative" status landed in the latter category, but not always. Sometimes guys (and even a few cis lesbians) would offer me the backhanded compliment that they didn't care about me not having a vagina or "not being a real girl." That kind of crude reduction to my genitalia and sex assigned at birth would leave an acerbic taste in my mouth. But it was almost like I should be grateful they even looked my way. And the thing was, I knew these folks weren't usually trying to be disrespectful. This kind of treatment was largely the result of living in a society where women like me, people like me, were novel.

On the dating apps, all of that complexity was heightened. As a trans person, I fell through the digital crevices of a technological landscape informed by cisheterosexist desire. Among the stalagmites, I had to gamble on which path would lead me out of the cavern of loneliness. I used the "straight" app because I assumed there would be more value placed on my gender than my sex assigned at birth, whereas the "gay" one could easily turn up someone who valued the opposite. For me, the latter felt more disconcerting because I didn't want a relationship or situationship where my sex was center stage. Regardless, it felt like I was screwed in whichever route I chose and not in the way I would've wanted.

I was adamant about mentioning my transness in dating profiles at first, hoping guys would respectfully receive my authenticity. Matches flooded in, but often after a few messages the tiny images of the guys would disintegrate. I figured they'd finally read my profile after a mindless swipe and decided they couldn't handle my identity. And when that didn't happen, guys might ask what I meant by saying I was "trans," weaponizing ignorance and hoping I'd help them come to terms with their attraction. And sometimes I did. "Being into me doesn't make you gay," or

"I'm still a woman; that's why you were into me," I'd reply. Other men would suggest I was joking or reduce me to a sexual experiment or object, possibly some comical anecdote they'd throw out when they were drunk with their buddies one day or that they'd only reveal to the next trans girl that they claimed was the first they encountered. The worst guys berated me, then reported me. If that happened enough my account would be banned, and I'd have to dig up another email address and start the cursed process all over again.

After dealing with the constant rejection, I felt like I had to try something else. I was intoxicated by the idea of not having to disclose my identity. It felt like, all things being equal, that if I were cis I could let my images really do the heavy lifting and keep it moving. So, in time, I tried it. I figured if they could just get to know the real me, ostensibly some version of me that was everything except my transness, then we'd be good. At least I could get them to engage with me, then tell them a few messages in. But sometimes, I loved the conversation so much or was so attracted to the guy that I aborted the mission. I became riskier. I rationalized meeting up with guys without telling them my T ahead of time. After all, once they met me, I figured they'd see my womanhood and not give a fuck anymore. And it worked sometimes. There were would-be suitors who misgendered me despite my explanations, others who loved that I had a penis more than anything else, and still others who saw me as a woman-like creature to whom they'd never be able to commit. I think I hated the latter the most, the one who reminded me that girls like me could only be loved in the dark. Every experience became an experiment, and eventually I stopped putting my identity front and center. The desire to be desired won out.

* * *

AFTER TAKING THE key out of my car's ignition at Damon's apartment complex, I just sat in the darkness. Aided by illumination from a nearby streetlight, I popped down the sun visor mirror to check myself. I swiped at the creases of foundation forming under my eyes. *Damn, maybe I should have redone all of it.* I tried to ignore the thought as I reglossed my lips. After smacking the mirror up, I texted that I'd arrived. Before I knew it, a door on the second floor swung open and a guy looked around. *Damon.* I took that as my cue and approached him. *Walk naturally, girl. Loosen those shoulders. Sway those damn hips.* A half-smile appeared on his face, which was plumper than I anticipated. His photos must've been a year or two old, because he certainly looked different. Still, he was undeniably attractive. As I made it up a staircase, he scrambled back inside, leaving the door ajar. *Okay?* Maybe he had to do some last-minute tidying.

Well, I made it this far, I thought as I approached the door. But Damon's vibe was off as he analyzed me and smirked awkwardly. We said our hellos, and he closed the door. Hearing the deadbolt click loudly from his deliberate force sent a jolt of fright through me. *That's a little extra.* Before I could completely give in to fear, he offered me a glass of water and I softened. The room's walls were mostly bare, but in his coarse voice he reminded me that he'd just moved from Chicago. And he had the major furniture: a huge floral couch he said his grandmother gave to him before she died, a coffee table, and a television on a stand. When he came back with our water glasses, he gently handed one to me as I perched on the edge of the sofa. His swag emanated even with this minute gesture, and I felt almost precious, titillated even. But instead of sitting near me, he took to a chair several feet away. His eyes scanned me as his legs settled into a wide position. As I sipped the tepid water, I resisted looking at the way his basketball shorts clung to his thighs.

"You know what I want to ask you, don't you?" he said, sipping slowly and leaning back.

My grip around the cup tightened and I stared at him with narrowing eyes. He had an unfamiliar look than all the other guys that I'd met up with recently. There was an unsettling knowingness about him. I had almost forgotten what this brand of confusion and curiosity looked like. It was one of uncertainty, as if I was some sort of alien. Not in a sexual objectification kind of way, or at least not entirely. No, there was something a bit more xenophobic in his eyes. I tried to hide my alarm when I realized that his chair was between me and the door. *What if I needed to get out? How would I escape?* If I ran, he'd catch me.

Moisture coated the perimeter of my face and the advice about surviving a bear encounter appeared in my head. No sudden movements. *Do I tell him or keep omitting the truth? Eventually, he's going to demand proof that I'm not . . . No, just pretend like you don't know what he's talking about. You'll be fine.* We verbally sparred about his inquiry, but I kept deflecting. *I live and work every day as the woman I know myself to be. I'll be damned if I let this nigga question me.* I knew I was gambling as my pride roared, but I refused to let him suggest I owed him an explanation about my identity. Even if he threatened my life, I wouldn't give him the satisfaction of dismissing my truth.

I'd read a *Guardian* article not long before about two Black trans women who had been killed in Baltimore.[1] Mia Henderson and Kandy Hall were found in an alleyway and a field, respectively. When Reggie Bullock, an NFL player and Mia's younger brother, spoke out, I'd felt hopeful that things were changing. But I hadn't integrated those grisly narratives into my life. Despair overcame me but sometimes danger seemed so distant. Yeah, Black trans women were killed every day, but that wasn't me. My isolation from other trans women of color had given me a warped sense of immunity. Sometimes Momma would tell me she worried about my safety, and Chet even gifted me a taser for protection, but this part of my life, this underworld of hookup culture, was something I never talked about in detail with anyone. The most my friends wanted to know was if I had my back blown out, enjoyed it, and whether I'd be seeing the person again. So, with little space to process, the gamble felt worth it.

"You look strong," Damon said, scanning my body. I couldn't tell if it was a look of lust or loathing.

"I played tennis for a few years," I shot back. The lie flowed so smoothly through my lips.

"You have an interesting swag," he prodded again.

"Well, I knew it'd take a minute to get here so I just threw on something quick." *What did he mean by that?*

He gave me a blank, unbelieving look. My stubbornness had often been a saving grace, but he was slowly wearing me down. I stared back, daring him to fight me on it. *You're so stupid. Why did you even put yourself in this situation?* Then our conversation skittered as he dove into his phone and shot back bite-sized responses. *What was he doing?* He told me he was looking at fight techniques. *Liar.* No, he had to be searching for whatever he wasn't getting from my lips. Maybe he was googling information about girls like me. *What was he typing in the search bar?* I imagined there were only seconds until his digital inquiry "How to tell if a woman used to be a man" was answered. Then, he'd get more ideas on how to pick my womanhood apart. So I tried a new approach. If I kept a soft voice and talked him down, I might have a chance at living. But his detached responses continued. So I grew impatient.

"What do you want to ask me?" I pushed.

"You know what I want to ask you," he repeated. "Don't you?"

"You're scaring me," I said as I crouched into the corner of the old couch.

"Why am I scaring you? You know what I want to ask you."

"No. Why don't you just say it? Tell me what you want to know."

"Why don't you just tell me? Or you can just leave."

My eyes lit up. *He's not for real, is he? I can leave? No, there's no way.*

"You know what I want to ask you," he repeated.

"I know." I surrendered. I imagined the worst but said it anyway.

"I'm a transgender woman." I emphasized the *woman* part, but that didn't ward off the bewilderment on his face.

"So you're a man?" His brows furrowed.

"No, I'm a woman, a transgender woman."

I awaited the debate about whether I was serious or just fucking with him. *How could I blame him?* He'd grown up in the same culture that I had. One in which the extent of his exposure to trans stories was probably some *Jerry Springer* segment, clandestine porn search, or a punchline in a basic ass joke. But he didn't push just yet.

"Do you know how lucky you are that I'm not, like, crazy?" he huffed. "Because I know plenty of guys who would really do some shit to you. I used to be a gangbanger. I've got a gun and everything."

I shuddered at the thought of hot metal hurling toward me. All I knew of guns was what I'd seen in movies, I'd never seen anyone shot in real life. I was sheltered as fuck. When my dad died was the first time I learned he had a wooden box with a firearm in it, ostensibly for protection. I knew my brother had one for similar reasons, but that was it. So, if my life was taken, then what of the aftermath? *What would Momma and my family think if I died here on this god-awful sofa?* I'd probably be called a man by the coroner and the reporter on the scene would blast the details of my genitalia to the world. They would shred up the last few years of my life as if my transition and all I had fought for had never happened. Ignorant transphobes and transmisogynists would make comments and posts online claiming I got what I deserved for my deception, punishing me for ruining my attacker's life. That's if he faced any sort of accountability in the first place. And I'd be reduced to another statistic.

"Why would you come here knowing I'm straight?"

"See, this is the thing. When guys are attracted to me, they can still be straight. They usually are. You think gay men are interested in me?"

"Why wouldn't they be?"

"Because I'm a woman. I'm not a fucking gay man. I go to work, walk around every day, and live my life as a fucking woman. And this is why I don't always say something immediately. I want them to get to know me, not what they assume they know about me from my identity."

"And you don't think it's fair for me to know this before you come into my house?"

I considered his point for a second. Perhaps I should've told him, but I refused to believe the fact that I didn't was inherently immoral. There were myriad things we could've discussed before I came over. We could've talked about our sexual orientation, STD status, or, like, what the fuck we were actually going to do together. He could have revealed that he was only attracted to cis women, as partially inaccurate as that was. *Why was the sex I was assigned at birth the information he got to hang his hat on?*

"Maybe, but I shouldn't have to wear my transness on my sleeve. That's not fair," I said, tearing up. "You don't have any idea how it feels to have everything that I've fought for, struggled with, or dealt with to be thrown in my face like that."

"No, shit. I know you've probably been through some things. Actually, I'm sure you've been through some things."

We sat in silence for a second before I fully realized he wasn't going to hurt me. He asked more questions about my experience. We discussed the complexity of identity, and he nodded along as I discussed how gender is more complicated than most people realize. He bargained with the remnants of attraction he still felt toward me. He licked his lips a few times in that way that only hood niggas do. I could tell he was considering how far he could go before spontaneously combusting. This part wasn't new to me. Whether guys knew I was trans before or after we met, many of them gave themselves pep talks, trying to make sense of their interest. Sometimes my conditional passing and pretty privilege tipped the scales in my favor at this point. The dialogue might shift to arguments like "Wow, you don't look like any trans woman I've ever seen" or "Well, you're still pretty, though." The back-handed validation from these exchanges was like a delicious beverage with an abhorrent aftertaste. But often, it gave them permission to indulge.

"So, what do you do with these guys when you meet them?" he asked. "Have you had sex with any of them?"

"I mostly make out with them, but sometimes we hook up. It's not uncommon."

He quickly ran his tongue over his lips again and squinted for the briefest second.

"And they know beforehand?"

"Yeah, I mean I'm not just going to get a guy to that point, undress, and there he is, seeing me naked."

I shifted my legs and leaned back on the couch for the first time, surrendering to this twist in uncertainty. I glanced at the growing mound in his lap. He managed a hum of affirmation. *Was he picturing himself in this scenario?* As quickly as we slipped into lustful gazes at each other, we fell out of them. His face broke and he said he felt betrayed. You know, because he didn't swing "that way." After all of this enlightenment and stimulation, that was where his mind settled.

"Well, I'd better go," I said, snatching my purse as I stood.

He got up too and made his way to unlock and open the door. In the silence, I looked back at my spot on the couch where, not long ago, I'd thought my life might end. As I turned back around, I noticed he hadn't opened the door all the way. He was inches away, just peering down at me.

"You know you owe me an apology, right?" he said.

"Wait, what?" My eyes darted in confusion.

"Yeah, I mean you came into my house and didn't tell me."

"You're the one who just said all this stuff about how you could've killed me."

He just stared at me, like he was waiting for something more than an apology.

"Fine. I'm sorry," I said, rolling my eyes.

"Like you mean it."

"I'm sorry," I said, swallowing my sighs.

Then he opened the door completely and I walked through. I didn't turn around nor did I care how square my shoulders looked or whether I was walking femininely enough. When I sat in the car, I noticed he watched for a bit longer before going inside. As I drove away, tears trickled down my face. I felt fortunate to be alive and pissed. *What did I have to be sorry for? That I had to fear for my life? That he was attracted to me? That society told him I wasn't a real woman? What was I to do in a world that so rarely produced men who could regard, respect, and cherish me?* This wasn't the woman I wanted to be, scrambling for scraps of affirmation. But it felt like no matter how beautiful, intelligent, independent, or successful I was, I'd have to accept that most men would only ever see me as a receptacle for their desires or a reflection of their insecurities. I hoped for a day when this labyrinth of desire wasn't so impossible to navigate.

14

Letter to Leelah Alcorn

The only way I will rest in peace is if one day transgender people aren't treated the way I was; they're treated like humans, with valid feelings and human rights. Gender needs to be taught about in schools, the earlier the better. My death needs to mean something. My death needs to be counted in the number of transgender people who commit suicide this year. I want someone to look at that number and say "that's f***ed up" and fix it. Fix society. Please.

—Leelah Alcorn

Dear Leelah,

The first time I saw your face served as an introduction and a farewell. It was posted with an article alerting the world of your death by suicide. In the image, you're trying on a cream-colored dress with a black satin belt. Your hand is softly, yet defiantly, gripping your hips just below a dangling price tag. I don't know if it was the first time you put on a dress, but it's clear you were feeling yourself. You had coiffed your short, dark hair to the sky, and etched a smirk across your face as if daring the world. It made me think of, just years before, when I was first gathering the courage to let my femme hang out. Often those little moments when I could be myself were my only source of freedom.

I wish I could have known you before you left this earth. I'm no superhuman with all of the answers, but I would've told you everything I wish someone would have acknowledged in my youth. I would have explained how trans folks like us are born amid an invisible war. On one side is the patriarchy and its special forces, cissexism, and heterosexism, which deploy no shortage of expectations and demands around our bodies and destinies. This complex gender enforcement system maps out our whole lives as soon as a doctor bares our genitalia to the world. We're told how to identify and who we're allowed to love. Along with our names, we're given a script of dreams, interests, and emotions we can experience, as well as rules on how our bodies can move and even how we should react to others who don't follow these rules. These edicts assert the false idea that our lives can be placed into neat boxes and that adhering as closely as possible to the gender binary will lead to fulfillment. But the patriarchy destroys our opportunities for connection. It relies on judgment and domination, the constant search for how we can prove certain people are more deserving of power than others. If we cannot comply, we become traitors who need to be snuffed out.

On the other side of the war is true freedom of expression. It's the side that people like us unwittingly come to represent because of our gender nonconformity and queerness. But it's also the force necessary to liberate our society from how the patriarchy fails us. This freedom allows women and girls their rights to bodily autonomy, self-determination, and inherent power. Our way of being has the potential to encourage men and boys to define themselves beyond the urge to control and dominate others while repressing their humanity. It exalts all who fall between these doomed ideals around manhood and womanhood and dares us to chart fuller lives. Our side often requires us to be the only ones raising our voice among a crowd of detractors. But it is a righteous and worthy perspective. Freedom of expression asserts authenticity, empathy, and vulnerability as superpowers. And darling, you deserved a life fueled by all those things.

As I reflected on your letter, tears streamed down my face and my eyes darted around my apartment. There was a high ceiling and gorgeous wooden shelves built into the wall. I was sitting on a hand-me-down couch that my mom let me have from my childhood home. And though my stocked refrigerator had many a to-go container, I never felt the threat of houselessness or hunger. In fact, I was just settling into a digital publisher role at a new workplace, HowStuffWorks (HSW). Even though I'd had a limited vision of what my future could be as a trans woman, I'd figured out how to navigate this far. You deserved a chance to see this kind of independence, to have a kind of control over your life. And you deserved your destiny.

I understand why, at seventeen years old, you felt so cheated and out of joy. I'm sure you were promised a world of progress in which all the great struggles around justice had been won. You were probably told that you were blessed to have a family and a home, that you should want nothing else, and that your desire for free expression was craven and selfish. All around us, the LGBTQ+ community celebrates the hurdles we've managed to clear, and there is an assumption that we no longer must hide. Sure, more of us are indeed visible than ever, but the risk of being ourselves hasn't lessened enough. All those strides we made didn't keep you here and they don't bring you back.

Leelah, your parents didn't know what to do with you. That is their failure, not yours. Most parents are ill-equipped to raise a queer child, much less a trans one. They're covered in the nuclear fallout of patriarchal expectations and take our truth as a slight against their dreams for us. Your school and society also failed you. And my silence failed you. I feel like I let you down, and there is no amount of apologies that can make up for not using my voice to speak up for you and our community sooner. While I was hiding away from the world, frightened of losing my career, you were suffering. With all my privileges, I could have been doing more.

I could barely fathom how you planned out your death when you should've been working on something as mundane as math homework. My first instinct was to blame you. *Why couldn't you just stick it out a bit longer? Why did you give in to their hate?* But that wasn't fair. Our society tells us that suicide is one of the most selfish acts one can commit, yet so little is focused on improving conditions and treating people with dignity so that they will want to stay on this earth. My next instinct was to scream, "Look at me! I made it. You could have too." But that was my survivor's guilt, my uneasiness with having a trancestor eternally younger than me.

Survival for people like us requires a mountain of fortitude. It requires finding refuge, people who understand (or at least affirm) our experience, and reprogramming all the negative, demonizing thoughts we've internalized. We must throw on a shield and sword to break down all these ideas around domination. I know you did what you had to do to hang on as long as possible, but I hate that you were stripped of your only sources of solace when you needed them the most. Your story is one of many that shows the world that it doesn't get better for everyone. You reminded me of the importance of community and I'm on a quest to find it.

Recently, a local advocate named Bellamy with a contagious

grin and ever-sparkling eyes became my gateway into the queer and trans social justice scene in Atlanta. They invited me to a meetup at an eclectic bohemian coffee shop in my neighborhood. Over a few hours, all these vibrant folks and I chatted about our varying backgrounds and passions and played icebreaker games. There were artists, nonprofit staffers, academics, and wellness experts—people who seemingly had their entire careers figured out and others still grasping for their purpose. About thirty souls took up space in that room, and between the discussion and laughter, I wondered how I had gone so long without that kind of community for so long. Even though it felt like a privilege to live long enough to see this part of my journey, it shouldn't have. This is the life that people like you and I deserve.

The words in your parting letter transformed me in an instant. Using your demise as a lesson demonstrated your warrior spirit. Even when you most needed support, you were thinking of how things could be different. I didn't know how I would heed your call to action and "fix society," but I knew I had to start. Struck by urgency, I decided to speak. I stacked boxes and books and plopped my laptop on the pile's apex. There was no plan; I just surrendered my heart to the moment, channeling my anguish. A younger me swam to the surface of my spirit. I told the world how I felt about you, what you had been through, and how I felt about the way people like us are treated. I ugly-cried, pleading to whoever watched to take our people seriously. It was the tiniest sliver of catharsis.

A day later, a BBC producer requested an interview about the video. I ecstatically agreed, but my sister reminded me that my appearance would require coming out at my new job. I had been trying to hold out as long as possible before I had to come out, if I ever did. But your story was a catalyst. So, the day of the interview, I anxiously approached my bosses. Without hesitation, they both expressed their support and gave me the green light to do the interview.

Your marching orders helped me cross that threshold and reminded me of the importance of living out loud. I thank you for that. I can only imagine what you and many other trans people we've lost along the way could have inspired had you been given the love and support you deserved. And that is the query you left us to ponder. You taught me I am obligated to others, my community, and younger trans folks to blaze a path. I can't bring you back or the souls of our siblings who similarly departed this world, but I'm vowing to do my part in an attempt to fix society. I will demand the liberation we deserve.

In love,
Raquel

15

Awakening to Black Liberation

A jolt of defiance shot through my body the first time I held a BLACK TRANS LIVES MATTER sign. It was Martin Luther King Jr. Day, and I had joined Bellamy and a few other activist friends for a counterdemonstration to the main celebration called #ReclaimHerDream. It had become de rigueur for young Black activists and organizers to shine a light on the sanitization of King's legacy by the U.S. government and the white masses. But we were also incensed about another dynamic that persists in the retelling of Black liberation movements: the erasure of women and LGBTQ+ folks.

Hours before, most of our ad hoc contingent of young Black gender-nonconforming, queer, and trans organizers attended an annual event created by Atlanta advocates Darlene Hudson and Craig Washington. The Bayard Rustin/Audre Lorde Breakfast, launched in 2002, honors the contributions by Black LGBTQ+ leaders fighting for liberation. They served as a bridge between our generations' aims and the overlooked work of Rustin, a formidable organizer and one of King's cherished advisors who is often credited as the chief architect of the 1963 March on Washington for Jobs and Freedom, and Lorde, a feminist activist, poet, and thought leader who led pioneering discourse on Black lesbian identity and intersectionality.

At the march, we assumed a funeral aesthetic, wearing a reverent all-black uniform. Several fellow protestors carried a small wooden coffin through MLK Jr. National Historic Park for dramatic effect. A sizable crowd watched us, soaking in the sacred demonstration and parting the way until we settled in an area to build a makeshift altar. All the while, we chanted words like, "None of us are free until all of us are free." I felt the scrutinizing eyes of our audience even more upon us. I could tell they were sizing up whether I was trans because of the sign I was holding. And I wondered how they felt about that.

After a string of cishet leaders spoke on the event's main stage, Bellamy gave a stirring address. They were admirably fluid in their gender expression, rocking a short beard, a dress adorned with a statement silver necklace. I'd first met Bellamy before I moved to Atlanta at a queer student conference in college when Misters Not Sisters led a packed presentation on the intersections of gender identity and drag performance. Afterward, Bellamy came up to us and shared that a lot of what we'd presented resonated with them. Naturally, we'd bonded over our queerness and, of course, being Georgians.

In this context, the role had reversed. Bellamy was the orator and I an observer. As they gripped the microphone with red-painted nails, they explained the necessity of Black cishet people being in solidarity with their queer and trans counterparts, how homophobia and transphobia often destroy familial relations and lead to intracommunal violence, and that Black communities would be able to demonstrate collective power by intentionally elevating the leadership of LGBTQ+ folks and women. We were captivated by Bellamy's words, and a few folks even shouted their affirmation. But, as my friend continued to speak, I thought about how stratified acceptance was for our community. The stakes seemed different for Bellamy to speak as a gender-nonconforming cis person versus a trans person. It seemed society had shifted to a point where the former's acceptance was growing, but trans folks were still shrouded in silence. I wondered what would have happened if a Black trans woman had addressed the crowd. *Would her words have been accepted as readily? Would she have been regarded with respect? Where would she have fallen within today's movement for Black liberation?*

By 2015, Alicia Garza, Patrisse Khan-Cullors, and Opal Tometi had worked with others to expand Black Lives Matter (BLM) beyond a hashtag and social media mobilization. It was now a complex apparatus including the Black Lives Matter Global Network and a broader coalition of numerous fledgling and legacy collectives, initiatives, and organizations focused on ending anti-Black discrimination, inequity, and violence. Despite the widespread involvement and leadership of women and queer people in BLM, the issues of homophobia, misogyny, and transphobia seem to be of negligible concern in this nascent movement's national discourse and work. Typically, cishet men were the subjects of actions and campaigns, and it seemed the only societal ill worth rallying around was police brutality.

Atlanta's social justice scene showed me that more nuance could be found on the local level, though. In fact, I found a bustling, decades-long organizing ecosystem. Legacy groups like Southerners on New Ground and SisterSong: National Women of Color Reproductive Justice Collective were at the forefront of Atlanta's presence, having prioritized a blended economic, gender, queer, and racial framework since the nineties. The former group was founded by Black lesbians (Pat Hussain, Joan Garner, and Mandy Carter) and white lesbians (Suzanne Pharr, Pam McMichael, and Mab Segrest) who had witnessed the sidelining of queer leaders within the Civil Rights Movement and the second Feminist Wave (which ignored the realities of non-white, non-straight women) and how the Gay Liberation Movement had focused squarely on cisgender white men. SisterSong, which began as a coalition of numerous women from color-led organizations and a volunteer network, drew its analysis from revered activist and thought leader Loretta Ross. She was instrumental in the theorizing and praxis around multiracial solidarity within the feminist movement and reproductive justice.

I was also fortunate to connect with a constellation of Black trans elders: Cheryl Courtney-Evans, the co-founder and executive director of Transgender Individuals Living Their Truth, offered sage advice on a very real tip; and Dee Dee Chamblee, who founded LaGender, Inc. and received a Champions of Change presidential honor under Barack Obama, and Tracee McDaniel, a leading local advocate of criminal justice reform, gave me a glimpse of the power that Black trans women can wield to improve conditions for our communities. In them and my peers, a deeper desire to find my place in movement took hold. The false narrative that I'd carried since childhood, that the South was defined solely by its oppressive history, unraveled with the quickness. In Atlanta organizers, I witnessed a pride in enduring and finding ways to thrive in the region where the systems of chattel slavery and Jim Crow were experienced and felt the most. There was a sense that if we could fight and win here, we could fight and win anywhere. The more I immersed myself in the Black queer and trans community in Atlanta, the more I saw the South's radical transformative power.

16

Between Visibility and Vitality

Blake Brockington, not unlike Leelah Alcorn, carved his way into my heart through an image in a news story. The young trans activist was wearing a long-sleeved black shirt with the names of young Black boys and men who had been brutally murdered: Emmett, Amadou, Sean, Oscar, Trayvon, Jordan, Eric, Mike, and Ezell. An ominous ellipsis concluded the list. As I absorbed this image, I recalled how invested my peers and I were in transforming UGA, how as collegiate organizers (though we didn't use that label) we fiercely believed that our society could be more equitable for folks on the margins. Blake blazed a path even before stepping on his college campus.

The year prior, as a student of Charlotte, North Carolina's East Mecklenburg High School, Blake became his state's first openly trans homecoming king and the country's first Black openly trans homecoming royal. He won among a cohort of young trans people who had started normalizing their experiences by vying for those titles across the U.S. I admired Generation Z's indomitable urge to dismantle binary ideals.

Blake's crowning received national attention. In interviews, he bravely revealed that he experienced outsized transphobic vitriol online. This dynamic, coupled with difficulties coming out to family and peers, only worsened his mental illness. For year, he'd battled depression and self-harm. Nevertheless, he continued to advocate for the LGBTQ+ community and against state violence with his newfound notoriety. In *BrocKINGton*, a short documentary about his journey, he said, "I honestly feel like this is something I have to do. Nobody should be scared to be themselves, and everybody should have an equal opportunity for an enjoyable high school experience."

On March 23, 2015, Blake, eighteen years old, died by suicide after walking onto the outer loop of Interstate 485 in Charlotte and being struck by several vehicles. When he was laid to rest a few days later, his estranged family continued disrespecting his transmasculine identity by deadnaming and misgendering him. Blake's death revealed to me how visibility doesn't necessarily lead to increased vitality for trans people. It didn't insulate him from the self-loathing that society had indoctrinated in him and the harm enacted by those who wouldn't fully accept him, including his family. In fact, visibility heightened it in many ways. Blake's and Leelah's stories of suicide were part of a larger web of anti-trans violence. According to data from the 2015 U.S. Transgender Survey (USTS), published in a separate report by the UCLA School of Law's Williams Institute, 81.7 percent of respondents reported seriously considering suicide in their lifetimes.[1] By mid-2015, there had also been a handful of anti-trans murders, mostly of women of color.[2] As a Black trans woman, I wondered why the macro-movements that claimed to fight for the lives of the most marginalized weren't pouring resources into keeping trans people alive. Blake, like countless other young Black trans people, were on the frontlines of organizing and protests, yet all their lives were relegated to the periphery.

* * *

DAYS AFTER BLAKE'S death, I joined a national contingent of trans leaders of color at the fourth INCITE! Color of Violence conference in Chicago. I was invited by Nadine Figueroa of Transgender Law Center (TLC), who discovered me via social media. When I got the email, I felt honored and surprised. After all, it was my first time attending such a major gathering, especially since I was just starting to be more vocal about our community online. But I asked for some time off at my day job and swiftly made plans to attend. I learned that INCITE!, a national women's, nonbinary, and trans folks of color collective and organization, was founded in 2000 specifically to address the needs of—at that time—women who felt their needs had been overlooked or sidelined in larger feminist and anti-violence advocacy spaces. With the recent suicides and deaths in the community, violence seemed like the most pertinent issue of focus.

At the event, I was struck by the fact that the space was gender diverse, intergenerational, and multiracial. I appreciated that there was a larger general convening where leaders of color discussed their work across identity groups, and there were designated rooms for specific communities. TLC established a track at the conference for trans people to discuss employment, healthcare, and justice. I felt energized as I witnessed trans people discuss their advocacy work at various nonprofits or in governmental roles. When I had to step out for a work call, a sense of frustration rose in me. I hated having my energy torn between my innocuous day job and this conference, where crucial conversations that impacted my life and people like me were happening. At least here I wasn't a token because of my Blackness, queerness, and transness.

Just like in Atlanta, I felt transformed when I met Black trans folks invested in our community's liberation. After years of reading the award-winning *TransGriot*, I finally got to meet the blog's creator, Monica Roberts. Since 2006, she had tirelessly documented the accomplishments and struggles of trans people—something that was still not happening in mainstream publications. I'd known of actress and advocate Angelica Ross ever since I followed her on social media in college. She seemed like an older sister in my head as she chronicled her professional experiences with her tech nonprofit, TransTech Social Enterprises. Perhaps most importantly, I met Miss Major Griffin-Gracy, a Stonewall riots–era legend, decades-long organizer, and designated community mother to many young trans activists. After being incarcerated throughout the 1970s, she moved to Southern California and became involved in grassroots community efforts. By the nineties, she'd settled in the San Francisco area and focused on HIV/AIDS advocacy. In 2005, she joined Transgender, Gender Variant, Intersex Justice Project as a staff organizer, later becoming executive director of the organization, which centered on support for currently and formerly incarcerated transgender women.

In between sessions, I spotted a gaggle of trans folks gathered around Miss Major in the hallway. She smiled warmly and gushed over her court of admirers from her motorized scooter. I timidly made my way over to her, taking this prime example of what longevity could look like for me as a Black trans woman if I were so blessed decades down the line.

"Hi, Miss Major, it's nice to meet you," I said, beaming with a wide smile.

"What's your name, baby?" she said with familiarity, like we already knew each other.

"I'm Raquel."

"And where are you from?"

"I'm from Georgia. Augusta originally, but I live in Atlanta now."

"Oh, you're one of my Southern girls."

"Yes, ma'am."

"Well, you hang in there, baby."

"I will."

It was a brief exchange, but I felt seen and held in a way I hadn't before. I wondered what it would have been like to know someone like her when I was younger. Perhaps I wouldn't have waffled back and forth on my queerness, or maybe I would have begun my gender transition sooner. She felt like a long-lost relative. I wanted to ask her questions my biological grandmothers would have never been able to answer. I wanted to soak up the wisdom from her life's stories, but our time was limited. Even though I didn't have an immediate opportunity to amplify her story, I silently vowed to chronicle her impact in some way one day.

Despite these warm moments earlier in the day, by the afternoon an argument broke out between various women from different backgrounds and regions. A leader shouted at some younger participants in the New York scene, who returned the sentiment. The non-Black Latinas, most of them also Hispanic, kept to their circle while Black trans women mostly stayed in ours. As people stood up and spoke their turn, they explained the different needs between the South, Midwest, East Coast, and West Coast. People discussed the immense poverty many faced in their communities, the lack of access to adequate and gender-affirming healthcare, and the safety concerns of engaging in sex work. Overall, I heard a similar theme: our disparate smaller communities had been underresourced and undersupported for decades, and there was much more work to be done before we fully coalesced as a national trans movement. I left the conference not entirely knowing my place within it. I was a journalist first and foremost, but it was becoming harder to see myself as simply an observer of my community. I'd learned those lofty ideals in college about objectivity—

that is, the idea that I should pretend as if bias doesn't exist, that I shouldn't consider how systems of oppression impact how or why certain voices are considered important or not, and that I should leave my lived experience on the cutting room floor. I didn't know where my career fit in all of this, but as I was figuring these things out, one trans narrative exploded in the media.

* * *

IF LAVERNE COX's starring role in *Orange Is the New Black* sparked the trans visibility era, then Caitlyn Jenner's *20/20* interview with Diane Sawyer in April 2015 was the climax. I was far too young to know Jenner's cultural impact in the seventies when she was most known as a gold-winning Olympic champion. I also hadn't watched a single episode of *Keeping Up with the Kardashians*, so I had little knowledge of her career and life. But, in the months prior, I'd followed the social media discussion of Jenner's changing appearance. I loathed the fact that her hypothetical womanhood had been reduced to accruing long hair, painted nails, and alleged plastic surgery. If she was trans, she deserved the chance to tell the world in her own time.

My stomach lurched as I went back and forth between Jenner's and Sawyer's conversation. I knew that millions of people were watching, and this exchange would serve as a "Trans 101" course for most of them. According to a GLAAD and Harris Poll online survey[3] later that year, only about 16 percent of adult Americans reported knowing a trans person. She needed to distill gender and queer theory to the general public. Otherwise, she could singlehandedly make things harder for the rest of the world's LGBTQ+ community. I didn't envy that pressure.

Jenner's story was both familiar and foreign to me. I related to the lifelong feeling of gender incongruence and not meeting the masculine expectations thrust on her beginning in childhood.

However, there was a significant gap between my transitioning in obscurity during my college years and her doing so as a senior citizen who had lived a very public life as a pinnacle of hypermasculine virility. Her wealthy, white identity had shielded her from the struggles that most trans people I knew faced, particularly in employment and healthcare. So I hoped her story wouldn't become a stand-in for all trans people. After all, there's a misconception among some that even being able to identify as trans is a privilege. While much of the language and understanding of trans identity emerged within academia over decades, people who defy gender norms have existed throughout time. Jenner's interview should have been an opening for the general public to hear from trans people who had crafted authentic lives rather than revolving around the privileges that Jenner had enjoyed. A conscientious media landscape, one that also elevated trans journalists and storytellers to steward this narrative, would have ensured this and forecasted the outsized impact of Jenner's revelation.

When her *Vanity Fair* cover was released in June, Jenner was styled with Lauren Bacall–highlighted locks and her arms behind her back in a white corseted undergarment, almost inviting the world to dissect her body as much as her identity. I didn't fully see the comfort and confidence that others saw. There seemed to be knowing defiance mixed with tortured coquette in her glare. In an accompanying mini-documentary on the cover-making process, *Vanity Fair* features editor Jane Sarkin said, "We discuss absolutely every detail of the surgeries that [Caitlyn] Jenner will endure to what [her] new name will be." With nearly consistent deadnaming and misgendering throughout the video, other publication staffers explained her journey as an older wealthy white woman living secluded on California's Malibu Hill coast as the true underdog story, and the choice of an appropriate aesthetic style and "presentation" as the most crucial part of her coming-out process. Perhaps these were authentic descriptions of Jenner's feelings at the time, but the hyperfocus on her body packaged in old Hollywood conceptions of femininity felt regressive to me.

Overall, the cover story, released during LGBTQ+ Pride Month, seemed well received. Celebrities like Ellen DeGeneres, Lady Gaga, Seth Meyers, and Kerry Washington expressed their support for Jenner's revelation. On social media and in an appearance for the Logo "Trailblazer Honors," President Obama lauded Jenner's courage to tell her story and the growing acceptance of LGBTQ+ Americans in the broader culture. On one level, he was right. By the end of that month, June 2015, the Supreme Court of the United States would rule in favor of marriage equality for same-sex couples in *Obergefell v. Hodges*. However, trans communities on the ground saw the cracks in America's so-called progress. At that month's White House Pride reception, a trans-Latina undocumented activist, Jennicet Gutiérrez, would interrupt Obama's address, opposing his administration's deportation policies and their impact on LGBTQ+ immigrants. Amid heckles and jeers directed at her from the primarily cis gay and lesbian crowd, she was escorted out by Secret Service officers. The distance between the reception of Jenner's glorified coming out and Gutiérrez's life-and-death battle cry couldn't have been greater.

The strides Black trans women like Laverne Cox and Janet Mock had made in expanding the discourse around trans identity seemed to unravel as well. Though Jenner mentioned both figures in the mini-documentary as pioneers, it seems she took few cues from their thought leadership. In recent years, Cox and Mock had utilized their platforms to assert that trans people were more than our assigned genders and names at birth and the state of our genitalia. There had long been a sensational stench in media coverage of trans people's bodies, prompting cis people to ask invasive, objectifying questions. Further, Cox and Mock had consistently made clear that there was a vital feminist element to trans people's sense of self-determination, how exceptional their stories were, and that most trans people, particularly Black, were facing tremendous systemic barriers that would never afford them the access and platforms Cox and Mock had gained.

It was also unfortunate to watch other Black trans figures who lived authentically be overshadowed by the media. Madison Hinton, better known as TS Madison, and Amiyah Scott revolutionized how trans people appeared online. After years as a staple in the adult film industry, Madison expanded her audience through videos demonstrating her raw and comedic personality. Scott pioneered the before-and-after gender transition posts that would destigmatize trans people's lifelong gender journeys while also being scrutinized by cis people. She also heavily influenced the Instagram baddie aesthetic, and images of her immaculately applied cosmetics and polychromatic wigs would regularly go viral, influencing celebrities—including the Jenners and Kardashians. Meanwhile, Carmen Carrera and Geena Rocero seamlessly blended community advocacy into their modeling careers. These figures built careers and carried the trans community along the way, opting to become educators on our experiences.

I admired these women for their trailblazing feats, and their work made it possible for me to live more openly, especially online. Since my role at HSW was focused more on social engine optimization and website maintenance, I was no longer writing regularly. So, social media became a necessary outlet. And let me tell ya, being an openly trans person on the Internet was dangerous and stigmatizing. Strangers would regularly discount what we said about our experiences, misgender us, and, if we made enough of a splash, dox us so they could find our deadnames and disseminate them to others. Once someone scoured my social media for a baby picture just to post it on their own account to show that I wasn't a "real woman." Nevertheless, because of the bravery that other trans women of color demonstrated, I began to share my thoughts on culture, identity, and politics online. I dreaded that those trailblazers would become eclipsed by Jenner, who was aligned with one of the most powerful cultural brands and media dynasties. Then, of course, she'd become a de facto spokesperson for the community despite lacking the brilliance that trans women of color had carried in the media for years.

Weeks after the *Vanity Fair* cover story was published, *The New York Times* ran "What Makes a Woman," an opinion-editorial by filmmaker and journalist Elinor Burkett. She argued that Jenner's concept of womanhood was gender essentialist and reductive. Burkett rejected Jenner's statements about having a more "female" brain and being more emotional since fully delving into her transition. She critiqued her traditionally feminine clothing choices and expression, asserting that because Jenner had been assigned male at birth and navigated most of her life being seen as a man, she shouldn't get to "define" womanhood. Interestingly, what most grabbed me was Burkett's denouncement of Jenner's womanhood because she assumed she hadn't experienced gender-based violence, the gender wage gap, sexual objectification, or the fear of an unplanned pregnancy. In the world's leading publication, this piece elucidated how Jenner's story could become a stand-in for all trans women's stories. Burkett couldn't even consider, for instance, that someone like me, who socially transitioned at a much younger age than Jenner, could experience most of those circumstances. She stated that womanhood should be defined by a finite list of "accrued certain experiences, endured certain indignities and relished certain courtesies in a culture that reacted to you as one." Burkett was being just as essentialist as she accused Jenner of being by conflating gender and sex. And her assessment was peak white feminism because I could easily see a suffragist from the early twentieth century denouncing Black womanhood with a similar line of argument. Burkett's op-ed gave voice to the growing ire from a segment of cis people who felt uncomfortable with Jenner's visibility and, by proxy, the trans community.

Though there were significant critiques to make about the rollout of Jenner's identity in the media, for me it was more important to denounce the transphobia surrounding how people discussed her. Whenever someone deadnamed or misgendered her, I imagined them readily doing that to me or any other trans person. I shuddered the few times when I revealed my trans identity to people, usually cishet men, who asked, "Oh, like Caitlyn Jenner?" It was great that the cis public was exposed to a trans narrative, but it wouldn't necessarily lessen the systemic barriers that the rest of our community was bound to face. I was inspired to do work that would lift the names of the trans people of color we had lost that year or before. I wanted to reassert the importance of historic movement heroes like Marsha P. Johnson and Sylvia Rivera. Visibility was rising like a determined rocket in the sky, but the vitality of trans folks on the margins was being wholly eclipsed.

17

Slouching Toward Liberation

Dear East Point Police, I will not give you my courage. I will not give you my dignity. I will not live in fear of you, and I will not let you shame and humiliate me into submission. I heard what you think of me and my community, with all of the names you called me. . . . And I will unapologetically tell you who I am. I am not an "it," I am not a "thing." I am trans, and you don't have the right to arrest me for being trans.

—Juan Evans

* * *

I would still be an aimless advocate if it wasn't for Juan Evans's influence.[1] The proud Black trans activist galvanized local community members after East Point, Georgia, police officers stopped him for allegedly speeding and not having identification documents in October 2014. While hurling dehumanizing words, the officers demanded a genital search to verify his gender. But Juan rebuffed the request. Afterward, when he maintained his arrest was for not complying, Solutions Not Punishment Collaborative (SNaPCo), based in East Point, led a contingent to rally for his justice. When the police department released Juan without charges, the collective further called for accountability and change. One fruit of the collective's labor was the creation of an internship for Black trans leaders and I felt honored that Juan considered me for it.

It didn't take long for SNaPCo to become my political home. The coalition was an arm of Atlanta's Racial Justice Action Center, dedicated to criminal justice reform and prison abolition in the metro area. And the internship served as a deep dive into community organizing with an emphasis on political education and creating a landmark survey on trans and gender-nonconforming (TGNC) people's interactions with the Atlanta Police Department. I secretly dedicated my HSW work-from-home days to attend sessions at the SNaPCo headquarters, which we called the Blue House. Whenever I entered that place, I felt a sense of familiarity, safety, and security.

Camaraderie came easily with the advisors for the program, especially community elders like Dee Dee Chamblee and BT. The former was the group's divine auntie, who always met us with her dazzling smile and its glorious gap. Her mellifluous voice could fill a room and your heart all at once. When we first met, she said she'd noticed me weeks before the internship at a rally where I took the microphone. That I spoke brazenly about being trans and how the primarily cishet audience needed to connect with our community impressed her. BT was the complementary uncle figure, an ever-encouraging OG who imparted lessons to younger trans folks in navigating their medical transitions and the healthcare system.

With her Senegalese-twisted hair and inviting demeanor, Toni-Michelle Williams welcomed us as the internship coordinator. She invigorated our weekly meetings and became a quick friend with whom I could compare notes on being an openly trans twenty-something in Atlanta. Her admirable leadership was fueled by empathy, and she could gracefully dissolve moments of conflict and confusion in mere minutes. Though Toni-Michelle was the leader, I always felt a mutual exchange of information. Her raw, street-smart understanding of the world and the remnants of academia I'd carried since college helped us concoct a unique blend of Black trans feminist praxis and theory.

The other participants' lived experiences also challenged my educational and socioeconomic privileges. Together we gained a deeper analysis of ableism, anti-Blackness, mass incarceration, serophobia, sex worker stigma, and state violence. I was no longer the sole Black person in a predominantly white space, nor the sole Black trans woman surrounded by white transmasculine folks. In this dynamic, I contended differently with the mosaic of oppression and privilege and how everyone carries some mixture of the two depending on positionality. During our discussions, we traversed historical and political contexts that seemed familiar given my collegiate background. But I realized the academic language that had soaked into my pores was largely unfamiliar to many in the room and within our wider community. None of these theories or words were flawless and often they stood in the way of meaningful communication and connection. The importance of accessibility would be top of mind by the end of our first month together.

By July, we'd picked up a major internship assignment to build a workshop for the first-ever Movement for Black Lives (M4BL) convening in Cleveland, Ohio. This 1,500-deep gathering would define the contours of a sprawling coalition of organizations and individuals focused on Black liberation across the United States. At the center was the Black Lives Matter Global Network (BLMGN), which skewed to younger folks, particularly millennials. Still, it drew an array of organizers. Our crew's goal was to connect with other leaders while highlighting Atlanta's crucial work.

As we piled onto a bus with about fifty people from various local groups, I stared hopefully out the window. As far as I knew, there had been no other gathering in the history of Black liberation movements to draw a noteworthy amount of trans and queer people or be so impressively led by Black women. I was still an organizing neophyte, but Black movement space felt hallowed in a way that LGBTQ+ or feminist spaces weren't. Other movements, despite their complexities, felt more within reach, even with their own histories of internal struggles. There wasn't as much documented about queer and trans folks in Black liberation movements, but M4BL seemed primed to amend the fact that we existed.

I didn't assume that the convening would be completely affirming. It's not that I was under some illusion that Black people were more queerphobic or transphobic than any other group. I knew that white supremacy painted Blackness as ignorant, savage, and uncivilized. As if a history of destroying, displacing, and terrorizing entire peoples isn't the pinnacle of inhumanity. No, my nerves came, in part, from trauma. Because of social and physical proximity, I'd encountered hate more directly and often from people who looked like me. Of course, some of my earliest scrapes were with my Black family. Bullies of the same race were more likely to dissect or demonize my nonconformity than my non-Black peers. The patriarchy had convinced them I was an obstacle or a threat if I didn't reflect a "normal" gender or sexual orientation back to them. Beyond that trauma, I also had to contend with a media landscape that almost solely mainstreamed a white image of queerness and transness. This made it easy for many Black people to consider my queerness and transness as inauthentic "white things." Then, to white people, I imagine I was an amorphous figure of "other." I was already Black; the nuances of my otherness rarely mattered.

As a Black openly trans woman, my atypical gender experience added another layer of distance between me and Black cishet people. Often when I'd share my truth, I'd watch their faces morph from warmth into confusion, and our potential for genuine connection would slip away. Not unlike a hook-up, they might ask invasive questions about when I started my gender transition and what surgeries I might have had. Then, they would share backhanded compliments about my realness, how they would have never suspected, or claim to know someone "like me" (who many times wasn't even trans but a cis queer person). After our exchange, I might wonder if I had done the right thing by confiding in them. Even within the movement, my transness seemed to elicit an alienating response. *Why was this anxiety no different whether the interaction was with a nonactivist or social justice–oriented Black person or in a space constructed and crafted by, say, the M4BL?*

After our internship crew settled in at the convening, we took our seats among the other attendees for the opening ceremony. It was heartening to see that BLMGN hired a Black trans organizer who took the stage as a moderator, urging attendees to consider the diversity of our movement. I didn't know her, but her presence signaled our visibility in the space. Soon, a choir sang a rendition of "I Need You to Survive," the contemporary gospel standard by Hezekiah Walker, between testimonies from the loved ones of murdered Black people. Emmett Till's family led the roster, gripping the audience with an address on how Jim Crow and white supremacy contributed to his death. And the crowd thunderously applauded after families of other figures like Michael Brown, Rekia Boyd, and Eric Garner Sr. shared their stories. Then, Miss Major took the podium encouraging us to nurture ourselves in our lifelong social justice fights. Her exaltation was gratifying to behold.

After the event, I noticed an awkward sense of self-segregation. Trans folks mostly kept to ourselves, while cis folks, particularly straight ones, seemed to do the same. A few even complained about a perceived overpresence of trans people in the program and how unwieldy it was to have to be vigilant about identities and pronouns. Those dynamics hit a fever pitch at the welcoming party that night. After a few hours of socializing at the venue, attendees learned that security personnel had stopped Martin, a trans man, for using the men's restroom. Apparently, the bouncers didn't get the memo that they needed to suspend their gendered assumptions for our crowd. Martin said they called him a woman, attempted to physically remove him from the club, and then called the police after he resisted and rejoined the other attendees inside. *Fucking unacceptable.* Eventually, we all poured outside in solidarity, ending the event in protest. As the police gathered outside the venue, we all chanted our resistance, cutting through the blue and red lights. Not unlike with Juan, I noticed an undeniable power in Martin's refusal to be disrespected.

The restroom debacle loomed over the rest of the convening. While attendees had left the party in solidarity with Martin, the incident asserted that movement leaders might not be equipped to build trans-affirming spaces. I'd noticed since my arrival a feeling of dissection and a desire to hide behind passability. It felt dangerous to throw people together without a shared commitment of respect. We assumed every attendee was committed to Black liberation, but even if that were true, it didn't mean liberation meant the same thing to all of us. Leaders professed championing a Black queer feminist political lens, but it was unclear how it confronted cissexism and gender essentialism. Much like the movement, the convening was tailored to Black cishet people and many trans people felt unsafe because we knew many attendees had never even encountered a trans person before, much less the issues we faced.

Undeterred by the collective tension, our internship crew delivered our workshop, "Why Do Black Trans Lives Matter," the following morning. It was even more prescient now. We shared critical case studies of Black trans folks like Juan; CeCe McDonald; Ky Peterson, a Georgia man who was imprisoned after killing his rapist in self-defense; and Monica Jones, an Arizona State University student and activist who an undercover cop arrested after being accused of manifesting prostitution. The presentation was well received, though we wished our turnout was more extensive and comprised more of our intended audience, curious cishets. Most of the people in our workshop were other trans folks, and it felt like we were preaching to the choir.

Afterward, I heard rumblings about the convening organizers wanting to address how trans folks were feeling after the incident that Martin experienced. Alicia Garza gathered a sizable group for a healing circle, serving as a valiant effort to rectify many of our discomforts. Still, a foul taste about the night before lingered in many trans attendees' mouths. This led to the formation of an ad hoc working group to discuss the intentionality behind TGNC inclusion in the movement and how to improve relations. I appreciated the small meeting room full of over fifty Black trans people from all over the country. Before the meeting, I didn't even know so many of us were there. And soon, we mapped out what a contingent of us would discuss on the main stage. Our disappointment motivated us to draw up a list of demands for the movement, particularly for our cis counterparts. We knew we couldn't cower in silence and that we were stronger together.

When would a contingent of trans, gender-nonconforming, and nonbinary folks in a similar position hold the larger Black cishet masses accountable?

It seemed impossible to detach the discrimination that happened on the leaders' watch from the violence that Black trans folks faced on a regular basis. Patriarchal violence, particularly of the domestic-partner and intimate-partner varieties, was ignored in the Black mass movement. Focusing on state violence was strategic because it gave us a neater villain to tackle: white supremacy. While propping up this system of oppression as the most significant drew all Black people closer together, it also ignored the other issues that threaten Black lives, particularly women and LGBTQ+ folks. Confronting cisheteropatriarchy would require acknowledging that Black people wield systems of oppression over one another. Cishet people, in conforming to gendered expectations, feel entitled to being regarded as the default. When queer and TGNC people assert our existence and value, cishet people often feel denied their "rightful" place. Focusing only on white supremacy dilutes our understanding of positionality, allowing us to ignore trauma and how we harm others in our communities. It doesn't protect any of us from being exploited and dominated by patriarchal violence, and it doesn't liberate communities. Why does it matter that we defund police or abolish prisons if we go home to other violent conditions? Without accountability, cishet people operate as another form of law enforcement in our lives, encouraging our parents, families, communities, and movements to police us.

Hours after the trans organizing session, we shared our discussions with the audience on the convening main stage. I initially declined to speak, fearing the judgment of the audience. But I agreed after other organizers, including Toni-Michelle, urged me to take to the stage. Drawing on our experiences organizing in the South, Toni-Michelle and I implored cishet attendees to recognize that regardless of their understanding of our identities, at the very least they should be able to regard Black trans people as family. And our comments drew a few nods. After the last speakers gave their spiels, we presented our list of Black trans demands, which included political education on gender identity for the network, a working group of TGNC folks to represent our community within M4BL, and resources for trans-led organizations. Most of the audience seemed to affirm and applaud our messages, but many still seemed confused about our presence. Others approached us speakers and shared what resonated with them. Addressing unspoken tensions allowed many of us to open up and connect on a deeper level.

The convening was challenging, but it served as a turning point for M4BL and gave legs to an as-yet-undefined national Black trans liberation movement. Commanding the stage encouraged us to acknowledge our collective power as Black trans people. We weren't just decorations shoved in a corner, trotted out whenever the movement needed to seem more progressive. We were an inextricable element of liberation. I left with a new resolve to get our people to understand that Blackness is inherently gender nonconforming. A white supremacist cisheteropatriarchal concept of gender serves none of us. Black men will never be white men—assuming a supreme mantle of resources, unchecked power fueled by exploitation and domination, and wealth. Black women will never be white women—afforded the cursed fragility, softness, protection, and adulation. And though Black nonbinary folks may be most primed to embody Blackness in its most expansive form, they won't get their rightful place in the communities to which they belong until we all dismantle these systems of oppression that stifle us.

In an article for *The Nation* released after the convening, journalist Mark Winston Griffith said: "For a gathering that, up to that point, had set its sights mostly on external forms of oppression, it was a revolutionary moment of inwardly focused accountability, community building, and course correction. Queer and trans folks were not working at the margins of the movement for black liberation but had moved, quite literally, to center stage, where I suspect they will remain."[2]

18

Nobody's Savior

Weeks after the Movement for Black Lives convening, our TGNC contingent planned a national day of action concerning *afrotransphobia* and *afrotransmisogyny*, the antagonistic brutality that Black trans people and transfeminine folks experience, respectively. It was timely, as the National Coalition of Anti-Violence Programs would report a 14 percent increase of hate violence–related homicides of LGBTQ+ and HIV-positive individuals by the end of 2015.[1] And of the twenty-four recorded victims, half were Black trans women.

We called the observance Black Trans Liberation Tuesday (BTLT) and coordinated rallies coinciding with Marsha P. Johnson's birthday on August 24. By now, Black trans folks and the wider LGBTQ+ community had exalted her as a spiritual foremother. The historical lore of Marsha's presence on the front lines of the 1969 Stonewall riots and subsequent community organizing with another foremother, Sylvia Rivera, cemented her as a key inspiration in our work. Marsha's revolutionary insights and innovations were our connection to an often-buried narrative of trans and gender-nonconforming resistance. Another synergistic element of her story was her fate: a mysterious, untimely death in 1992.

On our first BTLT national call, I volunteered to work on the communications and social media team. Beyond flyers and graphics, I sought a unifying symbol for the day. After researching, I realized there were no visual descriptors of the Black trans experience. The original trans flag designed by lauded activist Monica Helms in 1999 was an indisputable signifier for the wider community. Inspired, I crafted a version that replaced the white stripe with a black one. Not only would this design draw attention specifically to the Black trans and gender-nonconforming experience, but it declared that nonbinary Black folks and those with more expansive gender experiences possess the most potential for inspiring collective liberation. I didn't even expect its use beyond that day; however, my peers loved it, and it gained traction in some corners of our emerging movement.

Once I fulfilled my national support role, I realized that there weren't yet plans for a local mobilization. Other groups had mapped direct actions for Dayton, Ohio; New York City; San Francisco; Washington, DC; and several other locations. I still felt fresh to the Atlanta scene but knew we couldn't drop the ball down South. So I collaborated with Toni-Michelle, Bellamy, and a gender-diverse group to organize a sign-making party and plan the speaking portion of the event. I would host alongside Holiday Simmons, a transmasculine two-spirit activist who worked in LGBTQ+ legal justice.

We hosted the event at the Metropolitan Atlanta Rapid Transit Authority (MARTA) station in the Little Five Points neighborhood of East Atlanta. It had been a site of afrotransmisogyny for years. There had been a recent instance of harassment and, more notably, two Black trans women had been attacked the year prior. In a viral video that would garner more than a million views, one woman tells two ostensibly cishet men to stop targeting them. Then, one man sends a kick in her direction and a brawl ensues. By the clip's end, one woman's wig has been pulled off, the other woman is nude, and the surrounding crowd is jeering at the woman's genitalia without intervening. Afterward, one of the victims, Janell Crosby, told reporters that MARTA officers took no action after they got off the train.[2] The attackers were later arrested and charged with disorderly conduct, despite some calls for the incident to be considered a hate crime. SNaPCo, in abolitionist fashion, released a statement emphasizing public education on gender and community service and dialogue between the victims and attackers rather than a lengthy jail sentence.

Our rally aimed to assert afrotransphobic violence as a systemic issue worthy of the city's attention. In one of the last evenings of the Georgia summer, our impassioned lineup commanded the crowd's attention. With care and reverence, Holiday and I alternated holding a parasol as Ms. Cheryl Courtney-Evans spoke as an elder who had witnessed discrimination for decades, Toni-Michelle gave a heartwarming speech about solidarity with our cis community, and Bellamy urged MARTA to release a set of policies focused on protecting and respecting TGNC riders. Our event defied expectations, drawing a crowd of nearly one hundred and local news coverage. We certainly didn't draw the same amount of attention as other rallies, particularly the one in New York, but we took pride in our modest showing. And it was most gratifying to hear elders describe our rally as the first of its kind in Atlanta. My confidence in organizing grew, and I left eager to further transform our local community.

* * *

NOT LONG AFTER the rally, Toni-Michelle enlisted me to help collect community responses for our report, *The Most Dangerous*

Thing Out Here Is the Police. It was our capstone internship assignment, and so far, we had already captured a stirring snapshot of the fear, frustration, humiliation, and sadness in TGNC people's interactions with the Atlanta Police Department (APD). By the project's end, we'd find that 80 percent of trans women of color reported being approached or stopped by APD, with approximately half being profiled as sex workers. Toni-Michelle and I had already gathered responses at Black Pride events and LGBTQ+ clubs, but tonight would be the first time she took me to "the stroll." This colloquial name refers to a location, usually a particular thoroughfare, where sex workers find clients. Often, there's a specific strip for cis women, queer cis men, and trans women.

On this dimly lit street, some women worked in pairs, but many worked alone. I shuddered with apprehension about our safety, not from our sisters, but from the clients we might encounter. Most of what I knew about sex work came from television shows like *Law & Order*, and even *Grand Theft Auto: Vice City*, a video game I enjoyed as a teenager. In those depictions, sex workers were rarely characters with whom I was expected to identify. If anything, there was an insistence to associate these, usually women, simply with annihilation. The *Paris Is Burning* scene in which house mother Angie Xtravaganza describes her daughter, Venus, being found strangled to death is also forever etched in my mind as an expected fate of sex work. I tried to shake those thoughts, following Toni-Michelle's lead to our first respondent. Perhaps we looked suspicious with our folders stuffed with questionnaires and pens as we approached a small, scattered collection of Black trans women. They dripped in allure even from a distance. Honestly, I felt underdressed.

"Hey, girl." Toni-Michelle motioned to a woman. She looked skeptical, not fully making out her face in the dark.

"Oh, hey, girl." She giggled. "I ain't know who that was."

"How you been?" Toni-Michelle said.

"Oh, I've been good. You know, working," she said, monitoring the street.

"I hear you," Toni-Michelle responded. "Well, I'm not gon' keep you, but this is my girl, Raquel. She's new to SNaPCo, and we're working on this report about the Atlanta Police Department and just got a few questions to ask you."

"You are so beautiful," the tall woman blurted out. "I thought you was fish."

"Thank you," I said, not trying to appear like I loved the idea that she couldn't discern my transness. Plus, now I was wondering what gave me away. Anyway, the woman skimmed the first page of the survey as Toni-Michelle held it out, then she looked back at us.

"Well, hey, girl, can I do this another time? I really gotta hit it tonight," she said.

"Oh yeah, we'll be out here," Toni-Michelle said. "But I'ma hold you for next time."

"Alright, girl," she said before sprinting across the street as a car headed her way.

Toni-Michelle and I continued walking up and down the street, talking to the women we passed. Most were wholly uninterested in our cause. As I saw them waving down cars, I teared up imagining what happened once they went off with their would-be Johns. *If we came back a week later, who would still be there? Would we be responsible if something happened to one of them and we hadn't intervened?* I tried to hold back my emotions, but Toni-Michelle noticed my silence when we made it back to her car.

"You OK, girl?" she said as she cranked up the car.

"They shouldn't have to do this. They deserve so much better. They should have more options," I blurted out, streams now flowing down my face.

I assumed she'd agree with me and that we could devise a plan to recruit them for another career.

"You know what, baby? You can't save anyone. That's not your job," she said after listening intently. "All we can do is support our girls by bringing them into this work when we can. But you aren't anyone's savior."

Is that what I was giving? I tried to search the filing cabinets in my mind for something I had learned about oppression from my women's studies courses to make sense of this moment. *Should I retort about their patriarchal working conditions or how sexualization was dehumanizing?* But as I looked out on the street and took in Toni-Michelle's words, I felt a revelatory flash of insight. *Just because my path had been different, why did I think I was uniquely primed to shift the trajectory of these women?* My sister-friend was right; I was on some savior complex bullshit.

Sharing a similar gender experience with the women we'd met didn't mean I knew them or their stories. I'd never had to consider being a sex worker. Besides, I was being judgmental as hell. Toni-Michelle's raw confrontation humbled me, urging me to think more deeply about my privileges and how they colored my lens as an organizer. My gut reaction was to focus on external solutions, but truthfully, I had work to do internally too. I needed to confront and deconstruct my classist and elitist notions of liberation and expand my understanding of agency, autonomy, and self-determination.

* * *

A VOID WAS left when my SNaPCo internship ended and I realized how unfulfilled I was in my HSW role. By 2016, I yearned to devote as much of my energy to social justice as possible. This desire came right as we neared the next presidential election where it seemed we'd either elect the first woman president or a bigoted blowhard. Hillary Clinton, though not a favored candidate by many in progressive organizing spaces, at least seemed to continue the representational trend that Barack Obama had eked out. Donald Trump had built a hateful campaign demonizing Black people, immigrants of color, Mexicans, Muslims, and protestors who opposed him. Both candidates had complex sociopolitical histories and documented moments where they or those they associated with further negatively impacted the lives of people on the margins. With these prescient conversations and continued news of anti-Black brutality, I felt demoralized with a job that simply focused on maintaining a company's bottom line.

To inject a renewed sense of interest in my work, I scheduled a meeting with my boss, Wanda. She was a reserved older Black Caribbean woman who was rarely receptive to ideas on how to improve our work processes. Still, I pitched a podcast idea centering dispatches from contemporary social justice movements. As I channeled my passion, relaying experiences with M4BL and community organizing, Wanda just furrowed her brow, tightened her mouth, and squinted with derision. My words seemed to fly right past her. When I finished, there was a sliver of silence. She gave me an "I don't know. Maybe later. For now, you just do what we pay you to do" response and that was that. So I returned to my desk, determined to find another job.

With a growing interest in the national LGBTQ+ rights landscape, I joined Georgia Equality's board of directors. Founded in 1995, the organization served as the leader for political advocacy and representation of the statewide LGBTQ+ community. For decades they had been instrumental in electoral victories, including encouraging more inclusive language in civil rights bills, lobbying for protections, and leading public education and volunteer efforts. It impressed me that the executive director had been a formidable HIV/AIDS activist in the eighties and nineties. After a weeks-long recruitment process, I joined the board as, perhaps, the first openly trans woman member. I realized this at our introductory retreat near the North Georgia mountains when, after hours of networking, a white cis gay board member grilled me on my gender transition. He treated me like I imagined cishet people probably treated him, with a creepy curiosity, while gushing about this being his first-time conversation with a trans person. He made me wonder how this board had ensured the best interests of trans and nonbinary people when our existence seemed to be purely hypothetical for some of its members. *Were our values actually aligned?*

I'd ask this question again later when we began a key obligation of endorsing candidates for local offices. After assuming an abolitionist framework from my time with SNaPCo, the expectation to cosign sheriffs and district attorneys disturbed me. I didn't fully believe many of the candidates would indeed reduce harm, especially for Black and brown people. Nor did I think a group mostly composed of unlikely victims of the prison-industrial complex should decide on these office selections. In one endorsement cycle, an incumbent white cishet man connected to mainline law-enforcement organizations like the Fraternal Order of Police was positioned as a more favorable candidate over a Black cishet woman who seemed to have a deeper grasp of diversity as a member of several groups focused on communities on the margins. Luckily, I wasn't alone in my concerns, and we held a deeper conversation fueled by those who opposed. Still, I wondered if I could truly be an abolitionist if I embraced a role that required this level of compromise.

Despite my reservations, I continued to explore the possibilities of electoral organizing. I volunteered for the campaign of a friend, Park Cannon, in a Democratic run for the 58th District seat of the Georgia House of Representatives. She ultimately won and took the reins from Simone Bell, the first African American lesbian to serve in a U.S. state legislature. Bell had tapped Park for succession, ensuring that the seat stayed in the hands of someone with a queer political lens. Witnessing Park achieve this goal reassured me of the importance of Black LGBTQ+ voices in politics and encouraged me to dig my heels into working on behalf of our community.

Soon after, I interviewed for positions at a few national LGBTQ+ organizations—knowing little about the decades-long context of some groups sidelining the trans community. I expected these nonprofits to be hella white and politically less progressive than my peers in Black grassroots organizing. Still, I wondered if I could be a facilitator of transformation once I got through their doors. At the National Center for Transgender Equality, I was cordially greeted by the staff. Then, as if I was being cross-examined, a white senior staffer interrogated me about my work with SNaPCo.

"Do you really believe in abolition?" they said, with a tone akin to rolling their eyes.

"Well, I think we can't discount how mass incarceration disproportionately ravages communities of color," I said, searching the faces of my other potential colleagues' faces around the table.

"OK, but what do we do with people who do harmful things?" the person pressed.

"Well, I think we focus on alternatives to just locking people away," I responded, praying the line of questioning wouldn't continue.

I wanted to delve deeper into how the folks most at risk for losing their rights were Black and brown people, not their white ass, but I held it in, feeling my chances of getting the job slip away. Perhaps I would have been a solid candidate if I was more politically moderate and palatable. Being filtered out as too "radical" or too much of a liability felt discouraging, but I also worried about this organization's outsized power on Capitol Hill. *How could they be so out of touch with the most marginalized people in our community and claim they were fighting for civil rights for all of us?*

After a few failed interviews with organizations, Bellamy became a saving grace yet again. They urged me to apply for a communications role at Transgender Law Center (TLC) that would require moving to Oakland, California. The location wasn't a deterrent, but I'd never imagined living that far away from home and didn't know anyone who lived there. The tipping point for me was attending a fundraising party TLC hosted weeks later in Atlanta. After reconnecting with Nadine Figueroa, who had invited me to the INCITE! conference the previous year and learning more about the national organization's work centering on the South and communities of color, I was sold and nailed my interview. Even though I wouldn't be making that much more salary, the benefit of working on behalf of my community was worth it. Plus, I'd finally experience life elsewhere, and it seemed only natural to spread my wings beyond the contours of the South.

* * *

ON JUNE 12, 2016, a month before my move to Oakland, I awoke to social media ablaze with posts saying "#PrayforOrlando," "#WeAreOrlando," and variations of "Pulse nightclub." Scattered facts from the tragedy flooded my mind. One shooter. A three-hour standoff. Many victims were dead or injured. Most of them were Black or brown. I absorbed the video clips of police surrounding the site's perimeter and tributes featuring the faces of the victims. It felt close to home as so many of my formative experiences had happened in queer clubs, on liquor-lacquered floors, between the throbbing bass of dance mixes and power anthems. These were the first places I felt glimmers of beauty, desire, power, and value.

As I imagined the victims' final moments, I saw shards of memories. I wept for all the versions of me I'd found in similar spaces: the young queer boy standing against the wall, eager to be a proper adult; the drag queen under the watchful eye of the audience, shimmying away inhibitions; the curious gender-queerling remixing my expression; and the self-assured trans woman relishing her winding road to authenticity. These identities clung to me like glitter on paraded streets; any of them could have been in Pulse that night.

It was impossible not to think about the rich history of the LGBTQ+ movement and how bars and clubs had been some of the only spaces where queer and trans folks could be ourselves. I saw the gender-nonconforming performers of the Harlem Renaissance and the mélange of drag queens, trans folks, cis gay men, and lesbians of the Stonewall riots. I saw the glorious elders who did and didn't survive the early HIV/AIDS crisis. It seemed like communities nationwide felt that connection too. In Atlanta, a vigil emerged organically at an intersection with Piedmont Avenue, where a collection of gay establishments existed. I joined a diverse group of folks who came out to light candles, sing songs, and chant about togetherness.

Just a year before, many had been celebrating the Supreme Court's decision in *Obergefell v. Hodges*, which guaranteed marriage equality. Just like the morning of Pulse, I'd awakened to the news in a contrasting mood of accomplishment and hope. In fact, Momma had called to share her own encouragement and excitement. Yet here, after so much death, we had a stark reminder that so many other problems had been left on the back burner. The news reports and social media posts glossing over the queerphobia inherent in this attack, focusing on the shooter's Muslim background and alleged ties to Iraq and Syria, enraged me. While the geopolitical implication warranted attention, we needed to scrutinize how our society, rife with anti-LGBTQ+ sentiment and a lack of empathy, stokes violence. When I saw the victims' faces, I thought of all the other queer and trans folks slain that year. *Where was the collective reaction when scores of our people were murdered every day or died by suicide? What was our community going to do to prioritize our safety?* I was eager to explore these questions in a more national context and TLC felt like that chance.

Weeks later, I left the first community where I felt like I could be my entire self, in all of my Blackness, transness, and womanhood. Staying in Georgia much longer than I'd intended—totaling at a quarter century—stoked introspection and revelations. A part of me felt like I was abandoning all that I'd reclaimed. The Southern social justice fight felt noble, partly because there was less of a progressive cushion than in many other places. *Still, who would I be to pass up this opportunity for growth and developing a new perspective?* After all, it wasn't as if I was running away from all that had helped my budding commitment to social justice. In fact, I knew I'd carry it with me. This departure and the personal evolution it'd beget felt necessary.

PART III

Pruning

19

An Era of Reckoning

There was an undeniable ease to my start at Transgender Law Center (TLC) in July 2016. A staff retreat just before my official start date served as the first taste of this new workplace experience. It had all the hallmarks of a typical professional function: overflowing coffee cups, concise agendas, dry-erase boards, and corny icebreakers. But as I connected with my new coworkers, I sensed similar desires to improve conditions for the trans and gender-nonconforming community. We talked about what was at stake for our people—isolation, limited access to healthcare, education, and employment, state violence, and the threat of conservative politicians. And I was energized after learning about how our era would build upon the organization's history.

Founded in 2002 as a project of the San Francisco–based National Center for Lesbian Rights, TLC provided legal counsel for and prioritized public education to trans Californians and their allies. In a *National Jurist* article announcing the initiative's opening, writer Christine Willard favorably described its emergence in "arguably the nation's most transgender friendly community," while citing a 70 percent unemployment rate among trans folk.[1] A few years later, TLC supplanted its state-based profile with a national scope through its impact litigation efforts. I noticed that this often meant representing white trans people in crisis despite ample evidence that Black and brown trans folks are most at risk of being devoured by the various systems around us.

But I, and several other younger colleagues of color, seemed to be entering TLC at a unique time. An Asian American executive director had recently taken the helm, playing a major role in shifting the composition of the organization from being predominantly employed and led by white and cisgender people. At that first retreat, I encountered a brilliantly diverse configuration spanning various ethnic, racial, and gender identities, abilities, and citizenship statuses. What struck me the most was that there were more Black employees than ever in the organization's history. Beyond Bellamy and me, there was Teju, a Nigerian trans brotha, and a gender-nonconforming lesbian director named Pilar. Both seemed like older siblings who had long stormed through nonprofits and had a wealth of knowledge to shower on the rest of us.

TLC's evolution aligned with the long social justice arc I'd associated with the San Francisco Bay Area. Since my teenage years, I imagined the location as the pinnacle of LGBTQ+ acceptance. Harvey Milk's audacity, bravery, and the fact that we shared a birthday astonished me. After a few unsuccessful runs for the SF Board of Supervisors, he was elected to the 5th District seat in 1977. With that win, he became one of the first openly LGBTQ+ folks elected to political office in the United States and the first in California. That an openly gay person could run for office and win, especially in the decade just after the Stonewall riots, felt transformative. Unfortunately, the hope I gleaned from Milk's story was reduced upon learning the grisly details of his assassination less than a year into his tenure. Incensed by a political divide that led to his resignation and then a protest to return to his post, one of Milk's conservative colleagues, Dan White, murdered Milk and

San Francisco mayor George Moscone. This tale was devastating, yet SF was still reputed to be a place where queer and trans people, fleeing less welcoming areas, could be their true selves.

Later in college, I learned that our community's resistance had existed even before Milk's political era. In the sixties, Vanguard, an organization led predominantly by young white cis gay folks, picketed establishments that stoked the community's brutalization by local police. This group's efforts laid fertile ground for the 1966 Compton's Cafeteria riot in the Tenderloin district. In the documentary *Screaming Queens: The Riot at Compton's Cafeteria*, scholar Susan Stryker threads the contextual needle for the riot's spark by interviewing Aleshia Brevard, Tamara Ching, Felicia Flames Elizondo, and Amanda St. Jaymes. These trans women reveal the era's complexities and how the uprising broke out after a crowd of patrons at Gene Compton's Cafeteria, a restaurant, fought back against the attempted arrest of a trans woman. Despite continued discrimination, this event would embolden the local LGBTQ+ community to live more openly than ever before. I marveled at these elders' gumption to demand respect for their humanity.

While I knew SF to be a haven for the LGBTQ+ community, Oakland's distinction as the birthplace of the Black Panther Party (BPP) was undeniable. But I had very little understanding of the delineation between the Civil Rights Era's respectability and the militancy of the Black Power movement (BPM) growing up. In scattered mentions from media and Black elders, much of the latter's lore was reduced to the "Black is beautiful" refrain that inspired African Americans to appreciate more melanated skin and coiled hair textures. There was both inspiration in the BPP history and caution in how Black self-assurance made activists into targets. The numerous midcentury assassinations, from Malcolm X to Martin Luther King Jr. to Fred Hampton, served as examples that you could be, or in fact would be, eliminated regardless of how righteous you were in your cause. As I grew older, I associated Black militancy most closely with a cisheterosexist, patriarchal concept of nation-building, in which cis straight men were regarded as natural-born leaders, cis straight women as submissive child bearers, and LGBTQ+ folks as insignificant, if not a threat to the institution of the Black family. Fortunately, I dug deeper into the history of the broader BPM and learned about formidable women like Assata Shakur and Angela Davis. They became cultural heroes after surviving encounters with the U.S. carceral system and reclaiming their humanity and narratives. Meanwhile, Elaine Brown, Kathleen Cleaver, and Ericka Huggins uniquely sliced through the sexist mores of the BPP, leaving their marks and achieving varying degrees of prominence. And, for his part, BPP founder Huey P. Newton seemed to publicly champion a more progressive politics.

In Brown's memoir, *A Taste of Power: A Black Woman's Story*, she explains that there was some truth to some of my initial considerations of the BPM's patriarchal overtones. Brown describes the context she encountered upon being appointed to lead the BPP when Newton fled to Cuba to avoid prosecution for criminal charges. She says she resisted an "undefined" Black Power principle of Black women's deference to Black men's leadership lest they be accused of "eroding Black manhood" and hindering racial progress.

> *I would claim my womanhood and my place. If that gave rise to my being labeled a "man-hating lesbian, feminist bitch," I would be the most radical of them. I made it clear that no more discussion would be had regarding my personnel decisions. The women I had positioned would be accepted for what they were: the most capable. I would be very hard on those who questioned me on the basis of my genitalia.*

Brown gives nuanced credit to Newton for the grand act of elevating her leadership, which seemed in line with his publicly progressive views on movement solidarity. In "A Letter from Huey to Revolutionary Brothers and Sisters About the Women's and Gay Liberation Movements," published in *The Black Panther* newspaper in 1970, Newton wrote, "Whatever your personal opinion and your insecurities about homosexuality and the various liberation movements among homosexuals and women (and I speak of the homosexuals and women as oppressed groups) we should try to unite with them in a revolutionary fashion." Activist Sylvia Rivera would verify that solidarity in a *Workers World* interview with author Leslie Feinberg, in which she detailed a favorable meeting with Newton at the Revolutionary People's Convention in Philadelphia in 1970. Despite Newton's urging to the contrary, there never seemed to be a considerable LGBTQ+ presence within the BPP or the BPM. Even further, his overt displays of empathy didn't seem to always align within his interpersonal relationships. In *An Oral History with Ericka Huggins*, Huggins revealed that Newton violently raped her, adding a necessary dimension to his progressive public stances on the patriarchy and the harm he committed privately.[2]

Nevertheless, with this complex history in tow, I envisioned Oakland as similar to what I encountered in Atlanta, which commanded an exuberance about its place within Black history and an even more formidable social justice scene. While some of those aspects were certainly there, I mostly felt a sense of cultural mourning, of what could've been if formations like the BPP had been able to evolve and thrive. By the time I'd made it to the "town," the Black population had decreased by nearly 70 percent while the total population had increased. The larger conditions that the BPP had fought against generations before had proliferated and continued to plague those still there and beyond. It wasn't uncommon to hear Black folks of varying backgrounds describe how things "used to be" locally and lament the impact of continued state violence, gentrification, and increased cost of living.

That first week of July 2016 was particularly rough, so perhaps that also colored my experience in the Bay. In the sociopolitical background of the TLC retreat, we were struck by the back-to-back police killings of Alton Sterling in Baton Rouge, Louisiana, and Philando Castile in Falcon Heights, Minnesota, followed by Micah Xavier Johnson's killing of police officers and citizens in Dallas, Texas. While Sterling's death shook me, watching the live-streamed video of Castile being shot at close range in front of his partner Diamond Reynolds and their four-year-old daughter was even more unimaginable. Right there, in real time, was the evidence of how police dismantled Black families. I felt for Castile's daughter, wondering how anyone could hold on to their childhood innocence after witnessing such a heinous act. And while protests broke out in Black communities across the country, Johnson's spree gave ammunition to anti-Black Lives Matter sentiments.

Undeterred, Bellamy, an Atlanta friend Mel, and I joined two thousand protestors on a march through Oakland on the night of the Dallas tragedy. There was constant fatigue in the air, as many of us had been participating in direct action for years without reprieve. But there was a feeling, a spiritual animus to keep disrupting the status quo. At one point, we stopped to chant outside the Oakland Police Department (OPD), almost as if putting a curse on them. A few men struck the OPD headquarters door with limbs and other items. Their outrage made sense. It wasn't just about the most recent deaths in other cities; it was also about the corruption and violence at the hands of local law enforcement. A month before, OPD had cycled through three police chief resignations in eight days after allegations surfaced involving police officers having sex with an underage sex worker and texting racist hate speech. And it was only seven years earlier when another local law enforcement agency, the Bay Area Rapid Transit Police Department, drew national attention when their officer Johannes Mehserle killed Oscar Grant III on the platform at Fruitvale Station.

Soon, OPD officers silently lined the building, trying to intimidate us with their military-grade armor and weaponry. But the men who had taken their anger out on the headquarters doors began yelling at the officers just a few feet from their faces. My crew kept our distance. We knew that being Black and queer and trans meant we'd face even worse horrors than our cishet male counterparts if we were arrested. Still, I felt for them and understood their righteous rage. My memory bank was like theirs, full of countless deaths.

Our group later journeyed onto Interstate 880, blocking traffic in solidarity with organizers in other cities, namely Atlanta. Camplike circles formed in the crowd across the highway as some people played music, others chanted, even as more tried to process our moment. The ongoing police brutality was top of mind, but so was the insistence, mostly by right-wing media, that Johnson's killings be pinned on M4BL and all those organizing against anti-Blackness. The latter assertion was particularly enraging because he had been more connected with unaffiliated Black nationalist groups for years. Further, it felt like a contradiction for his radicalization to be blamed on Black movements when he had been trained by the U.S. military. If he were to be our poster boy, then he had to equally be considered Uncle Sam's. I couldn't shake how the loss of police officers was seen as more of a tragedy for some Americans, mainly moderates and conservatives, than the loss of Castile, Sterling, and numerous other Black people killed that year. The former was an atypical incident akin to a water droplet, while the latter was a gushing stream, the result of hundreds of years of systemic oppression.

The bombast of that first rally dissipated into a tepid atmosphere. I was struck by how mellow Oakland felt during those first few months. It was like I was floating in some worn yellow-orange-tinted photograph as autumn approached. My work, leading TLC's digital presence and handling other lower-level communications duties like drafting press releases and basic external communication requests, kept me steadily preoccupied. It was more fulfilling than my past jobs, mainly because I was learning so much through the new relationships I was building. I grew close to Marissa, who started along with me. In between our constant giggles and girl talk, she revealed how her undocumented status impacted her youth and career trajectory. Finn, a longtime community organizer and educator, expanded my understanding of ableism, particularly regarding mental health. From him, I became less dismissive about self-care days, mental health, and wellness.

This heightened consciousness raising coincided with the upcoming presidential election. I was convinced that there was no way in hell that Donald Trump could win over Hillary Clinton. I can't lie; I was excited about the promised cultural transformation that having a woman as president might inspire. There were lofty expectations for Clinton to carry the baton of equality (especially among white cis women and white LGBTQ+ folks), and I bought into that. I didn't see her as some incorrigible feminist savior, but I knew we'd be in a better place with her at the helm than Trump. White supremacy, misogyny, and xenophobia were unfortunate pillars of U.S. society, but I'd always believed that the masses shared a general level of common sense, one that would ward them off from voting for Trump. Everyone may not have all the theories to dissect systems of oppression, but that didn't mean they didn't see them, especially after the last eight years of white conservatives complaining about our country's first Black president.

When Obama won the presidency in 2008, I was several months shy of my eighteenth birthday. I lamented not being able to vote for him, but I did during his reelection. Like many others, I accepted and often applauded the centrist crumbs doled out by his administration. For instance, I'd followed his lethargic public transformation on marriage equality and embraced his executive orders to protect transgender youth in schools. Though, admittedly, a Black family's presence in the White House was a satisfying enough example to me that progress was inevitable. But I had also been ignorant and privileged in my assessment of Obama's impact, paying little attention to how he wielded state power to bolster drone strikes and immigrant deportations.[3]

Then, I witnessed a sinister backlash upon graduating, while working for the *Monroe Chronicle* and reporting on rural Georgia. A fleet of ignorant conservative Americans, primarily white, demanded a return to form, steadfastly showing up to the polls during nonpresidential elections. They grew less interested in cordiality and decorum and focused on diminishing the self-determination of people of color, LGBTQ+ folks, immigrants, and, of course, women. Some of that sentiment came through in my receiving hate mail seemingly more frequently than others because of the progressive opinions I shared in our newspaper. In time, I noticed those sentiments grow online. I was one of many Black feminists with a growing social media platform, who were being inundated by right-wingers and bots saying disgusting things to us whenever we critiqued Trump's presidential campaign. Even though recent history had taught us just how low conservatives could go, I still believed that their hate would never return to center stage in American politics.

* * *

THE NIGHT OF the election, I joined a distressed group of colleagues in a conference room to watch the returns on CNN. We knew our communities would be in dire trouble if Trump was elected. Conservative politicians were already increasing their efforts to legislate away our right to use public accommodations via "bathroom bills." Many trans students were already unprotected in their schools as bigoted teachers, staff, and administrators refused to respect their identities by insisting on not using the name and pronouns provided or blocking access to restrooms and locker rooms corresponding with their gender.[4] And there was still no widespread discussion or action on the issues closest to many of our hearts: addressing the murders of trans women of color, decriminalizing sex work, immigration reform, and prison abolition.

As I took in the words of confused commentators trying to forecast the election's outcome, I developed a migraine. So, with a foggy mind, I bid my colleagues adieu and rushed out of our workplace, retreating to my bed. My solution to almost anything was to take a nap. If I am in a bad mood, I take a nap. If my anxiety is getting the best of me, I take a nap. Maybe America needed a nap? Besides, I had to catch an early flight to a conference called "Facing Race." *How apropos.* At home, I popped some pain relievers, undressed, and sprawled across my bed. Hours later, I scooped up my phone and looked at Twitter. It was official: Trump was our next president, issuing a referendum on progress. My mind raced to solutions—maybe the Electoral College would present a stopgap on his ascension or some news would come out about how former FBI director James Comey's discussion of Clinton's handling of classified information had tipped the scales in Trump's favor.

I racked my brain as I hopped up and scrambled to pack a shabby brown London Fog suitcase that Grandma Inez had purchased for me in high school. It emitted a masculine air I had long stopped pretending to adhere to, but I rarely traveled, so I'd never sought a replacement. It'd survived all my college years, a cross-country move from Atlanta to Oakland, and even outlived the person who'd bought it for me. I remembered Grandma's kindness when she bought it, saying, "You gettin' older, boy. You need to have a nice set of luggage." That Southern Black practicality permeated every lesson she imparted. *What would she have said now about Donald Trump?* I imagined her saying, "Aww hell, you shoulda known those white folks would go crazy about the first Black president!" After all, she was in joyful disbelief when Obama started leading in the 2008 Democratic primaries. Her refrain until the last debate was, "They'll never let that Black man have it . . ." She wasn't a pessimist; she was a realist. She knew what white people were capable of. Maybe the fact that I didn't was the problem?

My eyes were heavy as I darted through San Francisco International Airport the next morning. I felt like I could burst into a heated fit at any moment. I leered back at white folks' perplexed looks as I walked to my gate. They often gave that look as if I was a creature that wasn't supposed to be in the same vicinity as them. Once I was on the plane, it was as if the worst thing I could do was sit by them and interrupt their peace. *But who was different now? Me or them?* I wondered which of them had voted a monster into the Oval Office.

As I got to my seat, squashed between a white man and a white woman, I hoped I'd make it through the flight without crying. I felt alone, worried about the future, and also foolish for being so damn emotional. Soon, though, the woman struck up a conversation. I gingerly mentioned the heaviness of the day, and she concurred with a similar sense of disappointment. The man, at one point, crossed his left leg over the other and made a forceful turn away from us toward the aisle, as if the conversation disturbed him. She asked me where I was headed, and I told her I was flying to attend a racial justice conference in Atlanta, which felt almost like a cosmic joke.

"What do you do?" she asked.

"Well . . ." I hesitated, feeling cautious of who might eavesdrop now that we were in Trump's America. "I'm a writer and activist. But I work as a communications associate at Transgender Law Center, so you know, working to make the world easier to navigate for trans and gender-nonconforming people."

"Oh, you all do such great work. We donate all the time," she said, stifling her excitement and gratitude—now also afraid of what others in the vicinity might hear.

Over the next few hours, I bonded with this woman over her partner's budding gender transition. She shared how she still loved them and that they were figuring out how to make their relationship work. I divulged my adjustment to living in California. With this brief, distracting camaraderie, I felt a glimmer of hope. Maybe I would survive this season of the Great American saga after all.

Two weeks later, I was reminded, yet again, of the enduring progressive spirit when Bellamy and I attended a Trans Awareness Week reception at the White House. It was weird to be invited into that space at the tail end of Obama's presidency. *How could we celebrate when we didn't know what lay at the end of this Democratic rule?* I prematurely mourned the progress we could have made if we'd gotten four or eight more liberal years. Under

Clinton, we might have seen more leaders on the margins elevated, civil protections for various communities regarding violence, the Equality Act passed, fewer attacks on the state level, and less state violence. Perhaps activist groups would have been more capable of applying pressure and demanding systemic change. Maybe Clinton would have had something to prove by lessening military strikes and deportations. Or maybe it was just the last whisper of a belief in toothless liberalism. We'd never know the alternative outcome. Now, we had to stop our community's hemorrhaging. We knew people on the margins would die, and the hate against us would continue to be stoked. I feared doxing on social media and an increase in suicide rates. But, even with my anxieties, I knew our community would forge a way forward, as we had done for generations. Just moments before we departed the White House, a glorious gaggle of Black trans women vogued across the floor as a house beat swept them up. It was a sight I never expected to see in a federal building. It was a reminder that even when our community is served crumbs, we figure out how to feed ourselves.

20

Testing My Faith

Every square inch of the nation's capital was covered in the white political spectrum on the morning of the National Women's March in Washington, D.C. Conservative folks were kowtowing to the seemingly apolitical stray animal the Republican Party had taken in, resembling ecstatic tailgaters at a college football game. The siren-red "Make America Great Again" caps contrasted with the woolen pink "pussy" hats worn mostly by white liberal women. That adornment would draw ire for its essentialist signaling that all women had the same biological configuration. But at the time, I hadn't draped an analysis of transmisogyny onto this supposed uniform of resistance; it simply seemed they were capitalizing on Trump's misogyny in the most reductive way possible.

Momma had been beaming all morning. I hadn't given it a second thought to ask her to join me on perhaps the most significant stage I would ever encounter. And she hadn't missed a beat in expressing support after I told her that I would be speaking at the march. It was so rare that trans people who weren't celebrities were welcomed on massive stages like that, plus I wanted our relationship to serve as a lesson. The world needed to see that I had the love of this brilliant, bold Black woman in my arsenal.

"My baby's going to be speaking at the march today," she said, with big ol' bright eyes to a woman sitting near us at brunch. "This is just such an important day. It'll be in the history books."

As they discussed their disbelief at Trump being elected, I soaked up the moment. It felt gratifying to witness Momma's pride. We'd come a long way since I started my gender transition, and she understood who I was on a deeper level, including my passion for social justice. Her high spirits made up for how drab our nation's capital looked through the large windows behind her. There, gaggles of mostly white women and girls walked by with protest signs. I wondered what this experience was like for them. *Was it easier for them to feel empowered because almost everyone looked like them?* I already felt like a token, as most organizers I knew, particularly the Black, queer, and trans ones, had preemptively disengaged from the day's events. The march just didn't seem like it was for them, and if I hadn't been asked to attend, I would have still felt the same.

* * *

I FIRST HEARD about the march about a month after the election, when the flame of collective fury seemed its highest. After scanning articles and social media groups about the event, I immediately clocked the lack of diversity among the organizers and attendees. It was primarily white cishet women expressing interest in it. While I understood that most of them were galvanized by Donald Trump's "grab 'em by the pussy" mentality, I couldn't help but be disturbed by how muted discussions of his ableism, queerphobia, xenophobia, and, most importantly, his white supremacy were in the discourse. *Did they care when he demonized Mexican immigrants as rapists and criminals in his campaign announcement speech, tokenized and incited brutality*

toward Black people at his rallies, or when he mocked disabled
New York Times *reporter Serge F. Kovaleski? As much as I under-*
stood that we needed to build coalitions and shore up solidarity,
how could I trust white women when they had overwhelmingly
supported this demagogue as a voting bloc? Sure, the women
drawn to this action weren't a monolith, but they were drawing
on a long feminist inclination of leaning into their privileges at
the expense of others on the margins.

* * *

IN ADDITION TO the finer points of my queerness and transness, my feminism was forged in college. In fact, prior to then,
I'd mostly heard the concept mentioned in punchlines about
women, usually white, who were considered too opinionated
or outspoken. The idea that those qualities were negative never
made sense to me, considering Momma was a lauded community
figure and career professional, my sister was one of my greatest
role models for life beyond our childhood home, and Grandma
Inez was self-sufficient and never clipped any of her words no
matter who was around. I only knew women who knew their
power, though they would have never described themselves as
feminists.

In my earliest women's studies courses, I dove beyond the
truncated grade-school curriculum that claimed women gained
the right to vote in 1920, learning about the first feminist wave
in the nineteenth century and how the fight for women's suffrage
heightened on the heels of U.S. abolitionism. Revered white
women like Susan B. Anthony and Elizabeth Cady Stanton in-
termittently worked with Black leaders like Frederick Douglass
and Ida B. Wells. But in time, they pivoted from deep solidarity work once momentum toward Black Americans' emancipa-
tion shifted toward solely prioritizing suffrage for men of color

and uneducated and economically marginalized men. In "White Suffragist Dis/Entitlement: The Revolution and the Rhetoric of Racism," scholar Jen McDaneld excavates the Stanton-edited National Woman Suffrage Association's journal, *Revolution*, for the rhetorical arguments she made from 1868 to 1870. McDaneld complicates how we've come to understand Stanton's racism and how she used the plight and victimization of Black women to demand universal suffrage while also demonizing Black men whenever politically expedient to position white women as a more deserving and palatable voting bloc.[1]

In *Women, Race & Class*, activist-scholar Angela Y. Davis describes "Anthony's self-avowed capitulation to racism on the ground of expediency" for women's suffrage as her dominant public stance at least until 1900.[2] While it is tempting to explain away the actions of these white feminist "heroes" as products of their times, it's clear that they made conscious and strategic decisions to render racial, ethnic, and class minorities disposable. From the rifts between the second wave's straight women and lesbian women, as well as cis radical feminists and trans people, and the third wave's articulation of feminisms that center women of color and focus on other international contingents, the approach of conditional liberation, exploitation of marginalized narratives, and scarcity persist today.

* * *

DESPITE THE HISTORIC exclusion of more marginalized groups of women from feminist formations, I was more hopeful when the Women's March leadership shifted to organizers of color: executive director of The Gathering for Justice Carmen Perez; Tamika D. Mallory, known for being the youngest-ever executive director of the National Action Network; and Linda Sarsour, former executive director of the Arab American Association of New York. I was heartened by these changes, though I had lingering critiques about the leadership, including their lack of diversity: those from the South and Midwest, those who were LGBTQ+, and even those who were key in the Movement for Black Lives were not represented.

On Twitter, I shared that my main reservation was the lack of clarity around trans and nonbinary inclusion. Shortly after, Linda invited me to speak, to my shock. Though we had met at a joint speaking engagement at UGA the year before, I never would've thought she'd remember me. At the time, the conversation felt premature, as she had long been doing radical work, and my career was just burgeoning. But I appreciated how she so graciously shared the stage without diminishing my spirit.

"Hey, sis! How are you doing? We would love to add you to our lineup! Are you available?" her message read. "We also have Janet Mock!" she added, like icing on top of the request.

As I considered my response, nerves set in. I wondered if there was potential in the opportunity, if it could be a site for calling in and reclamation of women on the margins. *Plus, would I be able to channel all of my conflicting emotions into a rallying cry?* I figured I'd try. After checking in with friends and family, I ran the request by my boss at TLC and our executive director, and they gave me the green light. There was only about a week for me to figure out how I'd get there, what I'd wear, and, more importantly, what I'd say.

* * *

As MOMMA AND I made our way to the speakers' area, a journalist stopped us for a photo of my ensemble: an ombréd violet and fuchsia dress with a rectilinear bodice and a long-sleeved black crop top jacket. "You know you have to make a statement,"

Momma said days before. Jessica had agreed, offering undying big-sister support. They scrambled to order something for me, as only Southern Black women could. Despite not embracing the feminist label, my mom and sister—my lifelong collaborators—showered me in love and support, tapping into the roaring femininity that connected us. I thought I looked quite lovely, going for a warrior-woman aesthetic adorned with big, curly, brown-blond hair and a golden goddess choker clasped around my neck. The knee-high black boots signaled a militant effect and comfort, too. While I had wanted to look stylish and feel confident, I hadn't anticipated being stopped for my fashion. This glimmer of celebrity treatment felt discomfiting and exhilarating.

At the speakers' tent, Momma and I encountered a notable figure with each step. We saw Congresswoman Maxine Waters and actress Ashley Judd sitting in their respective corners. Momma immediately pulled away when the chance to meet civil rights icon Jesse Jackson arose. I wondered what it meant to meet him, knowing she had witnessed him graze the Democratic party nomination in the eighties, a generation before Barack Obama was elected. I felt honored to shake his hand and witness his solidarity. Not long after, I ran into queer entertainers Hari Nef and Troye Sivan, then grabbed a selfie with Zendaya. Janelle Monáe's presence floored me, as she had been a staple on my college years' soundtrack. Then, Jidenna opened his arms wide, saying, "What an honor." I wondered who he thought I was and if he actually knew me. Nevertheless, I was convinced that the combination of his smile and cologne could cure any ailment.

We eventually encountered Janet Mock in conversation with two other women. I darted in her direction, finding refuge in someone I knew. I'd first met her at Agnes Scott College in Decatur, Georgia, while she signed copies of her first memoir,

Redefining Realness. She recognized me from a Tumblr post with a selfie proudly holding the book like a newborn. Reading the volume while I was still stealth in Monroe had made me believe that no career was worth hiding my most authentic self. Here, after she asked how I was, I unloaded my anxieties about speaking. But Janet assured me of the necessity of my voice, seeming so calm and unafraid. Then, she introduced me to Melissa Harris-Perry, another journalist I had admired for years.

As a revolving door of notables swirled in the tent, Momma and I waited for my call time. Then, an unforgettable flurry of flashing cameras, microphones, and news crews surrounded Gloria Steinem, possibly the most famous feminist ever. I took my chance and excitedly waited in a line that had formed to speak with her. One by one, women of all ages paid their respects and grabbed an image. When I made it over to her, I mentioned the weight of having to represent so many communities and worrying about not showing up as fully as possible. She quickly attempted to squelch my concerns, confirming that I was there for a reason.

"I'm also worried on a deeper level because I know so many people who initially felt like they weren't included in this mobilization because of the initial planning," I said.

"Well, no one should feel excluded. They need to just show up and not expect a special invite," Steinem responded.

I felt the intention, but I wanted to press further. Beyond celebrities, nearly every woman of color and LGBTQ+ person I knew had not felt that the Women's March was for them. Then, of course, as a Black trans woman I wondered how the attendees would respond to my presence once I made it up on that stage. I was quite sure what kind of support I expected from her or how I wanted or needed to be seen in that moment. But our exchange made me wonder how top of mind were the divisions between various groups of women for our leaders.

* * *

As THE WAITING time dragged on, I noticed the tent gradually clear out, with many speakers leaving or joining the crowd. The production assistants scuttled around, reassuring us despite having flown past our scheduled speaking times. Soon, it seemed that lineup decisions were being made on the spot. The PAs told me they needed to cut folks' time, and I reminded them that they had only a few openly trans folks speaking today and that I already had only three minutes. Plus, I had been alerted the day before that I would have to introduce myself, slicing even more of that time. I was assured that they agreed with what I was saying and that I didn't have anything to worry about. Among some remaining speakers, there was a theory that celebrities were being prioritized over activists and advocates, who seemed to be pushed farther down the speaker's list. This irked me. Celebrities can choose any given day to speak up and out on an issue, leveraging their platforms to reach the masses. *What did it say about our supposed efforts of resistance that we championed celebrity over everything else? Wasn't that a large part of why Trump had been elected in the first place?*

When I finally made it next to the stage, I was heated, the chaos was palpable, and the crowd seemed on edge. Everyone was ready to march rather than listen to more speakers, and I felt similarly. I just wanted to share my message and get on with the rest of the event. Soon, I was positioned behind the legendary Angela Davis, feeling too frustrated to even take in the glory of the moment.

"OK, Raquel's been waiting a while. She's next," a PA said to the organizers. Linda nodded with affirmation, quickly expressing gratitude for my presence. As I approached the podium, with Momma in tow, I felt my chest grow stronger and fill with pride.

Still, I flirted with the idea of abandoning this mission. *I could just turn around if my nerves got the best of me. I didn't have to do this if I didn't want to.* But I knew that even if my inner voice betrayed me, my body wouldn't retreat on its orders. "Give it up for Raquel Willis," Linda exclaimed in a thick New York accent.

> *Before I start, I want us to take a second and look around. Look at all of these people who are gathered here to take a stand. These are your partners in resistance and liberation, and today, y'all are making a commitment to each other and to a new vision of liberation.*
>
> *Now, when I was younger, my father always used to always tell me, "Walk like you know where you're going." I thought he was just trying to be deep; I didn't know what he was talking about. But when I was nineteen, he died, and I quickly learned what he meant. He was no longer my guidance and my safety net, and that loss pushed me to figure out exactly who I am and the life I wanted to live. I found my voice.*
>
> *And today I stand here with my mom as a proud, unapologetic queer Black transgender woman from Augusta, Georgia. I'm more than those labels. I'm also a daughter, I'm a sister, an auntie, a friend, a lover, a human, and a feminist . . . And so I want to stress the importance of us being intentional about inclusion. I think about, historically, trans women of color like Sylvia Rivera and Marsha P. Johnson, who lit the fire on the LGBTQIA rights movement, and they were quickly kicked out and erased. They share a common thread with Sojourner Truth, another revolutionary woman, and just like her, Black women, women of color, queer women, trans women, disabled women, Muslim women, and so many others are still asking many of y'all, "'Ain't I a woman?'"*
>
> *So as we commit to build this movement of resistance and*

liberation, no one can be an afterthought anymore. We must
hold each other in love and accountability . . .

Then, just before I hit the core of my speech, my voice stopped
reverberating. Half of the audience's attention was diverted elsewhere. *What's going on?* I sensed some commotion to my right,
where an organizer stood. I caught the tail end of her flashing
"go ahead" gestures to another staffer and I quickly realized that
my microphone had been cut! *Why?* My panic-tinged adrena-
line boiled into rage. I glanced at my mom to search her face for
a take, but she hadn't noticed what had happened yet. Then, all
became clear when the Indigo Girls' guitar riffs broke through
the awkwardness. This moment I'd built myself up for had been
shattered. Stupefied, I made an embarrassed, heavy-footed exit
from the stage.

My mother attempted to assuage my disappointment as I
gathered my thoughts, but I sensed her anger too. Several people
in the vicinity came over, offering consolation. Actress America
Ferrera expressed appreciation for the part of my story I was able
to share. Immediately after the Indigo Girls finished, band member Amy Ray came to acknowledge what had happened and her
reluctance to play at that moment. And queer musician B. Steady
approached and chatted with Momma and me as well. Eventually, two PAs came over and apologized. I told them that very
little could be done now, and that I was still considering what
accountability would look like. At the very least, I expected some
communication from the organizers.

At Momma's behest, I reached out to Janet. "She might have
thoughts on the matter," Momma said. And she did. In sage
big-sister fashion, she advised me to consider the impact of a
hasty reaction to my work. "These things have a way of sticking
to us and we become known more for the moment of tension

than anything else." I felt that. I didn't want to be defined by or reduced to this humiliation.

I left the march feeling angry, exhausted, and, most of all, naïve. *Had my participation been taken for granted so that the march could claim intersectional brownie points? Should I have trusted my initial skepticism?* I'd spent days smoothing over every syllable and sliver of nuance only to have my voice ripped away. And it wasn't some white male conservative villain who had silenced me, it was supposedly some of the most progressive women imaginable. So often in movements, we're consumed with holding external forces accountable, forgetting that we also have the capacity to harm. Truthfully? Women harm other women every day. Black folks harm other Black folks every day. LGBTQ+ folks harm other LGBTQ+ folks every day. It's a disservice when we consider ourselves immune to the allure of systems of oppression. I envied the other speakers, and the scores of folks—mainly the cis white bourgeois women—who came away from that day feeling empowered rather than disposable.

Though I left the event dispirited, I hadn't completely given up on the idea of solidarity. None of us really knew how we'd fare under the thumb of this new presidential administration, but we were getting clues. Just after Trump and his vice president, Mike Pence, were sworn into office, the White House website scrubbed all mentions of LGBTQ+ issues. Weeks later, Trump signed executive orders targeting immigrants at the Mexico–U.S. border, his Departments of Education and Justice abandoned protections for trans students, and his Department of Housing and Urban Development deprioritized access and safety guidelines around gender identity. As the attacks rolled in, I grappled with how the Women's March appearance elevated my stature as a thought leader in social justice. More importantly, I asked myself critical questions about my work: *Am I using my energy well? Is the femi-*

nist movement and its ideology redeemable? Are women who are more privileged than me, with more power than me, redeemable? Would change come from working solely with other trans women of color? What would a truly inclusive feminist movement act, feel, and look like? I imagined a feminism in which imperfect politics were expected but not excused.

21

Letter to Chyna Gibson

It was the fault of the earth, the land, of our town. I even think now that the land of the entire country was hostile to the marigolds that year. This soil is bad for certain kinds of flowers. Certain seeds it will not nurture, certain fruit it will not bear, and when the land kills of its own volition, we acquiesce and say the victim had no right to live.

—*The Bluest Eye*, Toni Morrison

Dear Chyna,

A premature death never felt more inevitable than when I read your story. It was after-hours at the Transgender Law Center's headquarters and I couldn't tell how dark it was outside because our offices were on the building's basement floor. The pitiful echeveria on my desk was the starkest reminder of the absence of sunlight. But now, that concern felt frivolous as I fixated on an article that took an uncharacteristically humane approach to your story.[1] Usually, cis journalists would feature a singular quote from a loved one or a community member, but rarely anything of note beyond a trans victim's grim demise. I'd expect a birth name, incorrect gender, or a disparaging mention of a criminal record. But no, this piece was distinctive.

I learned that there had been five Black trans and gender-nonconforming folks reported murdered in the nation that month. Louisiana, the site of your death, had become ground zero, and you were one of the state's three victims. You were a Southern girl, too, having grown up in New Orleans before being displaced by Hurricane Katrina. To survive one of the worst natural disasters in world history only for a mortal to strike you down was incomprehensible.

As a bounce music–loving teenager in Atlanta, you assumed the mantle of performer. I was never a "Dancing Doll" like you, but reading that fact transported me back to when I found drag. It gave me purpose and release. Later, I watched one of your numbers online. You were at The Jungle, once a staple gay club in the ATL scene, and you embodied defiance and grace. With every lilt of your arms and shift of pelvis, I saw myself and our trancestors. That performance was recorded just a year before my first visit to the venue and any gay club whatsoever. We'd just missed each other's presence, and I wondered who I'd be if I had seen my sista living her truth then.

In time, you made a name for yourself across the United States. This fact made me consider the limitations of visibility, and how it didn't necessarily translate into safety for you. I wondered what it meant for us Black trans women to be valued only as spectacles when we're mesmerizing folks on a stage. *Where was the care and consideration when the spotlights were dimmed and the curtains were drawn? And who would take care of the community you left behind?* The sisters, siblings, and brothers who felt differently about their fates in your absence, who felt mortality hurling toward them. *And what about your family in California, particularly your mother, who expected your trip back to your home state to be brief?*

I thought of your future—all the places you had yet to perform and our similar timeline for gender-affirmation surgery. You were just a few weeks off from reaching this milestone, and it made my stomach turn. It made me vengeful. Your murderers were still out there and the chances of them ever being held accountable felt slim. They'd return to communities with widespread support, probably even more transmisogynistic and protected than before. So many people they knew would probably justify your death and blame you, asking what spell you put on them to cause their violence. They'd encourage other fragile, insecure people to uphold these disgusting beliefs and take more of our lives.

I can only imagine the fear you always carried with you. *Did you mourn yourself before the attack like I am now?* Sometimes I feel the premature grief of our sisters immediately, and it consumes my energy. Other times, I power through, refusing to let the emotions take hold. I'm constantly mourning people I don't know and people who probably would have justified my death. We live acutely aware that danger doesn't come just from the State; it comes from our communities, families, and lovers. Black trans women carry the deaths of Black cis boys and men, Black cis girls and women, and we carry those of our own trans and nonbinary community. We see our humanity as inextricably tied to theirs, while we're treated as otherworldly by comparison. I often fear that I'll be next, and the world will make a mess of my story if I'm murdered.

I feel lucky and guilty to be alive. It's insulting when people insist that this "trend" of violence is new. It's not new just because more people than ever are paying more attention. Our elders faced similar threats and had their concerns brushed farther under the rug than ours. Now, so many Black trans leaders are just trying to survive. And those who push to find solutions often lack the respect and resources to make it happen. We toil with all of our brilliance at the whim of non-Black and cis people who can't comprehend what's at stake; and if they do, the willingness to put in that action isn't there.

We constantly fall through the cracks of social justice movements. Here I am at my nonprofit job. This is supposed to be a heralded position for a so-called social justice warrior. But I'm wondering why our organization, our movement, is doing nothing to keep our Black family alive. Advocacy. Capacity building. Impact litigation. So much jargon is thrown around as if it means anything to those of us being shot, shanked, and murdered. *What good is an organizational strategy if none of the people you aid are Black and trans?* Press releases and social media updates don't do enough to transform the culture and make society safer now. I keep thinking if I just pay my dues and do what I'm told then eventually I'll be able to champion Black trans lives in this environment. Sometimes I want to scream that keeping our people alive should be the priority.

Chyna, you should be here. Every time I speak your name, I feel like I'm not doing enough, that I never could. I want our Black trans sisters to live freely, to be revered for embracing transformation, for defying the stifling boxes of essentialism. We are grand possibility models, but we also deserve our humanity. We are not satellites floating isolated in some dark sky; we are tethered to those around us. We have loved ones, families, and friends.

You make me believe that we change these dynamics by giving honor to those we've lost, caring for those still here, and building in the service of those yet to come. I will carry your name on my tongue and your legacy on my shoulders. I will keep wondering who you could've been if the world had loved you the way you deserved.

Your sis,
Raquel

22

Womanhood, Expanded

The Trump administration stoked an apocalyptic fear in the trans community. In fact, within that first week after the election it was reported that crisis and suicide prevention hotlines had received spikes in calls.[1] We had been so swiftly pushed into survival mode that Finn regularly advised our team to create "go bags." He truly believed that the world, especially in a fascist era, could descend into the kind of chaos you'd find in the pages of an Octavia Butler novel. While I was skeptical of his assessment, it felt very likely that Trump and his cronies would eventually restrict access to gender-affirming care. So, I mapped out the next stage of my medical transition.

One of the benefits of working for a major trans-led nonprofit (based in California, no less) was that bottom surgery, or vaginoplasty, became more accessible and affordable. Back in Georgia, I had a hellish time navigating low-paying jobs and horrendous health insurance options. There were times I'd call an insurance company only to encounter representatives who would give me conflicting coverage information. At HSW, I'd started the arduous process for approval, which included a flurry of virtual meetings with various surgeons, medical reference letters, and ignorant receptionists. After months of frustration, I was finally approved a day after I received my TLC offer letter. For the rest of that week, I debated whether to proceed with the surgery or take the position. I chose to forego the former, convinced that the job wouldn't be available by the time I recovered. Plus, I trusted that my new health insurance plan would cover it. And it did.

By March, I was all set for surgery in California and I had the hookup with full access to a gender clinic. Beyond having specialists in gender-affirming care, the clinic held group therapy sessions in which patients could ask questions about procedures and compare notes about goals and preparation. The staff also worked seamlessly with TLC to request the necessary time off and helped me apply for temporary disability assistance. *Was this a dream?*

With the technical part of the journey handled, I continued my self-work, examining my motives and weighing outcomes and risks for surgery. While I was excited to approach this milestone, I yearned to connect with others who had been through this process. But it wasn't easy to find them. Most of my peers, by choice or due to lack of access, had opted not to have bottom surgery. This just further illuminated the privilege of having a certain type of transition. Still, I grew so desperate that I called up a friend from my SNaPCO days for support. He connected me with one of his friends, and she graciously shared her story. She was an encouraging elder who'd had a vaginoplasty decades earlier. There were absolutely no regrets on her end, and she reified what I already knew—that getting a grasp on the mental aspect of this adventure was crucial.

On some level, I felt like I was genuflecting to the cisheteropatriarchy, letting the world and its expectations win. *Hadn't I evolved past that?* Yes, I had long felt uncomfortable with that extraneous flesh between my legs. That organ became nothing more than a nuisance, baggage I was carrying around, trying my best to ignore. *But as a trans activist, wasn't part of my overarching message for my people, my values, to love ourselves as we were? Did my opting for surgery betray that aim?* I didn't want to feed this narrative within and outside the trans community that "real" trans women "go all the way." That's what had been fed to us for so long. Plus I envied my sistas who were at home and secure in their womanhood with no deep sense to "complete" their journey. I thought their perspective was beautiful, perhaps more liberated. *So why did I desire this? Who was I really doing this for? Was I trying to prove something?*

* * *

DURING MY SURGERY preparation, Nigerian feminist author Chimamanda Ngozi Adichie became a trending topic on social media after being interviewed by Channel 4's Cathy Newman. Adichie was someone I had admired for years, even before her words were sampled in the skittering, electro-trap of Beyoncé's "***Flawless." Her TEDTalks, "The Danger of a Single Story" and "We Should All Be Feminists," came into my life at a crucial point in my feminist and gender journeys. Unfortunately, I recoiled at her words on trans women:

> *So, when people talk about whether trans women are women. My feeling is trans women are trans women. And I think if you've lived in the world as a man, with the privileges that the world accords to men, and then sort of change or switch gender, it's difficult for me to accept that then we can equate your experience with a woman who has lived from the beginning in the world as a woman and who has not been accorded those privileges that men are. I don't think it's a good thing to con-*

flate everything into one. I don't think it's a good thing to talk about women's issues being exactly the same as the issues of trans women. What I'm saying is gender is not biology, gender is sociology.[2]

*   *   *

WHILE ADICHIE COUCHED her opinion in a polite, matter-of-fact tone, I couldn't help but imagine a nineteenth-century suffragist saying something similar about Black women: *"So, when people talk about whether Black women are women. My feeling is Black women are Black women."* On the surface, there seems to be an acknowledgment that women with other qualifiers are still women. But there's also an invalidation of them as being so thoroughly different that we shouldn't ever consider them a part of the general category.

Whether wittingly or not, Adichie was simply rehashing decades of transmisogynistic rhetoric pushed by a contingent of mostly cis lesbian and queer radical feminists. In the 1970s, a new era of lesbian-only collectives sprang up after being sidelined by cis gay men in the LGBTQ+ rights movement and by heterosexual women in the women's liberation movement. Early prominent radical lesbian feminists like Mary Daly and Adrienne Rich critiqued their cisheterosexual oppressors and simultaneously demonized a marginal trans experience. In the latter half of the decade, Daly would advise Janice Raymond in her dissertation-turned-seminal-tome, *The Transsexual Empire: The Making of the She-Male*, which denounced trans people who opt for gender-affirming surgeries as a threat to the feminist cause and urged the restriction of transition-related healthcare.

Adichie's remarks made me consider all the ways that folks had tried to diminish my womanhood over the years. There's this assertion that *real* women are defined by having a particular body type (certain chromosomes, female reproductive organs), a set of bodily functions (the ability to menstruate or get pregnant), or a certain set of experiences (usually categorized under misogyny). If anyone considered this checklist for more than one second, they'd see the cracks in the theory. For many cis women, at least one of these qualifiers would present an impossible standard to meet: cis girls and women don't all have the same capacity for reproduction, and some may never experience menstruation or pregnancy. Nor do all cis girls and women experience the same degrees of misogyny. While it may be unlikely, women can express that they've never experienced discrimination based on gender or sex. (Conservative women often make this argument in an attempt to undercut progressive aims.) Plus, no one could tell me that the average cis person would refrain from acknowledging the assumed girlhood of the newborn assigned female with the smallest well of experiences in the world. To be clear, cis girls' and women's gender identities are typically respected without knowing whether they have had particular bodily and life experiences, not to mention their chromosomal composition, which most people would only really know if they were tested.

Witnessing Adichie platform this line of transmisogynistic thinking hurt because I expected her to understand, as a fellow Black woman, how feminism has not always welcomed more marginalized narratives and voices. Many cis people think that trans folks, particularly trans women, are claiming that our experiences are exactly the same or insinuating that they must be to be valid. I don't believe that is true. But that also doesn't mean our embrace of womanhood diminishes their own.

Even further, while it may be true that many trans women experienced some form of privilege in being perceived as boys or men at varying points in our lives, it ignores the spectrum of experiences that people assigned male at birth have. My cishet brother experienced a greater degree of privilege than I did as someone often perceived as a feminine, queer person growing up—and even more so once I was open about my sexual orientation. Even further, there is a privilege that all cis people share in actually identifying with and being consistently affirmed in their gender from birth than those of us who have dealt with some kind of incongruence throughout our lives.

Either way, privilege and oppression are not binary concepts. They exist on a spectrum and must be treated with nuance. Black feminists like Audre Lorde, Barbara Smith, and Patricia Hill Collins have long illuminated this truth in their own ways. If only Adichie championed this existing legacy in Black feminism and feminisms of color, one that brought women on the margins together rather than drove them apart. Many Black feminists have constantly broken down that discussions on male privilege among our cis counterparts are more complex for us than the broad stroke that white feminists have often painted. We know within communities of color that men of color, although still privileged, don't experience the degree of privilege that white cis men do. It is beautiful to notice and discuss the nuances of the average cis woman's experience and the average trans woman's experience. However, it gets dangerous when we place all these requirements for one group of women to be valid versus another.

This public discourse reminded me that even if I'd had bottom surgery, I would still not be fully considered a woman by many. In fact, people might consider my medical gender transition a desire to fulfill a patriarchal conception of womanhood. But honestly, this idea ignores that everyone, on some level, is seeking a life in which they are comfortable with their identity on their terms. Cis people have long opted for surgeries (breast and buttock augmentations, labiaplasties, rhinoplasties) and procedures (hair transplants, hormone replacement therapies) that are gender-affirming and haven't been considered menacing for it.

I firmly embraced that my vagina would not define my womanhood, for I was a woman long before I even had the prospect of accomplishing this part of the journey. This transition milestone, like all the others, would be for me, not to fit into a "real woman's" club, not men or partners, nor the cisheteropatriarchy. I just wanted to feel at home in my body. If anything, having surgery would open me up to focus on the rest of my life. Plus, my desires for myself shouldn't hinge on others' judgment.

* * *

I OPENED MY eyes to blurred vision and a hazy mind in a San Francisco hospital bed. I slowly looked around, taking in the generously sized room I had all to myself. I tried to remember the last thing that happened before the anesthesia took hold of me. There was brightness. There was the nurse telling me to relax, which I was already doing, thanks to the Valium. I tried to think about more particulars, but the morphine had my mind scrambled. That's why I had the audacity to claim, "That wasn't that bad," about what most would consider the final step in my transition. In a chair nearby, Momma sat, looking up at me from the newspaper she was reading. She smiled expectantly.

After my hubristic declaration of victory, I started to inspect myself. I turned my arms over on the thin, baby-blue waffle-textured hospital blanket. There was a plum-colored dot of dried blood under the clear bandage where they had placed the IV. There was also a dull ache. I compared it to my other yella elbow crease, which was hardly ever considered viable for injections. The vein had a personality all its own. Whenever a nurse tapped it, it would slide from beneath their finger pad, refusing to succumb to its fate.

After what felt like an eternity, I looked down toward the pièce de résistance. Oblong, bulging cotton sacks filled with ice cubes lay perpendicularly between my thighs. Somewhere underneath all that fabric and ice (including the thin, cotton panty they had slipped on me) was a brand-new vagina. And what awaited me was removal of my sutures, learning to dilate, returning sensation, and the rest of my life.

23

Girls' Night Outing

After months of recovery, I was eager to get back into the world, have a night out, lap up some libations, and maybe flirt with a cutie. My girls, Constance and Maxine, obliged, and we set out to serve the trans girls of color version of *Sex and the City*. I'd met them out and about in the community, commiserating over our nonprofit jobs at different organizations. Constance was a few years older and dark-skinned with a signature East African golden complexion. She was a staunch environmental justice advocate. Maxine was slightly younger and passionate about reproductive healthcare access. She was a light-skinned Latina with long, shiny jet-black hair and a palpable naivete. Constance and I were constantly sharing stories with her about our early twenties, having lived openly trans for a few years longer.

Our trio settled on a downtown Oakland bar called The Layover. I'd become a fan in the months before surgery because of its unique atmospheric blend of a club, dive bar, and lounge. It wasn't the largest space, but each part had a distinctive feel. As usual, the designated dance floor was dimly lit and full of tightly packed, writhing bodies. Opposite that was an area featuring couches obscured with piles of jackets, purses, and whatever else people didn't want to hold. It always struck me how trusting folks seemed to be in there. To round out the venue was a long bar where single men congregated and surveyed the dancing crowd, no doubt hoping to get lucky. Cishet Land felt tribal in this aspect, almost like a game. I still got a thrill from it all. Even though I was queer, I felt like I'd drifted far beyond the desirability that was prized in those spaces. Perhaps my aesthetic and vibe were too stereotypically feminine. But also, generally, queer spaces also prioritize cis men or cis women, and if gender-nonconforming, nonbinary, or trans folks get to play, it's usually non-Black ones. There's an uninterrogated way that Black trans women are seen as untouchable spectacles in those spaces, only valued if we're performers or serving immaculate beauty. At least in my adventures in Cishet Land, there was a chance of really being approached. It didn't always feel safe, but I felt like I knew the stakes.

Would things feel different now? Would I be more confident? I wondered. In the past, whenever I danced with a random guy, I imagined a timer counting down until my transness disrupted our connection. *Would he sense a rigidness to the motion in my hips, get intimidated by my "sturdy" frame, or notice the effort it takes to make my voice flutter over the boisterous crowd? Or would I survive until the not-so-luckiest scenario, where I get to reveal my identity like it's a murder confession?* Once a guy feigned acceptance, only to leave the club with his friend once I was out of sight. Another time I whispered my truth to this tall basketball player type, and he responded, "I'll try anything once," as if hooking up with me took as much gumption as sky-diving. Still another time, while I was out with another friend, these two guys pushed up on us before asking, "Why do their voices sound like that?" and slowly backing away as if we were 1970s' slasher-film villains.

Those kinds of negative interactions used to spark self-loathing, but maybe now was different. I felt like I'd done all I could to transition on my terms, like there wasn't anything I needed to prove to anyone else. I knew it was still risky being visible, having my "T" spilled for me. But if anyone wanted to clock me, I'd have to let it slide right off my back. Besides, I felt sexy with my strawberry-blond ombré box braids gathered in a high ponytail. I was also wearing a new black lace bodysuit with dark blue jeans. The design of the top traversed my torso in a way that suggested I was baring more skin than I actually was. It felt daring to wear something so constricting with this newer version of my body. It might not have been prudent, but I did what needed to be done.

As my crew posted up near the bar, we chatted as our eyes scanned the place. It would be great if our girls' nights out lived up to a bell hooks's feminist ideal of simply being about communion with one another, but rarely was that the case. The unspoken desire was to find an attractive guy with which to waste any amount of energy and time. We yearned for normalcy and validation, things we rarely experienced. Maxine would be the first to experience this fantasy. A guy with a mahogany complexion around our age started chatting her up, and it wasn't long before a toothy smile appeared on her face. She didn't signal to us that she was OK or to let us know she'd find us; she just walked near the dance floor mesmerized by ol' dude. It wasn't surprising that Maxine caught an eye right away. She was undoubtedly an attractive young woman, but, of course, she also benefited from the fact that non-Black girls seemed to be the hottest commodities in the Bay. While colorism is a near-universal dynamic, it seemed deeper here than in Atlanta. I'd also heard many Black cis women espouse that assessment. Perhaps the location's racial heterogeneity made it easier for Black men to pursue all types of women. But there was a clear hierarchy, and my darker-skinned Black sisters were often even more overlooked.

As Maxine got her life, I continued to hang with Constance. We sized up the trade, stole swigs of our drinks, and swayed our bodies to the music. The Bay Area would never play out Too $hort's "Blow the Whistle" or Kamaiyah's "How Does It Feel." As I soaked up the vibes, a taller, impressively toned guy approached, asking my name and burrowing his eyes into mine. I immediately glanced over at Constance, feeling a wave of guilt about the imminent whisk away.

"You good, girl?" I asked.

"Yeah, I'm going to get a smoke," she said as she swiftly made her way to the door.

"OK," I said.

It's annoying to be the last girl standing, and I wanted to be cognizant of that. I hated that we spent so much time vying for fleeting moments of attraction. These men didn't deserve our presence, and it was only a matter of time before they knocked us down a peg for not being "real" women; then we'd be crawling back to each other, commiserating. But even though I wanted to resist the urge to talk to the guy, I didn't. He was cute enough and seemed friendly.

As he led me to the dance floor, we exchanged names and our professions. His name was Vic, and I gave him my old alias, Rebel. He vaguely said he worked in tech and I flippantly shot back that I work in nonprofits around women's rights. He didn't deserve a deeper explanation. It's not like the connection would translate into anything after the night was over anyway. So, I just tried to be present for the time we had together. I fixed my eyes on the outline of his pecs peeking through his light blue T-shirt just below a gold medium-length chain that kept hitting his collarbone. As our bodies drew closer, I averted eye contact and wrapped my arms around his neck. But even with this new lease on life post–bottom surgery, the fear of being clocked snuck up on me. So, I held on to his body like a shield.

After a while of wordless dancing, I had had my fill of his attention and took the opportunity to flee once we began moving on different rhythms and the DJ switched up the mood. "I'm just checking on my girl," I said, which was partially true. I felt the relief of leaving the sticky club air for outside's coolness. Constance was on another smoke break, poking at her phone. She didn't look up, but I knew she sensed me nearby. A few scattered groups of people loitered, and a line had formed outside the pizza spot next door.

"How are you and Mr. Mans?" she said, with a dwindling cigarette in hand.

"He's OK, girl. We'll see," I said, swatting the suggestion that this could be a spark of anything serious.

"What about you? Did you find anybody?" I asked.

"Oh, yeah, I talked to some dude for a bit," she said, looking out into the street. "But you know how they are."

"Yeah," I agreed, glancing over to Maxine and her guy on the sidewalk. "Well, I guess she's getting her life."

Constance looked over, and we both noticed Maxine walk around a corner with the man. Something felt odd, but I figured she was giving him head or something. It wasn't her typical behavior, but wilder things have happened on a girls' night out. Nevertheless, I stayed outside chatting with Constance, putting off the unspoken obligation to go back and dance with the guy. I desperately wanted to ward off his eventual requests to come home with me. I half-hoped he'd find someone else to fixate on, but he eventually came out looking for me.

"Your friend good out here?" he asked.

"Oh, yeah. She's just smoking." I smiled. "Now, I'm just keeping an eye on the other one." We looked over to Maxine and her guy, who were now yards away.

"I'm sure she's good," he said, smoothly moving closer to me. Maybe he was going to ask for my number, or if we could meet up for drinks on another day—we'll never know. Before anything else could happen, an exasperated Maxine darted toward us, followed by the guy she'd been talking to all night. I thought they were moving as a unit, but soon he pushed past her, making a beeline back toward the bar. He looked at my guy with frustration on his face.

"They're all men," he exclaimed as he paused.

"No way," my guy shot back before dubiously glancing at me.

I froze, trying to register everything that was happening, and the guy I was talking to slightly shook his head in disbelief. Then, he gave me a once-over, reached out, and forcibly grabbed my vulva through my skinny jeans. His rigid hand engulfed me, and I looked through him. Perhaps the feeling was amplified by the areas that were still healing and numb, but it felt like he was holding all of me at once. I froze.

"See," he said with satisfaction. "That's not a man."

All that mattered to him at that moment was safeguarding his heterosexuality. It was validating that he didn't think I was a man and that I no longer had any evidence that would have proved his investigation wrong. But the assault communicated its intention: I wasn't even a person. I was an object, a prop for his masculinity. It took Constance saying, "Girl, we gotta go," and pulling my arm for me to snap back into my body. Seconds later, we disappeared around the nearest corner.

In the days after that incident, I wondered if my body would ever truly be mine. I'd felt so vulnerable after being groped. At least before I had a vagina, I supposedly had genitalia that would give the average cis guy pause if he got me in a compromising position. Now, I had yet another entry point for domination. I imagined maybe this is how many folks assigned female at birth felt all the time. Still, I wondered if there truly was a difference from the vulnerability I'd felt before. Surgery or not, the patriarchy threatened and was threatened by my existence as a trans woman.

I felt foolish for thinking I'd finally be in control of my body when it had always been in someone else's hands. It started with being assigned a gendered box that never worked for me. Then it was the nonconsensual circumcision. Then it was my father and peers critiquing and coercing my behavior, movements, and voice. It was the times when that older neighborhood boy touched me or when I was coerced into sex during my first semester of college, or, more recently, when a guy I dated for a few months penetrated me without protection because he "just couldn't help it." And most of all, underneath many of these powerless moments lay a twisted desire for validation. I just wanted to be the right person, the right woman, so that people would understand that my autonomy, life, safety, and security mattered.

* * *

A MONTH LATER, after I buried the incident deep in my mind, I was reminded of the widespread disregard cishet men have for Black trans women's lives. While promoting her second memoir, *Surpassing Certainty*, Janet Mock appeared on the New York–based Power 105.1 radio show *The Breakfast Club*. The show's hosts—Charlamagne Tha God, DJ Envy, and Angela Yee—had a track record of platforming offensive narratives and stunts about Black women and LGBTQ+ folks, like pushing rapper Lil Mama to tears with their teenage lunchroom bullying tactics, asking invasive questions about the medical transition of reality television star Sidney Starr and shaming DJ Mister Cee for his multiple arrests for hiring trans sex workers.

Mock had crafted a seemingly unimpeachable image in the media after coming out publicly in 2011. It was risky for her to join that show, but there was no denying the reach of *The Breakfast Club*. It attracted Black and Latine audiences rarely exposed to our experiences. Perhaps she could be the one to crack the code on redeeming the show from its problematic history. After all, she'd gone toe to toe with conservative personality Piers Morgan on CNN, so these hosts might be lesser adversaries.

I watched the interview a few hours after it was officially posted online. Overall, it seemed to go well. Sure, there were invasive questions about her medical transition, but she masterfully pivoted from them by quipping that they should read her first book. The episode was solid, a good look for her book's press, and the trans community, by proxy, seemingly survived with minor bruises. Days later, though, *The Breakfast Club* hosts discussed Janet in an interview with comedian Lil Duval. His appearance started with typical, harmless radio show banter. Then, Charlamagne randomly asked Duval what he thought about President Donald Trump's ban on trans people serving in the military. He tried to brush away the inquiry, clearly thinking of something derisive to say about trans people but sidestepping the joke. Still, Charlamagne kept goading him, and his co-hosts joined in, laughing all through the line of questioning. Then, DJ Envy held up Janet's book and, ultimately, her existence as a prop. The conversation quickly devolved into questions about how Duval would react if he encountered a trans woman.

"This might sound messed up, and I don't care, but she [is] dying," he said.

"You can't say that," Yee yelled in between hearty giggles after Duval made a quip about "trannies."

"So, you couldn't come up with a good joke," Charlamagne asked in a throwaway line. But in it, he reveals his intention to prompt Duval into making light of trans people. As the banter continues, Charlamagne quips about how there should be legal repercussions for trans people who don't disclose their identity to romantic and sexual partners. Then, they ask Duval about political correctness and comedy. As if being expected not to dehumanize and justify the death of a group of people on the margins is just a matter of oversensitivity.

"That's the good thing I like about being me. I can say what I want and do what I want," Duval said. "[The fans] know I'm not coming from a place of malice. They know I'm just speaking my mind."

The problem is that comedians and their words carry weight like those of any other celebrity or public figure. Though we were supposedly living in the Transgender Visibility era, many trans people still existed solely as rhetorical fodder for conservative politicians, jokes by unimaginative comics, and hypothetical fantasies and threats to the general public. Most didn't know a trans person in their personal lives, so often the only time they encountered us was in the media. There's a confirmation bias when ignorant cis people talk about us. They underscore historically destructive ideas about trans people being predatory, undesirable tricksters and the average person runs with them. Instances like this *Breakfast Club* debacle signal to other people we shouldn't be taken seriously or worse, that we deserve harm and violence. These cishet folks attempted to cut down the accomplishments of one of the few lauded trans figures. This is why many Black trans people don't trust Black cis people or cis people because many will claim to respect us to our faces and then turn around and dog us when we're not in the room.

Lil Duval's video garnered millions of views on YouTube, whereas Janet's, in all its authenticity, received a fraction of that attention. Transphobic takes, not unlike Chimamanda Ngozi

Adichie's months prior, have an outsized impact on our media landscape. Imagine how many of those viewers went on to further the discrimination and violence of trans people in their everyday lives. In fact, it wouldn't be surprising if Duval's evil rhetoric made its way to his hometown of Jacksonville, Florida, where four transgender and gender-nonconforming people (Antash'a English, Cathalina Christina James, Jessie Sumlar, and Celine Walker) were killed the following year.

To my knowledge, no apology was ever made for how *The Breakfast Club* treated Janet. In the aftermath, a contingent of Black trans folks and our allies tried to flesh out the discourse— noting the damaging notions about our experiences that the hosts and guests had perpetuated. A group of people tried to orchestrate a boycott of the show. It was a powerful aim and one I supported, but the community was David and the show was Goliath. The latter just had too much support for this mini-action to put even a dip in their popularity.

On Twitter, I asked trans people and allies on social media to make personal statements on their platforms about how trans people should not be treated as comedic fodder. I crafted a hashtag, #TransFolksAreNotJokes, and made a call to action for people to make videos supporting Janet and the community. A noticeable amount of people joined in, and it felt beautiful to see even a smidge of resistance. Most importantly, I was empowered by Janet's response to the fiasco in *Allure*.

We must navigate difficult conversations about desire and identity, about the fact that trans girls exist, and for as long as we've existed we've been desired by men (including high-profile ones who won't ever own their desires) who are not working toward gaining the tools to deal with their attraction. And just so

we are clear: Just because you find me and my sisters attractive
does not mean we desire you.
You never could.[1]

The Breakfast Club incident was difficult to witness because
it provided a mirror. I saw these people try to diminish someone
I admired, a possibility model, a Black trans woman who dared
to demand dignity. If she could experience that, then how could
I be so shocked that I was groped outside of that Oakland club.
So many cis men are entrenched in a violent, oppressive idea of
masculinity and their desires that they have no idea where the
next human begins. That a Black woman, particularly a Black
trans woman, could be a victim is considered impossible to them.
In fact, we are perpetually painted as the villain, the culprit, the
disease, the predator, the liar, the harmer, the fool, the alien, and
the untouchable in our society. When cis folks view us as anything other than human, they strip us of agency, power, and self-
determination. And I can't help but think of all the people who
face this treatment in silence and don't have access to outlets,
platforms, or even therapy to process these things. When that
man grabbed me, it felt like my identity, my womanhood, had to
either hoist up his manhood, his masculinity, his sexuality, his
entitlement to domination, or be demolished as a threat. And as
dangerous as it is, I'd prefer to be the latter.

24

I Have a Right to Show My Color

After about a year into my time at TLC, a familiar feeling of being stifled in the workplace returned. It was a dizzying time, as I'd ventured into a thriving independent lane of work that drew me to speak at colleges and universities while I felt over-looked and underestimated in my communications role. I wanted to do more dynamic work that allowed me to connect face-to-face with the community rather than from behind a screen. Luckily, after providing technical support to TLC's Programs team on a few political education webinars and other digital strategies, the department director, Nadine Figueroa, took notice and put a meeting on the calendar for us.

She had been nondescript about this discussion as if we were concocting some top-secret plan. After ordering drinks and engaging in some quick banter, she asked me to join her team. Apparently, my leadership outside of the organization had impressed her and she thought I'd be a complement to her department.

As the lavender notes of Earl Grey tea traveled across my tongue, I pictured moving from my current white cis-led office to one helmed by another trans woman of color. There had always been a bit of an awkward air with my current boss as if I was some beast that intimidated them. I never quite felt like they knew what to do with me. So, this prospect felt promising. But I needed a salary increase, as I would have to do more traveling and carry more duties than my current position. Unfortunately, Nadine halted that inquiry immediately. She told me it wasn't a promotion but more of a lateral move and that I'd keep the same rate. Hiding my disappointment, I tasted the bittersweetness of having someone I expected to be like a sister to me as a boss, but not having an advocate for increased compensation for increased work. I figured we could revisit it down the road, but for now I was thrilled about becoming a national organizer.

* * *

WHEN I JOINED the Programs team, I was immersed in a collective of folks who wore politics on their sleeves. In the communications role, we had to make the organizational voice palatable. Our attorneys often leaned more respectable, a necessity of navigating the legal system. In this department, however, we could be as passionate and raw as we wanted. My earliest work involved co-facilitating workshops for our National Training Institute. Many of them focused on capacity building, lobbying, and policy for gender-affirming healthcare and public accommodations for campaigns in the Pacific Northwest.

By the summer of 2017, anti-trans legislation had been introduced in at least twenty-nine states, with nearly two-thirds being Midwestern or Southern. It felt like we were directing most of our efforts to established fights instead of prioritizing the communities most in need. Further, most of the workshop attendees were white. Nadine had impressively shored up support for trans Latine immigrants at the Mexican–U.S. border, and Cecilia Chung, a longtime HIV advocate and policy wonk, helmed a project for trans people living with HIV/AIDS. But as I audited the department's reach, I knew that the ongoing epidemic of violence, mostly plaguing Black trans women, was unaddressed.

I even took stock of TLC's most significant impact litigation cases. In *Norsworthy v. Beard*,[1] we'd represented Michelle Norsworthy, a white trans woman who had been held in a California men's prison. While incarcerated, she had been denied gender-affirming surgery and access to legally changing her name, despite psychological recommendations in favor of them. Ultimately, TLC argued, "the prison system's discriminatory actions violated fundamental constitutional guarantees, including the Eighth Amendment prohibition of cruel and unusual punishment and the Equal Protection Clause." On April 2, 2015, federal district court judge Jon Tigar ruled that Norsworthy's denial of care violated her right to medical care under the Eighth Amendment of the U.S. Constitution. This case proceeded under the watch of then-California attorney general Kamala Harris, who initially joined other state attorneys in dismissing "Norworthy's plea." While this was a major victory, the approach wasn't without critique. This case centered on a white trans woman although trans people of color are more likely to be criminalized. The National Center for Trans Equality's 2015 U.S. Trans Survey reported that Black trans women were nearly five times more likely to be arrested in the past year than their white counterparts. I was unaware of any Black trans people TLC had represented. I knew cases like that of Norsworthy were crucial, but it felt like the folks most at-risk were being left out of the organization's theory of change.

In a few meetings with Nadine, I'd asked why the organization wasn't doing more to end the murders of Black trans women. She said that getting Black trans organizers together was a risk and that the dustup at the INCITE! convening had deterred TLC from doing more. While I understood the complexities of movement drama, the response was insufficient. It seemed if TLC could go toe to toe with the U.S. Immigration and Customs Enforcement and call for its abolition, it could fight for the lives of Black and Latina trans women facing patriarchal violence beyond the State. But, in my newness to the department, I didn't feel comfortable saying this. Still, I wondered how we could chip away at this anti-Black mentality.

I found encouragement in external efforts, finding camaraderie in Echoing Ida, a Black women and nonbinary writers collective founded by another Oakland-based nonprofit, Forward Together. Through that initiative, I met Shanelle Matthews, who urged me to apply to her Black storytelling and media training initiative, Channel Black. Matthews had been instrumental in the Movement for Black Lives, serving as the network's communications director. Under her guidance, I studied messaging and political strategy, though there was very little data on what worked for trans communities. Still, our cohort examined the U.S. media landscape, its inherent anti-Blackness, and how we could be crusaders for more authentic portrayals of Black liberation.

I also attended a week-long intensive for Black Organizing for Leadership and Dignity (BOLD), a training institute for Black organizers. This experience immersed us in the Los Angeles Black Workers Center's "Do You See Me Now" campaign focused on elevating local cases of workplace discrimination. BOLD also introduced participants to somatics, a semi-meditative practice that strengthens the connection between the mind and the body. Individual and collective exercises required us to focus on breathing, excavate trauma responses, and uncover areas for growth, particularly around conflict resolution. I appreciated that we could share our experiences around multiple axes of oppression and develop plans for healing in our personal lives.

Even though the temperature rose behind my face as I discussed my experience as a trans woman in these mostly cis spaces, it felt like M4BL had become more affirming since the Cleveland convening. Lastly, I joined the first all-Black trans woman cohort of Auburn Theological Seminary's Sojourner Truth Leadership Circle under the direction of Lisa Anderson, Dr. Renée L. Hill, Carla Gaskins-Nathan, and Courtney Weber Hoover. They reminded my peers and me that our organizing work takes a toll and that we deserve access to spiritual replenishment and holistic wellness. These opportunities became necessary retreats from my nine-to-five.

* * *

By the fall of 2017, my feeling that TLC was sidelining Black trans people dovetailed with the organization's anti-oppression process focused on building a more inclusive culture. This effort, led by a white trans man and cis non-Black Latina, required separating our staff into a white caucus and a person of color (POC) caucus for regular discussions on our experiences, then bringing the groups back together every few months. Initially, very little was discussed in these meetings. There was an unspoken understanding that TLC was as equitable as it gets for national trans-led nonprofits. We had nearly as many people of color as we did white people and seemingly an equal split among our department heads. But many Black staffers felt uneasy about this myth. One day something broke open in a POC caucus meeting. As I sat around the table with a mix of Asian, Black, and Latine peers, we became more candid about our perspectives on TLC's culture work. Once again, mostly non-Black staff spoke up, sharing how great it was to work at a place with people of color in leadership. There was a very valid complaint from Marissa about needing more bilingual support for the organization's support hotline. As the question made its way around the table, something stirred inside me, a mix of passion and fury.

"I think working at TLC is great, and I couldn't imagine being elsewhere," I said. "But there are more dynamics to address than whether people are white or of color here. TLC is very brown, but it sure as hell isn't Black enough."

For a second, I wished I could have pulled the words back into my mouth, but in the silence and curious looks of my colleagues. Then, an ad hoc collective of Black attendees explained how so many of us were working in siloes, had few career and leadership development opportunities, and how the organization had no programming centering people like us. Other Black folks agreed, mentioning the lack of support across the board and the dismissal of many of their ideas. But most of all, we confronted the pats on the back that TLC had given itself for supposedly being on the right track for racial equity.

The solution to our grievances was creating a Black caucus, in which we also requested that TLC hire a Black facilitator who could support us. Initially, our contingent had a mountain of interest in having a space designated for our discourse. But after a few months, associate-level employees across the organization were hit with a wave of disillusionment regarding the racial equity process. If you weren't in a position of power, the meetings were still uncomfortable spaces to reveal your struggles, as many folks had issues with their bosses. The presence of directors and supervisors, even of color, neutralized any real discussion of how power was wielded at the organization. Over time, with seemingly few results, it felt audacious to be lectured on equity by our bosses and have mostly non-Black people impart "insight" on racial dynamics, especially to Black workers.

Non-supervisor staff found more release chatting with each other after the meetings when we weren't in earshot. I commiserated with Finn over the shortcomings of the Programs department. Both of us had experienced mistreatment in the form of belittling statements and even yelling in meetings. As Finn and I spoke with colleagues in the organization's other departments, we heard testimonials about increased workloads without adjusted compensation, micromanagement, and retaliation for leadership critiques. Eventually, the racial caucus was dissolved in favor of one for directors and supervisors and another for non-directors and non-supervisors.

Despite deteriorating morale among the staff, our national organizing team charged forth with new programming. Teju led the pack, developing a program centering Black migrants. The national program would work at the intersections of criminal justice, immigrant rights, and Black diasporic liberation. Observing his fierce determination helped me trust my instincts and leadership, so I secretly developed a program focused on Black trans women's survival. I reasoned that when a murder of a Black trans woman occurs, the Black trans women in her community experience fear and trauma. I wanted to create healing justice summits for us to share our stories and craft new solutions to end violence in their communities. Analyzing the data from that year of afrotransmisogynistic murders, I learned that Louisiana, Ohio, and Texas were the most impacted. So I selected New Orleans as the pilot location.

Months later, I presented my idea to our Program team at our strategic planning retreat. I called it Black Trans Circles, inspired by the restorative and healing justice circle process. While TLC leadership was interested, they weren't ready to fund the full idea of three local summits and one larger regional one for the South and Midwest. So I was encouraged to apply for the Open Society Foundation's Soros Equality Fellowship, a prize for midcareer professionals of the social justice variety. *Cue the right-wing obsession with the fellowship's namesake, George Soros, and his global philanthropic footprint.* Teju had been selected the previous year, using the opportunity for institutional support and seed funding for his project. So I applied, bolstered by advice from TLC's senior leadership. Impressively, Finn also planted the seeds for the organization's first-ever Disability Justice programming during that time. Even in the stress caused by the equity process, some strides were being made.

* * *

WITH NEW ORLEANS community organizers Nia Faulk, Syria Synclaire, and Cobella Bennett, the first-ever Black Trans Circles (BTC) commenced in March 2018. Each of my co-leads brought a different flavor. Nia was the crunchy-granola, spiritual one who always had an elevating, ethereal demeanor, Syria was the seasoned auntie who knew everything about the local community's history, and Cobella was the fiery ingenue who made sure our event had flair. They were a tremendous help with the outreach, leaning into their networks for participants while Bellamy, Finn, and the rest of our team graciously supported with curricula building, facilitation, and logistics. Ultimately, we gathered twelve Black trans women of varying experiences for a two-day summit that included sessions on embodied storytelling sessions, trauma, self-care, resource mapping, and survival. Attendees discussed incarceration, houselessness, sex work, and local politics. Some had known each other for years, while others were fairly new or had felt isolated from the community. As we shared our hopes for the space, people repeatedly expressed desires for sustained connection and support. Their stories pushed me to reflect on my journey and how meeting other

Black queer and trans people changed my entire life trajectory, giving me a purpose and a collective sense of liberation. Folks like Toni-Michelle, Bellamy, Constance, and many others gave a new dimension to my life. And I saw that in this room as attendees made plans to work on community initiatives together or to build out safety plans. One young woman, Mariah Moore, lit up throughout the event, brazenly chiming in with her perspectives. There was a spark in her, a possibility of what communion for women could inspire.

*   *   *

MONTHS AFTER THE convening, I was accepted to the Open Society's fellowship and began mapping out the program's future. Simultaneously, tensions between director-supervisor staff and non-supervisors at TLC continued to rise. The culture hadn't shifted quickly enough to address the issues that lower-level staff had brought to the fore, largely due to perceived inertia from the folks with power at the organization. In one last-ditch effort, non-directors drafted a letter to leadership urging them to address our concerns regarding the treatment of disabled coworkers, lack of transparency, retaliation after critique, and unrealistic travel schedules without a commensurate number of personal days. Despite an email back with a promise to address the letter in time, there was no major acknowledgment of the labor that nearly half of the staff had put into trying to get the organization to live up to its potential around equity. TLC was beginning to feel like a shell of its former self; what once felt like a close-knit family became more of a collection of jilted, twice-removed cousins. Numerous staffers plotted their exits from the organization; ones who'd only been there for several months dipped fairly early.

Though I was excited about the prospect of growing BTC, a program birthed from the experiences of Black trans women, the strain of the organization's equity process and the departure of colleagues I cared deeply about took a toll on me. *I'd had success, but at what cost to me mentally?* Following Teju's suit and earning the fellowship was no easy feat and certainly not guaranteed. I'd had to fight for a new title, greater compensation for an increased workload, program resources, hell, even an organizational credit card for expenses. It seemed there were endless hurdles that Black and lower-level staffers had to endure to prove our value. Where I'd once been excited to come into the office and even join staff calls, I began to dread them. *If people felt mistreated internally at this nonprofit, how could we claim to show up fully for our community externally?*

* * *

BEYOND MY MAIN job, I'd continued to freelance for various publications. Writing "The Transgender Dating Dilemma" for *Buzz-Feed* in 2015 was a transformational experience for me, mostly because I was able to cross paths with writer-editor Meredith Talusan. She was the first trans person to edit my work, which unlocked a different dimension of authenticity and vulnerability in my writing. We kept in contact over the years. In spring 2018, I visited Meredith in the Condé Nast offices during a work trip to NYC. Simply entering the building was a far cry from my experience in Oakland. First, it was a freaking glossy skyscraper in Lower Manhattan, complete with a long marble receptionist's desk, suited-up employees, and multiple layers of security. On the way to the upper floor where the *Them* team was located, I heard the click-clacks of heels I'd long foregone in daily dressing. No one got that dolled up in Oakland, much less at a nonprofit.

Taking in Meredith's office and the windows revealing the cityscape, I marveled at this boss bitch life. It was only supposed to be a brief chat, but she promised to introduce me to Phillip

Picardi, the chief content creator of *Teen Vogue*. As we made our way toward his office, we paused. I spotted the back of Anna Wintour's signature golden bob. They were in a meeting, and I took in the urgent air. We had to wait until they were done, so a few staffers took me to their product closet. It was just like a movie with piles of free testers and items they didn't mind gifting to me.

When Phill was ready, someone led me to his office. I first noticed his bright eyes and a magnetism that made it clear how he'd made it so far in his editorial career. He commanded immense respect within and outside of the corporation. We chatted a bit as I stared at the images of models and page mock-ups tacked to his wall. In that short time, he gushed about my Southern charm, and we commiserated over our tortured Catholic upbringing. We got along well right off the bat, and he even let me have a bomber jacket, as I hadn't planned for it to be so chilly in New York at that time of year. Soon after, he invited me to dinner with him and a few friends, and we had my first real night out in NYC. When I returned to my Oakland life, I couldn't get the experience out of my mind.

That summer, I visited Manhattan for work again, and this time Phill set up a clandestine meeting at a restaurant in Dumbo. I obliged. Entering the fifties diner–inspired spot, I soaked up the image of him and his partner looking cozy in a booth. We leisurely ordered some food, then he explained his plan to leave Condé Nast to revamp *Out* magazine, a longstanding LGBTQ+ publication. Co-founded in 1992 by editors Michael Goff and Sarah Pettit, it began with a mission of inserting a national community-focused glossy into the mainstream. The lore is that it delivered on equitable highlighting of gay and lesbian interests until Pettit was ousted in 1997. She would later sue for breach of contract and sex discrimination and reached an out-of-court settlement.[2] When it ascended to cultural relevance at the start of the millennium, the *Out* image unapologetically centered on cis gay men, usually white, well-to-do, traditionally fit and muscular, and class privileged. And anyone else in the LGBTQ+ initialism, especially trans folks, was utterly off the publication's radar.

Phill's petition centered on reclaiming *Out* for people on the margins and elevating voices that had long been overlooked in hegemonic queer narratives. He saw potential in me as his right hand, leading the print side of the operations, with my unique swirl of journalism and social justice experience. I'm sure he also sensed that the appointment might make a splash, as I'd become the first openly trans woman to join the leadership of a major national publication. Most of all, it would require another cross-country move—to the place that was still the city of my dreams. As I took in Phill's words, I didn't know what to say and didn't know whether I could handle the role. Even though I still free-lanced for national publications, I hadn't had a proper journalism job since I'd left the *Monroe Chronicle* years prior. Plus, I'd never been employed as an editor before. I didn't have a résumé that made sense next to Phill's. *Oh, and wasn't print journalism dying? And why me? Was I simply a diversity hire?* I knew on some level I'd always be that, as there were only so many trans journalists in the industry, much less Black. And at the heart of all my questions was a fear of leaving my burgeoning program at TLC.

I had hoped to at least see BTC become a pipeline for Black trans leadership at the organization, but that future seemed uncertain. I hated to leave TLC at a time when it felt so broken, but my peers and I had spent so much energy trying to shift our workplace culture. Perhaps it was destined for the nonprofit to go through these growing pains. After all, the Trump era had pushed everyone to reconsider institutions, hierarchy, and power. After I reflected on my role and had conversations with friends and family, it felt clear that I needed to take this new opportunity at *Out*. So I worked with my boss to map out the continued existence of BTC. In time, we'd hire Mariah, the energetic participant from the first convening, to lead the program. She'd shown interest in being more involved and had the charisma and connections in New Orleans to keep BTC afloat. As I said my goodbyes, I relished in pruning an environment that no longer fit and looked toward the potentially greater impact I could have on our community with this national platform.

PART IV

Blooming

25

A Peach in the Big Apple

New York's winter slapped me hard, reminding me that my jawline reduction was still fresh. In my last Oakland weeks, I'd somehow balanced packing up my life and recovering from what I imagined would be my final gender-affirmation surgery. It was a procedure I had wanted for a while, removing the last dysphoria-inducing feature I could feasibly control. Plus, I needed to take advantage of comprehensive health insurance before I left TLC. But the worst part of the recovery wasn't the deep aches or the layer of intense swelling just under my skin; it was inhaling the ever-present blanket of smoke from the Northern California wildfires.

That cataclysmic scene full of empty streets made the frenetic December energy of New York easier to accept. On the way to *Out*'s editorial office on the first day, I still managed to smile warmly at random strangers on the subway. It was like a Southern muscle memory. But, as expected, most didn't return my gaze. The frigid atmosphere on the C train made me doubt if I should've taken this editor role. *Was I qualified for this? How could I guarantee we'd elevate the stories of the most marginalized in our communities? Was this corporate role at odds with my social justice values?* Even though I'd dreamed of moving to NYC for a post like this, I feared I'd broiled in that Georgia oven too long and would never match this Northeastern glossy media bubble. And I remained unconvinced that my community organizing experience would grant me the cachet from others that Phill assumed it would.

As I tread the Bowery cobblestone alley to my new workplace, I felt like the bumbling interloper from every 2000s film or TV show about fashion publications. *What would my colleagues think of me? Had I worn the right thing? Should I even be worrying about this kind of shit?* Before I made it on the elevator, I received a few snooty looks from thin, chic white women. It reminded me of how out of place I'd felt in my earliest transition days at UGA. *Why did I care about what these randoms thought?* I wanted to say, "I'm an editor now, bitches!" But I didn't feel like one, much less look like one. I assumed most of the people I was passing in the hallways came from families of wealthy Northeastern stock, with careers buoyed by connections and access. They had the right pedigree. While they were carving paths for upper-echelon editorial jobs right out of college, I was covering city council meetings and community fairs in Nowhere, Georgia. They belonged here; I didn't.

My nerves were on one hundred as I tipped past the building's sterile white walls. I might have been slightly more at ease if I had received detailed guidance on how my first day would go from Pride Media's human resources officer. But he'd become harder to reach after I'd accepted the offer. I'd sent back-to-back emails only to get an ounce of tea. The responses were worrying. In one chain I was told that official job descriptions and an employee handbook were unavailable. Without a late-night call to Phill, I wouldn't have known when or where to show up that morning.

* * *

"How's everybody doing?" I beamed as I looked around the table, praying my Southern accent wasn't off-putting.

Going around, folks introduced themselves and filled me in on who wasn't present yet. When *Adweek* writer Sara Jerde[1] dubbed our motley crew the "avengers of LGBTQ media," no lies were detected. We boasted folks from across the gender spectrum and varying racial and ethnic identities. Some people came from a more hardline reporting background while others proudly claimed a penchant for cultural criticism. Still yet, others knew the ins and outs of the art and fashion industries. I certainly wasn't in Oakland anymore.

Soon, Phill turned the corner toward our table, with a long wool coat and black boots, no doubt designer. He sauntered like royalty, gliding across the floor. I'm surprised we didn't hear the crack of the muscles loosening from the lower part of everyone's faces.

"Hello, Ms. Willis. How are you doing?" he said.

"I'm great. Glad to finally be here."

"I can only imagine. Have you found a place to live yet?"

"Not yet, but I have a few places lined up. I'll look at a few when I get off today."

"Good. Once you find an apartment, it'll all fall into place." He drifted around the table.

In our first full-staff production meeting, I soaked up the current issue's pages that were collected and taped to a wall for review. I was disappointed that our debut cover story for this supposed new era seemed so typical, focusing on two white Hollywood cover stars. Sure, one was nonbinary and the other was trans, but it felt like less of a dramatic shift than I expected. It hardly stood out from *Out*'s first issue cover in 1992, which featured a white cis gay man and a white cishet woman model, as revealed by photographer James White in an oral history years before.[2] But I shrank away from sincerely critiquing. Our team had already worked tirelessly and here my ass was coming in at the eleventh hour.

I also didn't want to be a traitor to the people I'd organized with for so long or to myself. *Would they hit me with the "This you?"* Of course, I knew I wouldn't only be working on stories about people of color, but I hadn't anticipated moments like these when I'd have to uphold the status quo. *How would I know we were doing more help than harm to those I most cared about?* I was driven by my memories of being that kid who yearned to subscribe to gay publications like *Out* as a teen. Even though most of the scanned editorials I saw online featured men who looked nothing like me, I was thirsty for any representation. *But who would I be if I had access to Black queer narratives or even knew they existed?*

A later conversation with Phill gave me a sense of relief. He assured me that the next issue would represent my true debut with the publication. We both had much to prove. Phill needed to succeed outside the Condé Nast industrial complex and increase *Out*'s dwindling digital presence and relevance. We both needed to make diversity and social justice salient and glossy to our audience. Plus, we all needed some kind of clout. The fashion and media industries thrived on it and it was crucial to maintaining our community relationships. That latter piece would become clearer in the next issue's production. We had lofty goals to feature celebrities and public figures, but many of them seemed uninterested in being involved with *Out*. While the likes of former president Barack Obama, Beyoncé, and Lady Gaga had graced our pages, many of our requests went unanswered. Perhaps the post–marriage equality era had rendered us a bit obsolete or passé because even openly queer folks would neglect us entirely only to be featured in some higher-echelon publication months later. It seemed very little had changed since the 2007 *Out* cover story in which culture writer Michael Musto launched "The Glass Closet" into the zeitgeist to describe celebrities who lived openly behind the scenes. Many cis celebrities, in particular, feared being too attached to their queerness in the media.

* * *

AS PROMISED, PHILL turned over the reins more on our second issue. In my edit test for the role, I'd concocted an idea of a "Revolution" issue featuring the "Marsha P. Johnsons and Sylvia Riveras of today." I'd imagined an all-trans elders of color activist cast. Luckily, Janet Mock joined on as a guest editor for the issue, inserting an intergenerational approach for what would be "The Mothers and Daughters of the Movement" issue. For the matriarchs, we centered Miss Major, quite possibly the most revered elder of the Black trans movement, and award-winning Black lesbian activist-scholar Barbara Smith, who had been an integral part of the Combahee River Collective and coined the term *identity politics*. On the daughters' side, we had Alicia Garza, who had recently spearheaded the Black Futures Lab, an initiative focused on building Black economic, political, and social power; Charlene Carruthers, the inaugural executive director of Black Youth Project 100, a membership organization for young Black people; and Tourmaline, a community organizer-turned-filmmaker whose work had focused on uncovering the historical narratives of trans women of color.

The icing on the plan was dropping it in March for Women's History Month and exclusively featuring women and nonbinary femme writers, photographers, and stylists. This would be the first issue in *Out*'s history to achieve that feat and legendary Black lesbian photographer Mickalene Thomas was tapped to shoot the cover. This creative alignment shook my spirits, and I was excited to work with Janet, who was now a director, producer, and writer on *Pose*, a landmark primetime television show for Black trans women's representation. The opportunity was far beyond anything I could have imagined when I first read the article that served as her launchpad back in college. This was why I was at *Out*.

*　*　*

IN A CRIMSON blazer, high-waisted denim, and knee-high black boots, I tried to signal some executive realness for my first cover shoot. I took in the lights, screens, and backdrops in the Manhattan studio. A gloriously locked Mickalene engineered a living collage with layered tapestries full of vibrant colors and textures around the shooting area. Her statuesque partner, Racquel Chevremont, darted in and out of crevices between the luxurious furniture, showcasing potential poses for shots. Neo-soul songs were playing in the background, but otherwise folks were simply in a detached work mode, and the shoot needed to be familial and warm. I committed to being a morale booster, saying "hi" to as many of the folks working on set as possible: hair and nail stylists, the makeup artist, and the photography crew. No one knew quite who I was at first, but once I dropped my executive editor title, they conferred a level of respect.

Stylist Nicole Chapoteau's Afrocentric aesthetic beautifully enhanced Mickalene's vision. From the intricately braided strands adorning Alicia and Charlene's crowns to the squash, cherry, and plum layered fringes on Tourmaline's skirt-turned-dress, it all felt so lush. Barbara stunned in a Lafayette 148 carmine suit with a royal blue top just underneath. I smirked, thinking about her comment earlier in the shoot, where she'd proudly revealed that she hadn't worn lip color in decades. A true OG anti-patriarchal lesbian feat! On the other hand, Miss Major served all the glam. Ombréd black-and-gray curls draped her face above a Zero + Maria Cornejo coral plissé poncho. Forget cover shoot; this was a sacred ceremony.

Each subject's shimmering passion was undeniable. Mama Major revealed that the constant threat of violence and the mysterious loss of friends pushed her into activism in 1960s New York. She'd experienced bouts of incarceration that later led her to become a staunch advocate for TGNC and intersex folks who had experienced the same. Barbara regaled with stories of a youth stained by Jim Crow but buoyed by the promise of the Civil Rights Era. She also delved into how she founded the Kitchen Table: Women of Color Press, a grassroots publisher of women of color that served as an antidote to mainstream erasure. Tourmaline had been influenced by parents entrenched in the Black Power and Labor movements, Alicia channeled the resilience of her single mother, and Charlene repurposed her experiences at a predominantly white institution and political studies in South Africa.

As they shared insights on ancestry, joy, liberation, and each other's work, my pride swelled. I had known most of them for a few years but very little about their stories. In this capacity, I felt like I knew more about their stories than I might ever have had a chance to within movement spaces. I thought, "Maybe I could do this editor thing and not lose my values." After that day on set, I knew no other shoot could hold a candle to this one. But I was willing to chase that challenge as long as I was at *Out*.

26

This Ain't No Chick Flick

There was no *Devil Wears Prada* transformation sequence to prepare me for my first New York Fashion Week (NYFW). I had to be nimble with a Rent the Runway subscription that moved my wardrobe only slightly beyond my pre-NYC aesthetic. While some colleagues regularly strolled into our workspace with designer apparel, I wondered how I would survive. I'd often bug our fashion team, hoping for morsels of advice. Early on, one staffer bluntly explained the impossibility of fitting into anything that came into the office because I wasn't the cherished "sample size." Those words stung for months. To the team's credit, a few times they loaned me some jewelry, a Moschino coat embroidered with golden Roman characters, and a head-turning canary yellow Issey Miyake plissé dress for select events.

Nevertheless, attending NYFW made me feel like I had officially entered a new stage of my career. Top magazines had designated seats for editors and top-of-the-masthead staff, but who knew where *Out* fell in all that? Sometimes pubs would only get one seat, for the editor-in-chief or whichever representative was sent in their stead. I learned that I'd mostly get to go to the shows that our editor-in-chief and fashion director didn't feel like attending, but I wasn't too picky. The first show I saw was for U.S. designer Rachel Comey. I was all alone, so I pretended to know the protocol as I sat near a Black woman with statement eyeglasses and a half-updo of natural blown-out hair. As I took her in, I decided to break the ice.

"Hi," I said nervously, over the empty seat between us.

"Hi," she said. Looking around, perhaps for someone she actually knew.

"I'm Raquel."

"I'm Wanda." She smirked.

"So, where do you work?"

"*Essence*."

"Awesome. How long have you been there?"

"About two years. And who are you with?" Wanda said, professionally sizing me up.

"I just started at *Out*."

"Oh, with Phill. I love him. That's one of my dear friends."

"Oh, great!"

God, this is going to get back to him. What kind of impression is this?

The silence spilled over into the space between us, and the conversation dissolved. It was better to leave things where they were than small-talk Wanda into oblivion. I beat myself up for the gaffe of not knowing her, while I focused on the designs and the models coming down the cramped aisles. It was moving to be in this space. I loved the diversity of the models, including an older woman who stole the show with gorgeous, gray-streaked curls.

Not long after, a photographer snapped me for a *Teen Vogue* street-style roundup. I beamed as they told me they liked my rosy monochromatic outfit, complete with a tulle dress and a faux-fur patchwork coat. However, the next day I learned that the image was included in an article titled "The Best #FatAtFashionWeek

Style from NYFW." I appreciated that fat women were being covered in the publication, but that hadn't ever been a descriptor I'd used for myself. Just months after feeling chided for not being "sample size," I felt in over my head at Fashion Week. It was jarring to be seen so differently than I saw myself. I lamented having my agency stripped away by that reporter, but I also realized that I needed to interrogate how fatphobia played a role in my initial umbrage and proliferated in this industry. While I had silenced many insecurities throughout my transition, in this space I picked up new ones around my body and what I perceived to be a lack of style.

Later, at a show for 11 Honoré, a brand known for its inclusive sizing, I found a markedly warmer, more inviting atmosphere. The models of varying experiences, shapes, and sizes were captivating. Then, in a grand finale, Robyn's ethereal masterpiece, "Honey," permeated the atmosphere, and Laverne Cox glided down the runway with a majestic twirl in a flowing burgundy dress. The fabric whipped like hummingbird wings behind her. As she made her way back through the runway's center, confetti was released into the air like a dream sequence. Afterward, I went backstage to see Laverne with Ceval Omar, a young Somali-Norwegian trans curve model. It was a reminder that even in the unlikeliest places, our girls were there, leaving their mark. But even though we were there and I was the first or only openly Black trans woman editor in many of those spaces, what did it all mean? *How would I work through the powerlessness I felt in this space?*

* * *

As THE GLITZY veneer of fashion and media stirred uncertainty in me, the *Out* staff received an influx of questions about why contributors and freelancers from before our arrival at the publication hadn't been paid. Something didn't seem quite right with our parent company, Pride Media, and Oreva Capital, the private equity firm that owned it. Our associate managing editor alerted me that Pride Media hadn't been responding. And through conversations and articles, our team pieced together the problematic start to our editorial era.

In October 2018, days before I signed my official offer letter, *Women's Wear Daily* (WWD) reported on *Out*'s "editorial legacy"[1] of problems with compensation. Long before our team was in the picture, Oreva inherited and maintained an agreement that outsourced production and payment responsibilities to Grand Editorial, a company owned by *Out*'s previous editor-in-chief Aaron Hicklin. Then, Hicklin sold the company to the Evanly Schindler–owned McCarthy Media. This process was followed by Hicklin's departure and the termination of the relationship with McCarthy effectively dismissing an editorial staff that, toward the end of their run, had received no benefits, no full-employment status, and regularly late compensation. But it left contributor payments in limbo, too. Apparently, the stepbrothers who owned and operated Oreva, Adam Levin and Israel Maxx Abramowitz, also had a track record of donating to anti-LGBTQ+ politicians.

Our team was more alarmed when more than forty unpaid contributors, under the banner of #OUTOwes, published an open letter.[2] In it, the collective demanded open communication, a commitment to payment, cessation of any planned harassment or retaliation, and a public apology. They also started a social media campaign to draw awareness and stoke public pressure. It was their right, and our team completely understood the righteousness of their ire. Unfortunately, through our own sleuthing, we also discovered that the previous staff members were ousted only days after learning about Phill's appointment from an article. This only made tensions worse between all of us.

As we attempted to make sense of all this confusion, Phill tried to facilitate more transparency from our CEO, Nathan Coyle. He had been tapped by Oreva to revamp and steady *Out*'s ship. After a few canceled meetings, Nathan finally met with us, and we grilled him with questions. He claimed that McCarthy Media was responsible for our woes. But, to remedy the situation, we would need to accept sliced production budgets and across-the-board pay cuts. As we took in the gravity of the situation, Coyle and the Oreva executives assured us that a cash influx was imminent, said they'd be more responsive, and tried to woo us with future stock options once the company went public. With a sense of dread and skepticism about Coyle, our staff tried to trust the process and focused on maintaining the quality of our publication.

Weeks later, we heard that a payment plan had been implemented with the National Writers Union for past contributors. Meanwhile, our staff's paychecks were delayed without notice and Coyle bowed out of his position after less than a year at the company. The news hit the *New York Post* at midnight before we were informed. Our HR contact at Pride Media blamed the paycheck issues on a new payroll system, but our trust was severely damaged. It seemed like we were all on somebody's borrowed time. Despite promises from our chief revenue officer, who was named interim CEO, that he could rectify things, I wondered about my professional fate. *How could our staff be the future of queer media if we didn't even know our own futures?*

27

Our Ancestors' Wildest Nightmare

"That's mah baby" resounded in Times Square, buoyed by Momma's saccharine drawl. That June marked her first visit since I'd moved to New York, and I couldn't have been more thrilled for her to step into my new world. Her delight kissed my ears as we gawked at an electronic billboard just atop the Express store. Every few minutes video clips featuring other *Out* staffers and me flashed above us for the brand's Pride campaign. Our company's sales team had lined up the opportunity, coinciding with the fiftieth anniversary of the Stonewall riots, and I didn't know what to think as the walls continued to crumble around the *Out* staff.

We'd been assured that Pride Media's trajectory would straighten out but still hadn't received a capital infusion to handle our production costs. With each passing deadline, our work became more precarious. The press mentioned a potential sale of Pride Media to another company, a return to an all-freelance staff, and swirling speculation about a Chapter 11 bankruptcy filing. Meanwhile, staff morale hit an all-time low. People were griping at one another, flattened by the continued breakneck speed of production. Phill seemed physically elusive as ever, perhaps protesting against our perceived mismanagement by refusing to experience in person our fluctuating office situation due to rent costs. After a colleague was laid off, Phill supported others in placements at new jobs. He assured me I didn't need to worry about where I'd land just yet. But that only settled me so much.

If our Pride issue ended up being our last, it would be a glorious conclusion. Our staff collaborated on a "Then, Now, Next" theme, represented by activist icon Sylvia Rivera, Michaela Jaé Rodriguez of *Pose* fame, and Pete Buttigieg's landmark presidential campaign. My cover story chronicled Rivera's radical lifelong commitment to community organizing and how it influenced present-day trans-led social justice efforts. As a fierce trans-Latina who emerged from the Stonewall era, Rivera and her friend Marsha P. Johnson harnessed the early potential for organizing trans and gender-nonconforming folks, sex workers, and incarcerated and houseless people, and queer youth after initially working with the Gay Liberation Front.

Accompanied by Bambi L'Amour, Bubbles Rose Marie, and Andorra Marks, they founded Street Transvestite Action Revolutionaries (STAR). This activist organization unwittingly birthed a proto-intersectional politic and praxis for collective liberation. In the STAR manifesto,[1] the group demanded an end to intracommunal, medical, and state domination, exploitation, and violence. It also called for legal gender self-attestation, self-determination, and free clothing, education, food, healthcare, housing, and transportation for oppressed groups. The collective's most enduring work came from STAR House,[2] a shelter and gathering space for trans sex workers and "street" youth. Eventually, it established chapters in other cities. However, Rivera became disillusioned by the continued sidelining of trans folks in just a few years, and the original STAR House dissolved.

Tourmaline unearthed a video of Rivera at the 1973 Christopher Street Liberation Day Rally.[3] In it, Rivera critiques the early LGBTQ+ movement for sidelining trans people and others on the margins in favor of assimilation.

Y'all better quiet down. I've been trying to get up here all day for your gay brothers and your gay sisters in jail that write me every motherfucking week and ask for your help, and you all don't do a goddamn thing for them.

Have you ever been beaten up and raped and jailed? Now think about it. They've been beaten up and raped after they've had to spend much of their money in jail to get their silicone and try to get their "sex changes." The women have tried to fight for their sex changes or to become women of the women's liberation, and they write "STAR," not the women's group, they do not write "women," they do not write "men," they write "STAR" because we're trying to do something for them.

I have been to jail. I have been raped and beaten. Many times! By men, heterosexual men that do not belong in the homosexual shelter. But do you do anything for them? No. Y'all tell me to go and hide my tail between my legs. I will not put up with this shit. I have been beaten. I have had my nose broken. I have been thrown in jail. I have lost my job. I have lost my apartment for gay liberation, and you all treat me this way? What the fuck's wrong with you all? Think about that!

I do not believe in a revolution, but you all do. I believe in the gay power. I believe in us getting our rights, or else I would not be out there fighting for our rights. That's all I wanted to say to you people. If you all want to know about the people that are in jail and do not forget Bambi L'Amour, Andorra Marks, Kenny Metzner, and other gay people in jail, come and see the people at STAR House on Twelfth Street on 640 East Twelfth Street between B and C, apartment 14.

The people are trying to do something for all of us, and not men and women that belong to a white middle-class white club. And that's what you all belong to!

REVOLUTION NOW! Gimme a G! Gimme an A! Gimme a Y! Gimme a P! Gimme an O! Gimme a W! Gimme an E! Gimme an R! Gay power! Louder! GAY POWER!

* * *

INSTEAD OF CONSIDERING Rivera's critiques, many white cis gay men and lesbians continued to steer the movement toward joining oppressive structures rather than eliminating them. In the latter group, a contingent of radical feminists, precursors to modern-day trans-exclusionary radical feminists (TERFs), became some of the staunchest detractors of trans folks. Just before Rivera spoke, Jean O'Leary, founder of Lesbian Feminist Liberation, denounced drag queens' and trans peoples' place in the movement, purposely misgendering Rivera in the process. Two decades later, she would recant her treatment of "transvestites," stating that her opinions on the matter had shifted. Nevertheless, as the larger gay and lesbian movement became more mainstream in the eighties and nineties, trans and gender-nonconforming organizers were relegated to the back burner. They struggled. Rivera, for her part, dealt with chemical dependence and moved away from NYC for years. Johnson, who lived with mental illness, carried on, later becoming involved in HIV/AIDS activism.

After Johnson's mysterious death in 1992, Rivera returned to public activism with more erudite insights on the sprawling national LGBTQ+ nonprofit industrial complex, commonly referred to as Gay, Inc. She made her most potent indictment of the system when a young Black trans woman named Amanda Milan was murdered in June 2000. At this time, organizations like the Human Rights Campaign (HRC) had recently rallied around a national push for federal hate crimes legislation in the aftermath of the murder of Matthew Shepard. However, Milan received less than a fraction of attention. Rivera's theory of change foreshadowed today's assimilationist, ultracapitalist, and neoliberal LGBTQ+ movement. Yet despite all of Rivera's legendary and prescient stomping, none of us listened well enough. *What did it mean that I was smiling and dancing in an advertisement for a Pride Month that eschewed this history? What did it mean that I was working at a publication seemingly for our community, but had so thoroughly exploited it under cis straight owners?*

It was thrilling that my likeness was running in advertisements and physical stores across the country, but, most of all, I was validated by Momma's joy at seeing me "make it." I'd long felt I had to prove to my family and the world that my queerness and transness weren't liabilities. Aunties, uncles, cousins, and former classmates took snapshots of the campaign, expressing astonishment at my ascent as if I'd finally proved that I could have a successful, full life. But I wanted to tell them this wasn't more important than the often-unseen work that I and other organizers were doing in communities.

As I meditated on Sylvia's fight, I wondered what she would think of this time. I hoped there was some redeeming factor in trans people being seen in lofty places. After all, visibility seemed to render desirable lives that had once been discarded. But ultimately, these campaigns seemed to represent the chokehold that capitalism had on all of us. *Was there a way to ensure they actually changed the material conditions of marginalized people?* If I'd had my way, we would have been able to ensure that the proceeds went to grassroots causes instead of the short-list of sprawling LGBTQ+ organizations that rake in the lion's share of funding each year. I hoped, from then on, I could figure out how to leverage access and my presence with more control and intentionality.

* * *

DESPITE *OUT*'S TROUBLING forecast, Pride Media executives pushed forward with a "Legacy" celebration at the top of the Standard Hotel regardless. I arrived early, putting on a good face, dressed in a gold satin slip dress. The bronze rays of the setting sun shone as our team chatted with our amiable guests. By this point, it was public knowledge that Pride Media and *Out* were in hard times. But Phill called in favors from several guests, including floral sculptor Lutfi Janania, who masterfully assembled gorgeous arrangements on each table just before guests arrived. Still, the knowledge that our company hadn't yet paid many contributors, had reduced compensation for salaried employees, and seemed to have no idea whether we would even get the next issue out gnawed at my spirit. This event was a facade that everything was OK, that we were flourishing.

As our guests awaited dinner, Phill supplied us with an address akin to a benediction. He highlighted illustrious guests like renowned editorial executive Emil Wilbekin, model Leyna Bloom, *Advocate* editor Zach Stafford, and our special guest and previous *Out* cover star Lil' Kim. Then, Phill summoned me to stand. With clasped hands, I put on a pageant girl smile. I hadn't fully shaken the imposter syndrome that had occupied my mind since I'd moved to New York, but Phill's words of affirmation renewed a spark. He praised the work our staff was doing, despite the odds, to deliver a publication that spoke to our history. He deftly chipped away at any doubt that what we were enduring was in vain. As the night wore on and we partied, I surrendered to not knowing what the next chapter would hold for *Out*, our community, and our movement.

28

Letter to Layleen Polanco

Dear Layleen,

I learned your story before I knew your name. It was through an ominous text from Eliel Cruz, alerting me that a twenty-seven-year-old Afro-Latina trans sister had been reported dead at Rikers Island's Rose M. Singer Center. It wasn't uncommon for us to discuss such a tragedy. Eliel was the communications director for the New York City Anti-Violence Project (AVP), and we shared a history of community organizing. When he told me, a familiar feeling of depletion washed over me as I absorbed your demise. But I could tell that Eliel had a kernel of hope about getting you justice. What stood out to us was that you died in state custody, not at the hands of a romantic or sexual partner. It was one of those rare instances where it felt like there was a clear system to hold accountable.

* * *

A *VICE* REPORT[1] revealed that you'd been arrested in a New York Police Department (NYPD) sting operation, in which undercover police officers solicited you for sexual acts in exchange for money. After allegedly consenting, you were also found to be in possession of a controlled substance. If you hadn't been targeted and sex work wasn't criminalized, this momentum toward your death could've been halted. Unfortunately, your case was directed to the Human Trafficking Intervention[2] portion of New York City's Midtown Community Court, which claims "to promote a just and compassionate resolution to [sex trafficking] cases—treating defendants as victims who are often in need of critical services." However, due to three missed court dates and a 2018 arrest, you received a round of bench warrants, granting police the power to arrest you for violating court rules. On April 16, you were arrested again on misdemeanor charges related to an alleged assault of a cab driver after refusing to pay a fare in Midtown. Three days later, those charges were dropped, but you were held for failure to pay a $500 bail due to the prior bench warrants issued against you. That was the price the system had placed on your life.

Before most of this information came to light, Eliel sprang into action, contacting your family and working with an emerging collective of leaders who were just as outraged about your death. Within days a micromovement, hundreds deep, coalesced for a rally at Foley Square in Lower Manhattan. A few celebrities stopped by including actors and crew from *Pose*. I exchanged brief moments of comfort with Janet Mock and Indya Moore. The latter gave a stirring speech on the mic, sharing how you were a possibility model and demanding an end to the neglect that led to your death. Some organizers, including the legendary Cecilia Gentili, asked me to speak. Somehow, on the spot, I broke through my spirit's fatigue. Eschewing elegance and eloquence, I said:

I think at this moment, I can't be sad anymore. I'm saddened in an instant, and then I'm quickly fucking angry. I'm angry

*like the folks were angry at the night of the Stonewall riots—
that first night and the nights after. I'm angry like them. I ain't
gonna tell nobody to riot, but we got a lot to be mad about,
don't we? Fuck the respectability and the assimilation and the
ways that everybody wants to tell us to be like the straight folks
and tell us to be like the cis folks and tell us to be like the white
folks and tell us to be like the able-bodied folks, tell us to be
like everyone else who moves a certain way in the world. Fuck
that. We are who we are, we deserve to be here, and we are the
future literally.*

* * *

THE MOROSE ATMOSPHERE of the rally was no match for the
energy of your loved ones. Your House of Xtravaganza mother,
Gisele Alicea, and sister, Melania Brown, spoke candidly about
their anger but also their determination to do whatever is
necessary to find out the truth about what happened to you. I
admired your sister's strength and how her thick accent, drip-
ping of Bronx swagger, galvanized us. Like you, she was rare.
Instead of wallowing in despair, your demise ignited her. So
many trans people can't count on their biological family to
show up, but yours was on a crusade. Your story tragically collapsed many larger structures that fail Black trans people. You
had been incarcerated, a sex worker, and lived with mental illness. So much was stacked against you. I saw you as my sister.
I wanted to share your story with the world, so people could
know your humanity and that you were loved.

* * *

IN LATE OCTOBER 2019, when the sun's blessings came in spurts,
Out's photo editor Nic Bloise, photographer Elliott Jerome
Brown Jr., and I visited your mother, Aracelis Polanco, at her

Bronx apartment. Eliel helped me gauge your family's willingness to be interviewed and photographed for the annual *Out*100 issue. Naturally, I worried about being that interloping stranger, extracting tragedy from your loved ones. After all, it'd still only been a few months since your death. Luckily, Melania was determined to do whatever possible to get your story out. So she took the lead in choreographing the delicate dance between our magazine crew and your family. When I confirmed the visit a few days prior, she revealed that our planned date would fall on what would have been your twenty-eighth birthday.

A gold crown over one of your mom's teeth sparkled as she welcomed us. I'm sure you can imagine, but she was ready for a close-up. Her seamless beat and freshly straightened hair reminded me of the result of my own mother's beauty rituals growing up. As we entered, we also said our hellos to your niece Aliyah, community mother Ashley Chico, and family friend Amanda Collazo. Somehow, they'd all managed to keep going.

While Elliott scouted for the best shots, I gingerly walked to the olive-green kitchen to stay out of the way. My eyes swam over a stack of china dishes covering a table's surface like a crescent moon. "This used to be Layleen's favorite seat—right here in front of the window. She would sit there for hours and just look out," your mom said placidly. I appreciated that she broke the ice, lessening my stress about the official interview. Then, she gazed out the window, overlooking a mostly unobscured view of the upper Hudson River. I couldn't help but think of that body of water's significance: how it served as the setting for the death of Marsha P. Johnson and the scene in *Paris Is Burning* just before the audience learns of Venus Xtravaganza's demise. I wished death wasn't so common for girls like us.

Soon, Melania burst through the door, carrying the hectic

energy of having to drop her children off at school just before our visit. Exasperated, she welcomed us and plopped a few bags of warm Dunkin' Donuts on the kitchen counter. "I brought some snacks. Help yaself," she said, taking off her cross-body bag. Melania reminded me of my sister, Jessica, ever the coordinator for the right cause.

There was no putting on emotion as Elliott snapped shots of your family. Since there were images of you on various walls, it almost didn't feel like you were absent. We fumbled with pillows to situate them just right on the couch as your mom sank into place for what became the cover shot. Then, a few minutes later, she jumped up with energy. None of us knew where she was headed. I thought she'd grown too distraught and needed a second to collect herself.

After disappearing to another room for a few minutes, she re-emerged with a large, bulging suitcase. In the middle of the floor in a nearby bedroom, she gingerly unzipped it. As Melania lifted the lid, she looked at her mom in disbelief. "Wait . . . you kept all of this?" Your mother just beamed and nodded. Standing back, she watched as the younger women tore through the items of the suitcase, scrambling for remnants of their loved one. There was a small bottle of hairspray, a used electric toothbrush, a travel-sized Secret deodorant stick, and a batch of blankets—and, of course, there were so many clothes. At one point, Amanda held up a slate-colored T-shirt that read I'M GRRREAT to her nose, taking in the lasting particles of your scent. You were the only theme that connected these disparate, mundane things that death had transformed into mementos.

As the tender scene played out, I zeroed in on a small, round wooden table that had been fashioned into an altar for you. Your face was magnified on a poster that served as a backdrop for the space of reverence. I'd seen that picture of you before, but now, with the women who raised you, I saw more beauty in your angelic face, glorious dark locks, and determined grin. Above your head is a quote from Assata Shakur's autobiography:

You died.
I cried.
And kept on getting up.
A little slower.
And a lot more deadly.

I resisted tearing up lest I turn myself into the subject of your family's moment. Instead, I scanned the other objects on the altar: the golden urn (topped with an iridescent-colored unicorn figurine) that held the last atoms of your physical presence, two prideful rainbow mugs, one full of tepid coffee and creamer, a saucer with a quarter of a breakfast sandwich on it as an offering, the just-won award from AVP, and the pièce de résistance—a long, white candle with a solid and steady flame.

* * *

YOUR STORY BECAME the investigative centerpiece of the Trans Obituaries Project,[3] my attempt to resurface the humanity of my trans sisters of color. When our magazine staff began planning *Out*100, our most important issue of the year, highlighting the most influential LGBTQ+ folks in culture, industry, and society, I knew it was the perfect opportunity to elevate sisters like you and the organizers who are fighting to build a safer world for us. For so long, when I'd learn about another one of my sisters or siblings being murdered, the news article was accompanied by sensationalized headlines, with deadnaming or misgendering, and, even worse, readers justifying the deaths in the comments section. But I wasn't convinced my idea would be supported. I didn't know where it fit as colleagues rattled off celebrities as cover subjects. All I knew is that when I thought of our culture, I thought of the specters that linger over it, the trans women of color throughout time who rarely get a proper homegoing. I thought of how my sisters and siblings become martyrs and how that characterization strips away a level of your humanity. So often, the names trickle into a deluge as Trans Day of Remembrance approaches, and all that beauty, glory, and nuance is subsumed by tragedy. That couldn't happen again.

One day on a call about the ongoing financial dilemmas of Pride Media, Phill supportively pushed me to speak my mind. It sounded too ambitious of a project, but he urged me to follow my passion. So it was settled. Your tale would serve as the cover story, but it wouldn't be alone. I also concocted the idea to craft the humane obituaries that you and the other twenty-one sisters we'd lost that year deserved. It wasn't an easy endeavor. I spent months tracking down friends, family, and community members for each victim while keeping tabs on emergent cases. Sometimes their names were included in other articles. More often I had to dig on social media or the White Pages. One thing that drew everyone together was their willingness to remember the good times, the things that made my sisters tick. My organizing history informed so much of the process. It took everything in me not to get lost in melancholy because plenty of these interviews left me bawling and nervously pacing my apartment. But, over time, I found a deeper resolve. This was a way I could know them too.

One sister, Lorrissa Ashanti Carmon, was once houseless and had been a sex worker on Baltimore, Maryland's streets since her teen years. She fell in love with an endlessly supportive man and made plans to become an airline attendant. Just a month before her shooting, she'd even accepted a marriage proposal from her long-term boyfriend. I got the chance to interview him, hearing his deep love for her through the bouts of tears. Finally, he told me the grief had become too much and that he had to move away to start a new life. I wanted to console him, but I knew no words could fill the void in his heart. My heart broke as he recounted the story of their meeting and the joy of waking up beside her after finally finding the right apartment. After all, she was a girl who had found love only for someone to whisk her away from her dreams. Her fiancé revealed she had been a friend of Zoe Spears, a Black trans woman who was also on the list of sisters murdered that year. As I retraced these lives repeatedly, I encountered invisible villains, the systems that had caused or exacerbated your deaths.

Through my conversations, patterns emerged on how we could end the epidemic of violence. The result was a thirteen-point framework that combated many systems that constantly fail us, and I enlisted experts and organizers with a track record of showing up for our community to help flesh it out. Elders like Ceyenne Doroshow, Cecilia Gentili, and Monica Roberts imparted wisdom on everything from decriminalizing sex work to media literacy and accountability. My peers Eliel, Kayla Gore, Jennicet Gutiérrez, and Toni-Michelle Williams elevated the importance of investing in trans women of color leadership, reallocating resources to keeping our sisters safe, and decarceration efforts that include asylum seekers and migrants like twenty-five-year-old Johana Medina León from El Salvador who died in ICE custody just days before you. Last, with the help of contributor Serena Sonoma, we discussed honoring the history and legacy of our ancestors. For us, the Tenderloin, the world's first transgender cultural district in San Francisco, founded by Janetta Johnson, Honey Mahogany, and Aria Sa'id, modeled that beautifully.

Pride Media hosted a release party to celebrate the launch of *Out*100. We drew as many of the honorees as possible, including the organizers who fueled the Trans Obituaries Project. I had a chance to kiki with them, wishing you were there as well. It was an honor to be seen, to do right by our community. A life-sized version of each cover, including the one featuring your mother looking up at an image of you, had its own station with a spotlight. Melania fiercely vowed to take the cover home because she loved it so much.

As I looked around the room, I thought how, when I started the process, I worried if others would understand what I meant when I rallied around your influence. But perhaps no story had been as transformative for me as yours. It galvanized many of us in the fight to have Rikers Island shut down for its human rights violations. The battle for sex work decriminalization in New York ramped up. We considered mental health and how solitary confinement exacerbated conditions. Your story made it to the national stage, buoyed by politicians like NYC mayor Bill de Blasio, Representative Alexandria Ocasio-Cortez, and then Democratic presidential hopeful Senator Elizabeth Warren.[4] And there was some justice. Your family received $5.9 million from a lawsuit against the City of New York, the highest settlement concerning death in jail, according to David Shanies, the lawyer who represented your family. Four Rikers employees were suspended without pay, but the rest of the seventeen, including the captain initially named for accountability, seemingly received no repercussions.

Though shifts seem to be happening, the murders within our community haven't let up since your death. Trust that there are folks continuously fighting to ensure that what happened to you doesn't happen again. I know words in a glossy magazine can't bring you back or serve as an ultimate balm for the people wounded by your death. Still, I hope you accept it as an offering and a catalyst to change things for future generations.

In liberation,
Raquel

29

Falling Pillars

Riding off the high of completing the Trans Obituaries Project, I felt energized to fight for an extension of our *Out* era. Unfortunately, Phill had relayed some sobering news as I made my way to a Williamsburg studio in December. He'd been disillusioned for weeks, warning that his days at the publication were numbered. The few executives in our Times Square office (which our team had recently relocated to) carried a similar jumping-the-ship vibe. Most conversations with them were full of toothless assurances that we'd all be able to continue producing the magazine, just with half the number of issues per year than before and even smaller budgets. Thankfully, this conversation with Phill wasn't his goodbye, just more intel on the drama behind the scenes. Our owner kept claiming that another cash infusion was imminent, but neither Phill nor the other executives were confident he could pull it off. While I updated him on the current issue, I couldn't help but wonder why I was even here if everything could go up in smoke at any moment. Then, when I saw our cover subjects, Laverne Cox and Chella Man, I remembered. Just as was true a year ago, with my first *Out* shoot, I had an obligation to my community.

The studio, awash in natural light, was mellow. Our team had enlisted Camila Falquez to photograph this cover. I'd been taken by a quick study of her work before the shoot. It had a unique flair, pulling classical European composition with ebullient colors and textures influenced by Latin America. There was something simultaneously organic and intentional about her approach. On set, she engineered mini-stations full of random props. At one point, Chella, serving nineties-Leonardo-DiCaprio levels of heartthrob, allowed Camila to position a wooden horse on his head. It seemed ridiculous at first, but as Chella smoldered at the camera, the photograph transformed into something grander. Here shined Camila's innate sense of the avant-garde.

In between fittings, our fashion director and I murmured about our fates. And it was here that couture gave us something else to focus on, like the lavender-and-canary floral organza dress that whipped around Laverne's svelte frame or Chella's army-green gender-subversive satin Miu Miu two-piece. The beauty of the moment wasn't a given, though. For whatever reason, there were disagreements on some of the shoot's particulars. The slight tension, with the background of our editorial era's demise, gnawed on my spirit. But I leaned into an opportunity to mediate the opposing views being espoused and helped the shoot's crew move forward. Perhaps I most liked that aspect of my time at *Out*. Those moments when I could be a bridge and support the blending of varying visions. Afterward, I contemplated what I might do with a bittersweet offer to become editor-in-chief.

* * *

NEARLY A WEEK later, Phill called me again, sharing that he'd be out of the top position the following day. He also revealed that his dismissal wouldn't be enough to stop the company's hemorrhaging. Zach Stafford, *The Advocate*'s editor-in-chief, would also leave with a collection of staffers and executives, including our CEO of several months. I panicked a bit, as I didn't expect such a mass exodus. Nevertheless, our era was effectively ending the way it started, probably with some other clean-up folks in waiting. Phill assured me I wouldn't have to make any moves too soon because our team, or what was left of it, still had to finish production on the Culture issue. I was aggravated, but prepared. As soon as things started souring earlier in the year, I began saving as much money as possible to survive once the company's remaining executives pulled the rug out from under me. For now, I'd have to figure out how to lead the publication alone with minimal staff for an indeterminate amount of time.

In a turn of luck, the week after Phill departed, I was scheduled for a press trip to Cape Town, South Africa, sponsored by an airline and a luxury hotel chain. I couldn't pass up my first opportunity to travel to the continent. And I adopted the refrain: "I can't go to the Motherland without Momma." So, I finessed a ticket for her as my plus-one, squeezing out the last drop of perks from this role.

In tourist fashion, our first few days were spent traversing Cape Town with a gaggle of influencers taking in the penguins on Boulders Beach, wine tasting, and bus tours around the perimeter of the city. My favorite part came later in the trip when our group visited Khayelitsha, a vast township in the Western Cape. Our tour led by Malawian-Zimbabwean tour operator Juma Mkwela introduced us to the Black, mostly Xhosa-speaking residents. With the harsh sandy air whipping my face, I observed the sprawl of corrugated-iron shacks while our group planted crops in community gardens and painted murals with youth from the area. In between the joy, I was conflicted and remorsefully soaked up how white supremacy and capitalism had impacted yet another corner of the world. I felt guilty that my biggest concern was that my job was on the chopping block back home. *What immense privilege I had to journey to this region, mostly free of charge. Who had I become and who would I be once my editorial role disappeared?*

Toward the end of the trip, over a spotty cell connection, I exchanged concerns with the remaining *Out* staff. We were righteously fed up with the unreasonable deadlines and the broken promises from the executives. I kept it as real and transparent with them as possible, urging them to fulfill their current commitments and kick their job searches into overdrive. But I wondered what the C-suite and executives at Pride Media would do with me. *If Phill Picardi was expendable, then what was I? Would they try to keep me on as a figurehead of diversity? Would they swap some random person (probably another cis white guy) into Phill's role and keep me as second-in-command?*

* * *

WEEKS LATER, AS our team finished up production on the Culture issue, I received a call from our new CEO. She'd worked at the company and, particularly, *The Advocate* for years. She championed a working dynamic similar to how *Out* operated before our era. Undoubtedly under her reign, all budgets would be sliced even more, meaning fewer contributors and possibly little original photography. It felt like we were being asked to produce a much lower quality of work than what we'd created under Phill's tenure. I was unnerved at the thought of editorial decline, but I gave her time to make a case.

She got to the heart of the conversation, asking if I intended to stay at the publication. I said it depended on whether I would assume the editor-in-chief title, my salary would be commensurate with the increased role, and I'd have the necessary resources and support. She didn't have any immediate answers, which gave me a twinkle of hope. Days later, she assured me I could have whichever title I wanted, but that I'd have to take a 50 percent pay cut. Not to mention I'd have to continue operating with limited staff. I wasn't entirely surprised, and I knew there was no negotiating. Still, a numb disappointment gnawed at my heart. But my fate was sealed, and I planned my departure. For the first time since the start of my career, I'd be jumping into unemployed waters. A parting salvo validating my role was the Trans Obituaries Project receiving a GLAAD Media Award nomination. It made me proud that even though my experience at the publication had been full of doubt and fear, I could stick to my values. Our team put queer and trans folks from the margins front and center, as much as possible.

30

Revolution's Knockin'

U ncertainty defined my life before the COVID-19 pandemic struck. My dream job had shriveled up, and I had no real employment leads. But now, on my final day before the city and the world shut down, a new fear was awakened. It didn't take long before I regretted leaving my apartment and taking the subway. *Something really is off.* I remembered snippets of warnings in the news. As I held on to one of the hanging straps, trying not to be slammed into the door by the vehicle's force, a feeling of what-if took over me. *What if I wasn't one of the lucky ones who could endure this sickness?* Soon, I imagined contracting the novel coronavirus and losing control of my body—one it'd taken most of my life to reclaim. *I'd better get through this last day and stay my ass at home.*

The New York life that I'd always dreamed of puttered to a stop. Weeks of isolation thickened into months. I took on small freelance writing gigs and seriously considered making sense of my life so far in the form of a memoir. Like everyone else, I adjusted, venturing out only for eerily silent neighborhood walks with a new pandemic friend or for quick, mundane errands. I came to appreciate the silence and solitude. After a year of hustle, bustle, and precariousness, this felt like tranquility—until it didn't.

* * *

HELICOPTERS HOVERED IN the ether, sirens tried their damnedest to slice through the crowd's chants, and police cruisers slammed through metal blockades trying to intimidate us or worse. I felt small, but not insignificant, surrounded by other people who could hardly contain their outrage. Never had the New York streets felt so vicious nor so vulnerable than in the days right after the police killing of George Floyd. I hated that the brutality felt so ordinary—an agent of the State ruthlessly killed a Black man. Bystanders, who felt restricted from doing what was right out of the fear of losing their own lives, watched and screamed in protest. It made me think of what must have happened during enslavement, in which captive people simply stared at the whipping of someone they knew. Afraid of their own fates. This is what systems do; drive us apart and desiccate our senses. Derek Chauvin's knee crushing Floyd's neck collapsed centuries of violence and the unwieldy might of a white supremacist government into nine minutes and twenty-nine seconds. The tragedy snatched us all together. As thoughts flooded social media, I witnessed a connection that I only ever witnessed during popular television shows or sports games. I watched shortened clips of the video after it initially circulated online, but it took weeks to return and finish it. Even then, I skipped past the exact seconds of Floyd's life being snuffed out. I didn't need the visual evidence to integrate another Black death into my mind.

After public outrage ensued, New York and many other U.S. cities reanimated after the dormancy of COVID-19. Many an activist and organizer were born, and they joined seasoned ones in demanding change. It wasn't just about Floyd. Just weeks before, Ahmaud Arbery, a twenty-five-year-old Black man, was killed in my home state after being chased down by three white men. It seemed like after years of Black activists and organizers trying to shine a light on police brutality, the world had finally taken notice.

Initially, I felt hopeless and hollow. I was exhausted by the prospect of going out into the streets again, especially considering the silence about the recent murders of Black trans women like Monika Diamond and Nina Pop, which upset me. *How could people still have the energy to kill us during a global pandemic?* And I wasn't the only one questioning this. Many Black trans organizers I knew felt like showing up for yet another Black cishet man was pointless, that we'd never receive reciprocal concern. Our micro-movement had been showing up for years only to be ignored by our larger communities. *Why show up for the cishet folks when they never show up for us? Nothing will change, and if it does, it won't include Black trans people. I'm already just trying to survive.* I agreed to an extent and I was drained.

Then, two days after Floyd's murder, a police officer in Tallahassee, Florida, killed a Black trans man named Tony McDade. A *Mother Jones* article described the altercation and the events that led up to it as "murky."[1] The highlights revealed that McDade was suspected of fatally stabbing someone, accused by the police as being armed with a gun, killed without attempting de-escalation, and misgendered in initial reports. Days later, further information alleged that the incident occurred after McDade pistol-whipped Jennifer Jackson, a woman with whom he'd had an intimate relationship. He'd been brutally attacked by men in her family, including her son, who Tony ultimately fatally stabbed. Witnesses contradicted each other in saying whether Tony was asked to stop moving by police officers but agreed that they shot him even after he stopped moving and called him a "nigger." The case was undeniably complex, but more could have been done to ensure that another death hadn't occurred. There should be accountability after violence, but when white people commit lethal acts—like Dylann Roof in Charleston or Payton Gendron in Buffalo—they don't meet the fate that Tony did.

Online, McDade's demise engulfed the Black trans community as an example of how our experiences with State violence are obscured. Concurrently, the Louisville, Kentucky, police killing of Breonna Taylor in March 2020 resurfaced. Those instances mingled together as evidence of the erasure of Black women and LGBTQ+ folks from the national discourse. Unfortunately, I expected McDade and Taylor to be ignored. The scar tissue from years of screaming into the void with my peers had left me jaded. There was no glory in being a victim, but far less in harm being swept under the rug.

Days later, I ventured out with friends who lived near Brooklyn's Prospect Park, despite waffling on whether I should. The swirling helicopters seemed like an omen, a promise of violence. We heard the helicopters before we met the behemoth of a crowd taking over the streets. It was disconcerting but seeing other people with signs in hand reminded us of our righteous cause. We joined them in chanting, "No justice, no peace. Fuck these racist-ass police," and made our way toward Manhattan. Despite our fury and sadness, I felt a renewed energy and hope—not what I'd felt during my first summer living in Atlanta. There seemed to be a consensus of support and I had never seen so many white people out at a protest for Black lives. Even as we held up traffic, many drivers showered us in solidaric beeps. This contrasted with the dissatisfied looks I'd witnessed years before when organizers held up highways nearly every week for a while.

"Floyd" and other names filled the space in between the beats of an accompanying drumline. I waited to hear the names of Black trans victims, but they never came. By that point, more friends had joined the protest, so I felt more comfortable asserting my voice in our section of the crowd. As I shed the lighter, fluttering cadence I typically use to blend in with mixed company, my cheeks burned with vulnerability. My voice croaked out, *"Tony McDade,"* before steadying into an even, full-bodied tone. As one or two people looked back at me in the crowd, I wondered if they clocked that I was trans. But that old fear wasn't there anymore. People followed suit in shouting his name, and a sense of relief swept over me. I shouted more names: *Monika Diamond, Nina Pop, Layleen Polanco.* It was a bittersweet moment, and I felt fatigue. I wondered why we still, after all these years of being a part of movements that claimed to be progressive, had to remind everyone that we existed and that *our* lives mattered, too. Black trans people constantly showed up to add nuance, seemingly in ways beyond our cis counterparts. But it hadn't resulted in us necessarily being heard more after all this time, and that is a perpetual heartbreak that so many of us hold.

Protestors stayed out in New York, Atlanta, Seattle, Portland, Minneapolis, and more cities, not letting up for a single night. They persisted even as conditions at the marches became more violent, with baton beatings, rubber bullets, and tear gas being deployed. It was clear that everything the Movement for Black Lives had been fighting for years had found new momentum. And those who were once remiss to openly say Black lives mattered without qualifiers or discuss police brutality, abolition, or prison reform did. In this new world, supporting social justice was obligatory. And among friends and organizers, it really felt like the revolution was nigh.

In the LGBTQ+ community, Pride Month marked a major turning point from the heavily corporatized fiftieth-anniversary celebrations of the prior year. Opportunities for the queer community to come together had largely gone digital while discourse had, for once, largely been focused on Black LGBTQ+ folks. I'd appreciated the halt in Pride as usual. It seemed incredibly incongruous with the political moment. So, I was receptive when a friend, Fran Tirado, recruited me to join a collective planning a direct action for Black trans lives. The idea originated from a conversation between West Dakota, a Brooklyn-based drag performer, and her friend, Merrie Cherry. Quickly, they recruited a team with Fran and Eliel Cruz, who led communications, deciding what their approach would be as non-Black allies took the lead in crafting an event and platform where Black trans folks could simply celebrate, mourn, and be heard. It made sense to me. As Fran bombarded me with planning documents and emails, my heart welled with appreciation and warmth. In my years of organizing, I had never experienced such solidarity on behalf of Black trans folks. It felt like the pinnacle of allyship, and I was on board.

Rounding out the collective was Mohammed Fayaz, part of the famed queer nightlife trio, Papi Juice, who handled promotions and design for the event, and ebullient media professional Peyton Dix handled social media planning. Kalaya'an Mendoza, an expert in mutual protection, and Robyn Ayers, who was well versed in nonviolent protest design, led the safety team efforts. Alongside me, Black trans leadership came in the form of Ianne Fields Stewart, the founder of the Okra Project, a Black trans-led and trans-serving organization focused on food insecurity in the NYC area. We dedicated the action to various Black trans-led organizations including Black Trans Femmes in the Arts, the Black Trans Travel Fund, For the Gworls, GLITS, Inc., and the Marsha P. Johnson Institute.

I was honored to join the crew, a melting pot of folks with and without organizing experience. Many came from the New York media bubble that, I had often felt, lacked the range to champion social justice when I was at *Out*. However, they reminded me that the right conditions can urge us all to think and act more expansively. We planned to call it "Brooklyn Liberation: A March for Black Trans Lives," swapping the typical rainbow motif for outfits in hues of pearl and porcelain, paying homage to the Negro Silent Protest Parade that traversed the streets of Manhattan in 1917.[2] That action centered the ongoing violence of lynching and white supremacist rampages that Black people, largely in the South, faced. It was co-organized by the National Association for the Advancement of Colored People and other community leaders, drawing inspiration from silent multiracial suffragist demonstrations. Just like they drew national attention to their cause, we hoped on Sunday, June 14, 2020, that the world would take notice of Black trans folks' voices. We weren't sure how many people would attend a rally in the middle of a global pandemic, especially one that focused on Black trans people. But no matter how many folks showed up, we did our due diligence in getting the word out. A few days prior, we released an iconic poster on social media, hoping there wouldn't be a large NYPD presence as we intentionally didn't secure a permit for the space.

Unfortunately, more devastating news shook the national trans community days before the event. First, the Trump administration eliminated protections for trans patients against discrimination from healthcare providers, health insurance companies, and hospitals.[3] Then, reports about two Black trans women ruled dead by homicide spread through social media.[4] The body of twenty-seven-year-old Dominique "Rem'mie" Fells, who had been missing since June 8, was found in Philadelphia's Schuylkill River. She had incurred face and head trauma and had her legs severed. Then, there was twenty-five-year-old Riah Milton, who was fatally shot after being lured to Liberty Township, Ohio, to be robbed. As I read their stories, my heart sank all over again. The sadness, hopelessness, and disappointment returned to me, now with a sense of rage. These instances brought to mind Iyanna Dior, a young Black trans woman who was chased and attacked by a mob of Black cis men and women in Minneapolis on June 4, 2020.[5] Apparently, she'd struck several vehicles while trying to move her friend's car. Her story gained traction, revealing even further how disposable Black trans women are in our own communities. It seemed the media had outpaced our larger movements in the plight of Black trans people. For so long, I had held most of my critiques in, fearing that I'd be a traitor to the Movement 4 Black Lives or to the LGBTQ+ community or to feminist movements for speaking out too publicly and brazenly. But I was ready for us, as Black trans people, to stop coddling the cisheteropatriarchy and shying away from critiquing our movements that supposedly represented us. Even though Brooklyn Liberation was just days away, I needed to do something, say something, right then.

* * *

We mourn for you, do you mourn for us?
We cry for you, do you cry for us?
We rally for you, do you rally for us?
We imagine better for you, do you imagine better for us?
Here's another morning, after another long night of wondering,
"'What will it take for y'all to hear us?'"

* * *

ON TWITTER AND Instagram, with cryptic white text on a solid black background, I called our movements out for constantly erasing Black trans people from discussions on violence.[6] It was frightening, but I logged off unafraid of the consequences. Those posts would soon go viral, garnering the most attention of anything I'd ever shared on social media. Interestingly, I received an outpouring of support from people within and outside of the Movement for Black Lives. But there were no one-on-one discussions with cisfeminist leaders or cis non-Black LGBTQ+ leaders. I felt hopeful as I chatted with other Black leaders and worked with a collective of trans, gender-nonconforming, and nonbinary leaders to discuss how to make M4BL deliver on its promise to show up for all of us. It felt nice to know that I wasn't alone, that what I called out was seen by so many others. It gave me the confidence I needed for Brooklyn Liberation.

* * *

THAT SUNDAY MORNING of the march was extremely ordinary. I rummaged through piles, gathering all my white clothing. I hadn't thought much about what I was going to wear and how I was going to look on that day. My relationship with my body and aesthetic had shifted dramatically since the start of the pandemic. For the first time since I was a child, I felt comfortable with my bare skin and imperfectly coiled hair being seen. In fact, I'd grown accustomed to a few angles that my body still carried from life pretransition. So here I refused to spend longer than a few minutes deciding on my look.

I settled on wearing a fresh T-shirt emblazoned with I'M GONNA WIN in black letters by Phenomenal, a media and merchandising company founded by Meena Harris. She'd sent it to me as a part of a campaign that paid homage to a look that Diana Ross wore in the seventies. It had a vintage quality, and I appreciated the message. It reminded me that as long as I stuck to my values and believed in the potential of the collective, I couldn't lose. Paired with blue flared jeans, I was set.

Just before I walked out the door, I received a call from

organizers. I was asked to weigh in on a problem with one of our teammates who had been accused of sexually harassing two Black trans women in a local community. Those women intended to be at the rally but requested that the person be removed from their leadership post out of safety. I was enlisted, apparently as a respected figure, to deliver the complicated directive to that person and endure their response. I was anxious about being put in that position, but I heeded the request. The discussion wasn't positive, and they ended the call with a threat to derail the event. By some divine intervention, they called back shortly after soaking in my appeal that they shouldn't ruin the day for the collective and agreed to the terms. *What a start to the day.*

In the rideshare to the Brooklyn Museum, the site we'd chosen for the rally, I read over scattered notes that I had jotted down over the past week. For some reason, an eerie calm had washed over me despite not having a fully planned speech. All I knew was I needed to be as grounded and present as possible. By the time I arrived, I'd all but abandoned my notes, figuring I wouldn't retain them anyway. So I looked around, taking in the environment and making it familiar to myself.

Our organizing team was scattered across the museum's stone steps, rallying photographers and reporters, ensuring that people had food and water, and simply mingling. About twenty minutes until the start, our crowd was still spare, and a jolt of worry ran through me. Still, I calmed myself and continued to fellowship with the team. Then, the atmosphere opened up and people started gathering from every corner in the vicinity. Some hopped off the subway, others off their bicycles, and even more just walked up. There was a gentle orderliness to how people situated themselves, and all of them were wearing the uniform of white and masks per our request. Of course, they proudly held their protest signs: QUEERS FOR TRANS LIVES, ASIANS FOR BLACK LIVES, RESPECT MY EXISTENCE OR EXPECT MY RESISTANCE, NO PRIDE WITHOUT BLACK TRANS LIVES. As our anticipation grew, we just gazed at one another and the exponentially increasing number of attendees: 100, 200, 500, 1,000, and beyond.

All along the museum's dais, we speakers assembled, flanked by a frantic press and photo crew. *Having so many media folks on our team came in clutch, hunny!* Soon, our masters of ceremonies, longtime organizer Joshua Obawole Allen and drag performance artist Junior Mintt, took their places and kicked off the event. At the request of Ianne, Joshua commanded the allies to make space for Black trans people in the crowd to move to the center. It was a poetic display of what it meant for the non-Black people and the cis people in attendance to prioritize us. As Eliel and I took in the crowd's movement, I turned to him and said in astonishment, "We have more people with us than we realized." We had a glorious congregation that rivaled any place of worship, one drawn together by a sense of duty to Black trans people. Soon, one by one our speakers took to the microphone, baring their souls just beyond a giant rainbow flag.

Ianne, adorned with bright red flowers, served as our first speaker. I could barely focus as I tried to run through what I'd say in my head, but I felt the confidence she exuded. Our interpreter's deft fingers gorgeously moved in sync with her denouncement of white supremacy and transphobia. Then, Ceyenne Doroshow, a movement elder and founder of GLITS, Inc., addressed the crowd in sequined formalwear. For her, this gathering was a ceremony. I could sense years of survival as she exclaimed, "I want you to stand tall and proud and Black and live!" Then, before I knew it, Joshua announced my turn at the mic.

By now, I had resigned myself to abandoning my phone and simply speaking from the deepest part of my gut, allowing the words to flow out of me. I trusted that whatever I channeled that day, measured or messy, would be necessary. The crowd peered back as I walked to the edge of the dais. I locked eyes with a few people I knew from various points in my life: my days in Georgia, California, and New York respectively. I ignored the fact that this crowd had grown larger than I could count. And in a final act of submission to the moment, I threw my head back and relinquished my worries into the air. As I inhaled deeply, Marsha P. Johnson and Zazu Nova's energy coursed through me. I felt the defiance of Sylvia Rivera. Ida B. Wells-Barnett's and Anna Julia Cooper's formidable truth-telling. There was the prophetic poetry of Audre Lorde and the erudite rage of James Baldwin. I sensed all those victims I had mourned over the years, especially Leelah, Chyna, Layleen, Tony, Dominique, and Riah. I felt those victims who I knew the names of and those that I didn't. I felt the pride I hoped my father and grandmother would have in me. I let all those people, stories, and voices that had transformed me come to the fore. The impossible prayer, that I was enough in my Blackness, queerness, transness, Southernness, and womanhood, was finally answered.

In a moment of cosmic levity, the crowd's roar erroneously singing "Happy Birthday" brought me back to my body. For whatever reason, Joshua had told the crowd it was, and someone started singing. So, I quipped about it not being my birthday through a chuckle. Then I joked about it still being Gemini season, nodding to the hate that my supremely marginalized zodiac sign is known to attract. Nothing, however, could break my concentration. Then, I leaned over the dais, not for fashion or flair but because all my energy would go into my mostly impromptu speech.

"I am going to talk to my Black trans folks and model what it looks like to put us first," I said. "We have been told to be silent for too long. We have been told that we are not enough to parents, to family, to lovers, to Johns, to organizations, to schools, to our government, to the world, and the truth is that we are more than enough.

"We stand in the symbolic shadow of some powerful folks, don't we? Folks they tried to erase. They thought we'd not ever find their names, their stories. We know about Marsha, don't we? We know about Sylvia, don't we? We know about Miss Major, our living legend, don't we? We know about Ms. Ceyenne, don't we? And all of that glory that was on this stage today, don't we? And so let today be the last day that you ever doubt Black trans power.

"When they tried to erase some of these bold, beautiful figures, they built out infrastructure. They built out organizations on their foundation. They've had white, cis, queer (sometimes) people in leadership. You know, I might get in some trouble for saying this, and yes, the legislation matters, but white queer folks get to worry about legislation, while Black queer folk are worrying about our lives.

"All of this faith that we are told to have in a government that has demonstrated—through multiple administrations, not just Trump, because he is just one figurehead right now. Don't ever doubt the faith that you should have for yourself and your people, cuz we are the ones changing shit. And we are the lifeblood of everything they built and tried to lock us out of.

"And so, I want you, especially my Black trans folks, to hold every moment that you have been told you're not enough, that you're not worthy of love, and safety, and housing, and healthcare, that you're not worthy to be a leader of these organizations that these white folks are gatekeeping and these resources that they still gatekeep. I want you to know that you're more than enough.

"We have lost a lot of folks, haven't we? You know, people put Marsha up on this pedestal, but they never talk about how we don't know what happened to her, what led to her demise. They profit off of her history, her power, her legacy. They profit off of our history, our power, our legacy. I can't tell you how many of these mostly white organizations have us in their line items for their grant proposals and they have us in the rhetoric of their speeches and I want to know where is the money, and are the resources going to keep us alive?

"I don't care anymore about trying to be respectable, and trying to be palatable, and trying to be beautiful in their terms, and trying to sound the 'right' way. I'm supposed to be what I am right now at this moment. And so, today, I am saying, if you have an organization that has no Black trans leadership, if you have an organization that has no specific Black trans programming or funding, you are obsolete. If you are not serving Black and brown trans folks, if you are not serving our incarcerated and our sex workers and our detained and our disabled, you are obsolete.

"So I want you to take this feeling that you're feeling in this moment, because I'm feeling a lot of things right now, clearly. I'm feeling joy and filled to see all of your faces and your bodies in formation, hunny. I am feeling sadness and mourning for all of those souls that we've lost, but I know the spirit of Marsha and Sylvia, and the spirit of Rem'mie and Riah, and the spirit of Tony, and the spirit of our dear sister Layleen, and the spirit of Chyna Doll Dupree, and the spirit of all of those folks that we know, all of those names—I could go on for days. I feel that today, and the reckoning is here. The reckoning is here, y'all, so when you leave here today—we might be silent today, but tomorrow we're not going to be silent, right? So I want you to go and have that conversation with your loved ones about how you've been transformed because you know your power. I want you to go into any workplace, any of these organizations that claim to care about us and tell them that you know your power. I want you to be out on these streets long after today and tell folks that you know your power. And I want you all also to remember that whether you're Black and trans or not, you have a duty and responsibility to elevate Black trans power."

I'd known that I wanted to end with a chant, but it wasn't until I finished that line that I knew which word I had been searching for all along. *POWER.*

"I'm gon' ask you to do a little labor right now," I said before taking a quick breath. "Repeat after me." And I said, "I believe in my power." The crowd responded politely, "I believe in my power." Then, I chided them a bit to be fiercer in their conviction. "Y'all gon' have to be louder than that. We got a lot of souls to reach right now, don't we?" Then I repeated, "I believe in my power." The voices in the crowd swelled to match my energy, saying it back. Then, we traded shouts of, "I believe in your power." Then, "I believe in our power." Finally, I commanded the thousands in attendance to chant, "I believe in Black trans power," and my soul expanded beyond the borders of my body. I felt no fear.

After the first round, I asked them if they'd say it with me again and the crowd responded with cheers and affirmation. By the third time, we were all on a similar wavelength and it felt transcendent. It was a sacred moment, not unlike being touched by a song at church or realizing you've fallen in love or realizing your true identity. The solace I felt in my soul was undeniable as I gazed at the Black trans people in the front of the crowd. This day was for us to share our mourning, our healing, our potential, and our power. At that moment, I just existed with no pretense and no respectability. I didn't have to be an image, token, or agent to my oppressor's liberation. I was a vessel and it seemed like nothing was separating my soul from those in attendance. There was no question that I'd made the ancestors, trancestors, and future generations proud because I was something more than those magnolias that I longed to be like in my childhood backyard in Augusta. I no longer worried about being precious or pure; I was a wildflower fully bloomed.

As I put the mic back on the stand and turned to our beaming cadre of organizers, I tried to melt into the background. But the pride on people's faces was unforgettable. Right after, our attention turned to Melania as she spoke about Layleen's life and that justice won after her death. Eliel had ensured we include a victim's family member, signaling the support necessary to sustain Black trans dignity. It was a necessary call because her heart-wrenching testimony gave us a new, visceral dimension to why we had all gathered that day.

Soon the speaking portion was complete, and we descended downstairs to begin the march. Our speakers were handed beautiful little flowers as we proceeded toward the front of the crowd on Eastern Parkway. The audience looked at us in awe, but I averted my gaze. I was the least worried about being perceived that I had ever been, but I also wasn't ready to feel completely grounded again. I loved floating in this spiritual, adrenaline-filled space.

* * *

THE SUN PEERED through the clouds in a grand celestial display of optimism all along the route. Our safety team gently monitored the crowd with precision. And people handling provisions checked in and made sure folks were stocked up on water and sunscreen. Somewhere in the middle of the march, as we walked toward Fort Greene Park, Eliel pulled me aside and revealed that our attendee numbers were approaching the multi-thousand figure. He'd learned that the crowd was still leaving the Brooklyn Museum while our portion was near Barclays Arena. It had already exceeded our expectations. As we swarmed the streets, people repeatedly stopped me and thanked me for my speech, which warmed my heart. And I got my entire life while observing a voguing and dance break. Even in mourning, we were finding pockets of joy.

By the time the march officially ended at Fort Greene Park, my energy couldn't be depleted. Half of our attendees dispersed, but some lingered as if waiting for more directives. A few people took to the mic to share more thoughts. I was asked, but I had nothing else. I'd left it all on the dais. Afterward, I grabbed a bite to eat with several friends. We took in the glow of the evening sun, gushing about how well the march went. I could barely hear a word of what was being said, still caught up in the earlier moments of the day. We'd formed like the crest of a wave on that partly cloudy day. It seemed like nothing was standing in the way of connecting with one another's humanity: no particles, smoke, or haziness. I would never forget our passionate spirits committing to build a world without afrotransphobic and afrotransmisogynistic violence. It seemed like we were on the horizon of something new, but I wondered what would happen when the fanfare died, the protestors went home, the posters were discarded, we retreated to harmful institutions, another person's life was taken, and we were faced with the next obstacle. *Would we remember our clarion call for transformation? Would we continue to fight, digging deeper into liberation? More importantly, would we remember our power?*

Epilogue

Welcome to the Garden

> let there be new flowering
> in the fields let the fields
> turn mellow for the men
> let the men keep tender
> through the time let the time
> be wrested from the war
> let the war be won
> let love be
> at the end
>
> —Lucille Clifton

Brooklyn Liberation unfurled my petals and revealed an entire garden of wildflowers sprouting up through unjust soil. The lore of the march, with estimates as high as twenty thousand attendees, grew beyond anything our organizing collective could have imagined. It became an indisputable scene in the larger arc of social justice and, more specifically, in the fight for Black trans liberation. And the moment fell right in line with the revolutionary energy of the summer of 2020.

In time, however, the soil seemed to harden back around our

roots. I gradually returned to old patterns—feeling unheard, uninterested, and overworked. The promise of the end of the COVID-19 pandemic lured me into desiring normalcy, a bit of status quo. My disillusionment only grew as the upcoming presidential election washed away the collective consciousness that activists and organizers had been leading. The political demand to defund police was shredded by lawmakers, even liberal ones, who couldn't "break up with twelve," as Toni-Michelle Williams might say. And, gradually, the days of countless protests that we'd become accustomed to trickled to a halt. Attention turned to ousting Donald Trump and his cronies and reestablishing a neoliberal order that, for many, hardly looked different than the Christofascist one it claimed to differ from. Still, I joined many Leftists in getting Joe Biden elected, even though this meant supporting a toothless aim to heal "the soul of the nation" and a promise of "nothing fundamentally changing."

Now, in 2023, it feels like we're in the midst of a sociopolitical wildfire that is more daunting. There've been multiple waves of the pandemic (to varying degrees of survival), other emerging biological threats, a fascist insurrection at the U.S. Capitol, the striking down of *Roe v. Wade*, targeting of diversity, equity, and inclusion efforts, the banning of educational curricula and materials focused on communities on the margins, and increased legislative and physical attacks against the LGBTQ+ community. Now, you can barely turn on the news or scroll social media without being bombarded with a bigoted discourse about gender, race, and so much more, while war continues to rage globally, the environment continues to be neglected, technology continues to be mesmerizingly misunderstood, and communities, including LGBTQ+ folks, continue to face religious oppression.

The precipice of revolution that many of us thought we'd

reached in the Summer of 2020 is much farther away than we'd like. I wish I could provide a soothing conclusion where everything feels hopeful and bright, but it seems we will have to continue to hold the uncertainty of progress. We'll have to find the balance in those things that make our lives harder and those that make us hopeful. One thing is for sure: white supremacy, cisheteropatriarchy, classism, ableism, Christofascism, and other systems of oppression won't be eradicated unless we truly believe that we are the fruit of precious seeds.

Revolution isn't a singular event but a continuously unfolding phenomenon. The transformational energy we feel during seismic events doesn't dissipate. It stays with us, waiting to be reactivated so we can transform the institutions around us: the collectives, the industries, the organizations, the schools, the places of worship, our communities, our families, and ourselves. So, let everything you feel be fertilizer: anguish, anxiety, fear, grief, joy, love, mourning, rage, sorrow, wanting, yearning. And let us not be distracted or deterred from our duties in the garden of liberation: honoring our place, taking the risk to bloom again and again, planting seeds of resilience, and leaving the soil richer for generations to come.

I am constantly in awe of what our ancestors and trancestors were able to plant despite the wildfires they endured. They didn't wait for the perfect conditions or to be understood. They just knew they had dreams and—wittingly or unwittingly—crafted the scaffolding for our movements. Like them, we must continue to build sites of accountability, connection, dreaming, and healing even when the flames are the highest.

The older I grow the more gratitude I have for my roots. Sometimes I wonder what my father, my grandparents, and so many others who have gone on would think of me. Would they see my power now? There will always be a part of me hoping I can build a life of which they could be proud. I try not to have shame around the desire to be someone they could fully recognize and understand. I'm human and I want to believe that had they lived long enough to see who I've become that their love would have evolved alongside all of the others who make my life fuller.

To future generations, especially my transcendants, I want you to know what it took me so long to realize. You are a divinely crafted gift, and you are *really* cherished and *really* loved, and you *really* belong. I trust that you will carry on the light that our people—especially Black, queer, and trans—have held on to for so long. You deserve the blank canvas of your life, to make it your own and adorn it as you see fit. I consider it a victory that you might not label yourself, love, or navigate the world the same way that I do. Just always remember that our garden lies beyond the field of expectations.

ACKNOWLEDGMENTS

It is a privilege to share my life and my thoughts on liberation so far. I'm grateful for the wildflowers who supported me throughout life and this process.

Thank you to my editorial fleet: Anna deVries; Alex Brown, for being the initial shepherd of this work; and my publisher, St. Martin's Press, for giving my words a home.

My agent, Robert Guinsler, for running through the industry trenches with me. My team at the Katz Company for nourishing my professional life, especially during my creative retreats.

My residencies at Jack Jones Literary Arts and Oregon State University were crucial in gifting me space to surrender to the process. Thank you to Kima Jones, Peter Betjemann, Liddy Detar, and the staffs of both institutions. Shout-out to Hodgepodge Coffeehouse in East Atlanta, World Ground Café in Oakland, and Daily Press Coffee in Ocean Hill, Brooklyn, for the daylong escapes to create this volume too.

Thank you to Texas Isaiah Horatio-Valenzuela for lending your artistic brilliance for the cover and all others who assisted: Wazi Maret, Vassily Maximillian, Lexi Webster, Aya Tariq for the phenomenal beat, Ro Morgan for the hair wizardry, BVLGARI,

Prabal Gurung, KHIRY, Tanya Taylor, Alexis Bittar, Markarian, Savannah Engel PR, Stonefruit Botanical, The Wall Group, and Black Trans Femmes in the Arts for coming in clutch with the studio space and support.

To my movement elders who paved the way: Dee Dee Chamblee, Cecilia Gentili, Ceyenne Doroshow, Tracee McDaniels, Miss Major, Sir Lady Java, Eva Aubry, Duchess Milan, Cecilia Chung, Earline Budd, Barbara Ransby, Barbara Smith, Beverly Guy Sheftall, and so many others.

Immense gratitude to all the friends and chosen and origin family who hold me down and have forever transformed my lens on liberation: Toni-Michelle Williams, Aria Sa'id, Shamari Sylvan, Chase Strangio, Janet Mock, Phillip Picardi, J. Wortham, Christopher Guidarelli, Xairre Robinson, Marrion Johnson, Mariah Moore, Aldita Gallardo, Jadé Mora Gutierrez, Mickaela Bradford, Elliott Fukui, Charles Chaisson, Giselle Byrd, the Brooklyn Liberation crew, the Avengers of Queer Media, the Black Trans Circles sistas, Channel Black, Echoing Ida, Movement for Black Lives, Auburn Seminary fam, Misters Not Sisters, and too many more to name from my respective days in Georgia, California, and New York.

To those who have blessed me with romance and all its complexities.

My origin family that has loved and taught me the most about transformation: Momma, for your unconditional love. Jessica, for always being in the wings. Chet, for reminders that there's always time for laughter. Daniel and Jackie too! My nibblings, who I hope never forget they are precious and pure. And my sprawling extended Black Southern family—or my aunties, uncles, cousins and 'nem—who remind me of the glory of our roots. I love being a Devoe, a Willis, and so much more.

The departed, Dad, Grandma Inez, and Grandma Ida, who I

feel, hear, and see in my life and dreams all the time. And all the souls who continue to strengthen my spirit—including Marsha P. Johnson, Zazu Nova, Leelah Alcorn, Blake Brockington, Chyna Gibson, Layleen Polanco, Sylvia Rivera, Cheryl Courtney-Evans, The Lady Chablis, Crystal LaBeija, Venus Xtravaganza, Octavia St. Laurent, Monica Roberts, Ida B. Wells-Barnett, Bayard Rustin, James Baldwin, Combahee River Collective, Angela Davis, Assata Shakur, Toni Morrison, Valerie Boyd, and Octavia Butler. I would not be the Black, queer, trans woman and storyteller I am without you.

NOTES

EPIGRAPH

1. Elizabeth Appell, "Anais Nin and I are in lock step," *Elizabeth Appell* (blog), December 31, 2012, https://readelizabeth.com/anais-nin -and-i-are-in-lock-step/.

10. FOR WOMEN WHO HAD A BOYHOOD

1. Donovan Slack, "Biden Says Transgender Discrimination 'Civil Rights Issue of Our Time,'" *Politico44* (blog), October 30, 2012, https://www .politico.com/blogs/politico44/2012/10/biden-says-transgender -discrimination-civil-rights-issue-of-our-time-147761.
2. Ian Lovett, "Changing Sex, and Changing Teams," *The New York Times*, May 7, 2013, https://www.nytimes.com/2013/05/07/us/transgender -high-school-students-gain-admission-to-sports-teams.html.
3. ACLU, "LGBT Groups Challenge Medicare's Refusal to Provide Healthcare to Transgender Patients," press release, April 1, 2013, https: //www.aclu.org/press-releases/lgbt-groups-challenge-medicares -refusal-provide-healthcare-transgender-patients.

11. DESTINY'S DETOUR

1. Jeff Mays, "Transgender Groups Protest Handling of Islan Nettles' Death," DNAinfo New York, January 31, 2014, https://www.dnainfo

.com/new-york/20140131/central-harlem/transgender-groups
-protest-handling-of-islan-nettles-death/.

2. James C. McKinley Jr., "Man's Confession in Transgender Woman's Death Is Admissible, Judge Rules," *The New York Times*, April 2, 2016, https://www.nytimes.com/2016/04/02/nyregion/mans-confession -in-transgender-womans-death-is-admissible-judge-rules.html.

3. Michael Schwirtz, "Embarking on a New Life, Transgender Woman Has It Brutally Taken," *The New York Times*, September 9, 2013, https://www.nytimes.com/2013/09/09/nyregion/embarking-on-a -new-life-transgender-woman-has-it-brutally-taken.html.

4. Nicole Pasulka, "The Case of CeCe McDonald: Murder—or Self-Defense Against a Hate Crime?" *Mother Jones*, May 22, 2012, https://www.motherjones.com/politics/2012/05/cece-mcdonald -transgender-hate-crime-murder/.

12. PLAUSIBLE DENIABILITY

1. Amy Mitchell, Mark Jurkowitz, and Emily Guskin, "The Newspaper Industry Overall," Pew Research Center, August 7, 2013, https://www .pewresearch.org/journalism/2013/08/07/the-newspaper-industry -overall/.

2. Molly Ball, "Eric Cantor's Loss: A Stunning Upset," *The Atlantic*, June 10, 2014, https://www.theatlantic.com/politics/archive/2014 /06/eric-cantor-loses-in-stunning-upset/372550/.

13. THE LABYRINTH OF DESIRE

1. Ed Pilkington, "Fear and Violence in Transgender Baltimore: 'It's Scary Trusting Anyone,'" *Guardian*, August 1, 2014, https:// www.theguardian.com/world/2014/aug/01/murder-transgender -women-baltimore-heighten-fears-mia-henderson.

16. BETWEEN VISIBILITY AND VITALITY

1. Jody L. Herman, Taylor N. T. Brown, and Ann P. Haas, "Suicide Thoughts and Attempts Among Transgender Adults," UCLA School

of Law Williams Institute, September 2019, https://williamsinstitute
.law.ucla.edu/publications/suicidality-transgender-adults/.

2. "Addressing Anti-Transgender Violence: Exploring Realities, Challenges and Solutions," Human Rights Campaign, https://www.hrc
.org/resources/addressing-anti-transgender-violence-exploring
-realities-challenges-and-sol.

3. GLAAD, "Number of Americans Who Report Knowing a Transgender Person Doubles in Seven Years, According to New GLAAD
Survey," news release, September 17, 2015, https://www.glaad.org
/releases/number-americans-who-report-knowing-transgender
-person-doubles-seven-years-according-new.

17. SLOUCHING TOWARD LIBERATION

1. Dyana Bagby, "Transgender Man Alleges Called 'It,' Threatened
by East Point Police," *The Georgia Voice*, October 28, 2014, https:
//thegavoice.com/news/georgia/transgender-man-alleges-called
-threatened-east-point-police/.

2. Mark Winston Griffith, "Black Love Matters," *The Nation*, July 28, 2015,
https://www.thenation.com/article/archive/black-love-matters/.

18. NOBODY'S SAVIOR

1. National Coalition of Anti-Violence Projects (NCAVP), *Lesbian,
Gay, Bisexual, Transgender, Queer, and HIV-Affected Hate Violence
in 2015*, 2016 release edition, http://avp.org/wp-content/uploads
/2017/04/ncavp_hvreport_2015_final.pdf.

2. Dyana Bagby, "MARTA Police Arrest Suspect in Violent Attack on
Trans Women," *The Georgia Voice*, May 23, 2014, https://thegavoice
.com/news/atlanta/marta-police-arrest-suspect-violent-attack
-trans-women/.

19. AN ERA OF RECKONING

1. Christine Willard, "Two Open Transgender Law Center in San Francisco," *National Jurist* (Sept. 2002), accessed May 31, 2023, https://

web.archive.org/web/20031124050401fw_/http://www.transgender lawcenter.org/are/twoopen.html.

2. Ericka Huggins, "An Oral History with Ericka Huggins," conducted by Fiona Thompson, 2007, Oral History Center, The Bancroft Library, University of California, Berkeley, 2010, https://revolution .berkeley.edu/assets/Oral-History-of-Ericka-Huggins-excerpt-81 -103.pdf.

3. Jessica Purkiss and Jack Serle, "Obama's Covert Drone War in Numbers: Ten Times More Strikes Than Bush," *Bureau of Investigative Journalism*, January 17, 2017, https://www.thebureauinvestigates .com/stories/2017-01-17/obamas-covert-drone-war-in-numbers -ten-times-more-strikes-than-bush; Ana Gonzalez-Barrera and Jens Manuel Krogstad, "U.S. Deportations of Immigrants Reach Record High in 2013," Pew Research Center, October 2, 2014, https: //www.pewresearch.org/fact-tank/2014/10/02/u-s-deportations -of-immigrants-reach-record-high-in-2013/.

4. See, for example, *Whitaker v. Kenosha Unified School District No. 1 Board of Education and Sue Savaglio-Jarvis, http://transgenderlawcenter* .org/wp-content/uploads/2016/08/10-1-A.-Whitaker-Declaration .pdf.

20. TESTING MY FAITH

1. Jen McDaneld, "White Suffragist Dis/Entitlement: The *Revolution* and the Rhetoric of Racism," *Legacy* 30, no. 2 (2013): 243–64.

2. Angela Y. Davis, "Woman Suffrage at the Turn of the Century: The Rising Influence of Racism," in *Women, Race & Class* (New York: Vintage Books, 1983), 112.

21. LETTER TO CHYNA GIBSON

1. Beau Evans, "'A Hole in Our Hearts': Family, Friends Mourn Murder Victim Chyna Gibson," NOLA.com, March 2, 2017, https: //www.nola.com/news/crime_police/a-hole-in-our-hearts-family -friends-mourn-murder-victim-chyna-gibson/article_105599e9 -dc36-53a7-b8f2-9e2f3d5205f4.html.

22. WOMANHOOD, EXPANDED

1. Jessica Ravitz, "Calls to Crisis and Suicide Prevention Hotlines Surge Post-Election," CNN, November 11, 2016, https://www .cnn.com/2016/11/11/health/election-crisis-suicide-prevention -hotlines/index.html.
2. Chimamanda Ngozi Adichie, interview by Cathy Newman, Channel 4 News, March 10, 2017, https://www.youtube.com/watch?v =KP1C7VXUfZQ.

23. GIRLS' NIGHT OUTING

1. Janet Mock, "Dear Men of 'The Breakfast Club': Trans Women Aren't a Prop, Ploy, or Sexual Predators," *Allure*, July 31, 2017, https://www.allure.com/story/janet-mock-response-the-breakfast-club -trans-women.

24. I HAVE A RIGHT TO SHOW MY COLOR

1. "*Norsworthy v. Beard*," Transgender Law Center, n.d., https://transgenderlawcenter.org/norsworthy-v-beard.
2. Sarah Pettit obituary, *The New York Times*, January 23, 2003, www.nytimes.com/2003/01/23/nyregion/sarah-pettit-36-a-founder-of-out-magazine.html.

25. A PEACH IN THE BIG APPLE

1. Sara Jerde, "With Ex-Condé Nast Star Phillip Picardi at the Top, *Out* Magazine Looks to Expand," *Adweek*, November 15, 2018, https://www.adweek.com/performance-marketing/with-ex -conde-nast-star-phillip-picardi-at-the-top-out-magazine-looks -to-expand/.
2. Alex Panisch, "The Morning after the Night before: *Out* Celebrates 20 Years," *Out* magazine, https://www.out.com/out-exclusives/2012 /09/18/oral-history-magazine-celebrates-20-years.

26. THIS AIN'T NO CHICK FLICK

1. Kali Hays, "*Out* Magazine, Pride Media Rife with Challenges for New Editor," *Women's Wear Daily*, October 18, 2018, https://wwd.com/business-news/media/out-magazine-pride-media-challenges-new-editor-phillip-picardi-1202884718/.
2. #OutOwes, "#OUTOwes: Open Letter to *Out* Magazine," Medium, February 7, 2019, https://medium.com/@outwesopenletter/outowes-open-letter-to-out-magazine-22bbe9efbf15.

27. OUR ANCESTORS' WILDEST NIGHTMARE

1. *Street Transvestite Action Revolutionaries: Survival, Revolt, and Queer Antagonist Struggle*, Untorelli Press, n.d., https://untorellipress.noblogs.org/files/2011/12/STAR.pdf.
2. Leslie Feinberg, "Street Transvestite Action Revolutionaries: Lavender and Red, Part 73," *Workers World*, September 24, 2006, https://www.workers.org/2006/us/lavender-red-73/.
3. Chris Tedjasukmana, "Y'all Better Quiet Down," Videoactivism.net, August 12, 2016, https://videoactivism.net/en/yall-better-quiet/.

28. LETTER TO LAYLEEN POLANCO

1. Diana Tourjée, "'The State Is Her Ultimate Killer': How a Trans Woman Died at Rikers," *VICE*, June 12, 2019, https://www.vice.com/en/article/7xgdyq/layleen-polanco-sex-work-rikers-trans-woman-death.
2. Center for Court Innovation, "State Court Snapshot: New York State's Human Trafficking Intervention Courts," 2016, https://cjinvolvedwomen.org/wp-content/uploads/2016/12/HTIC-1pager.pdf.
3. Raquel Willis, "Introducing the *Out*100 Trans Obituaries Project," *Out* magazine, November 20, 2019, https://www.out.com/print/2019/11/20/trans-obituaries-project.
4. Sarah Lustbader, "Spotlight: De Blasio—The Circumstances of Layleen Polanco's Death Shouldn't Be So Perplexing," The Appeal, June 13, 2019, https://theappeal.org/spotlight-de-blasio-the-circumstances-of-layleen-polancos-death-shouldnt-be-so-perplexing/.

30. REVOLUTION'S KNOCKIN'

1. Laura Thompson, "The Police Killing You Probably Didn't Hear about This Week," *Mother Jones*, May 29, 2020, https://www.motherjones.com/crime-justice/2020/05/tony-mcdade-tallahassee-florida-police-shooting-death/.

2. "5,000 Negroes in Race Riot Protest March on 5th Ave.," *New-York Tribune*, July 29, 1917, https://chroniclingamerica.loc.gov/lccn/sn83030214/1917-07-29/ed-1/seq-13/.

3. Selena Simmons-Duffin, "Transgender Health Protections Reversed by Trump Administration," NPR, June 12, 2020, https://www.npr.org/sections/health-shots/2020/06/12/868073068/transgender-health-protections-reversed-by-trump-administration.

4. Madeleine Carlisle, "Two Black Trans Women Were Killed in the U.S. in the Past Week as Trump Revokes Discrimination Protections for Trans People," *Time*, June 13, 2020, https://time.com/5853325/black-trans-women-killed-riah-milton-dominique-remmie-fells-trump/.

5. EJ Dickson, "A Black Trans Woman Named Iyanna Dior Was Beaten by a Mob in Minneapolis," *Rolling Stone*, June 3, 2020, https://www.rollingstone.com/culture/culture-news/iyanna-dior-minneapolis-beating-1009736/.

6. Raquel Willis (@raquel_willis), "Cis folks of the Movement 4 Black Lives, the larger queer movement, and the feminist movement have long failed Black trans people. It's time for a reckoning on your collective silence and inaction," Instagram post, June 12, 2020, https://www.instagram.com/p/CBVOj4_gJwc/?hl=en.